COGNITIVE-
BEHAVIORAL
ASSESSMENT
AND
THERAPY
WITH
ADOLESCENTS

COGNITIVE-BEHAVIORAL ASSESSMENT AND THERAPY WITH ADOLESCENTS

Janet M. Zarb, Ph.D.

BRUNNER/MAZEL, *Publishers* • NEW YORK

Library of Congress Cataloging-in-Publication Data
Zarb, Janet M.
    Cognitive-behavioral assessment and therapy with adolescents.   /
Janet M. Zarb.
        p.   cm.
    Includes bibliographical references and index.
    ISBN 0-87630-685-7
    1. Cognitive therapy for teenagers.   2. Behavioral assessment of
teenagers.   I. Title.
    [DNLM: 1. Adolescent Psychology.   2. Behavior Therapy—in
adolescence. 3. Personality Assessment—in adolescence. WS 463
Z36c]
RJ505.C63Z37   1992
616.89'142'0835—dc20
DNLM/DLC
for Library of Congress   92-16165
                                                                                CIP

Published by
BRUNNER/MAZEL, INC.
19 Union Square West
New York, New York 10003

Manufactured in the United States of America

10   9   8   7   6   5   4   3   2   1

to George

Contents

Preface

In recent decades, an increasing number of mental health professionals have adopted a cognitive-behavioral approach to treatment of psychological disorders. The distinguishing feature of this approach is the simultaneous emphasis on the role of cognitive processes in shaping maladaptive behaviors and the endorsement of experimentally developed cognitive and behavioristic interventions. Although a number of books have outlined cognitive-behavioral approaches for adult clients, there are few specializing in the distinct set of behavioral, motivational, and cognitive features presented by the adolescent client. Furthermore, since adolescents are still under the daily influence of parents, as well as of peers and teachers, there is a need for a comprehensive approach that addresses the client's larger social system.

The purpose of this book is to demonstrate the application of clinically tested, cognitive-behavioral assessment and therapy procedures. A brief review of the core features of cognitive-behavioral therapy and of the underlying cognitive social-learning theory orientation provides the reader with a framework and rationale for both the general approach and the specific procedures to be described subsequently. A detailed assessment format is presented, with data collection instruments designed for each phase. Several cognitive restructuring and behavioral coping-skills interventions are then described in sufficient detail for replication by the therapist. These interventions are designed for individual sessions with adolescents, as well as for parent skill-training and family sessions. Final chapters address recurrent family, peer, and school-related problems characteristic of adolescent clients, along with adolescent depression and anxiety disorders which overlap all three areas.

A cognitive-behavioral approach to identification of targets for intervention is demonstrated for each problem, accompanied by suggestions for appropriate therapy procedures. The recommended interventions for each target are meant to provide a starting point for developing a treatment approach, rather than an exhaustive list of possible interventions. Interventions will frequently need to be adapted to fit the idiosyncratic features of a particular client's problem. Furthermore, new cognitive-behavioral strategies are continually being developed, and the therapist will need to be open to additional interventions not covered here.

This book is intended to be used as a manual by therapist practitioners working with adolescents. It is designed for use by psychologists, psychiatrists, social workers, and other mental health professionals and students-in-training working with adolescents and their families in clinics, agencies, therapeutic communities, hospitals, school settings, and private practice. It is not meant to be an exhaustive survey of adolescent psychological disorders. Nor is it meant to present an exhaustive coverage of individual and family coping-skills and cognitive-restructuring techniques. Instead, it is an attempt to demonstrate a therapy approach, and the application of several clinically proven cognitive-behavioral techniques to common problems of adolescent clients.

The assessment and therapy techniques described in this book have been found by myself and others to be appropriate and successful with adolescent clients and their families. References have been provided for more detailed descriptions of problem areas and interventions, if required by the reader. These techniques have been collected and adapted over a period of several years from journal articles, books, and discussions with other therapists. Care has been taken to give due credit to therapists and researchers who were originally responsible for developing each technique, but after years of practice it is sometimes difficult to identify the exact source. I apologize if I have unintentionally failed to acknowledge each contributor adequately in my references.

Case material presented is from actual therapy clients, including samples of client verbalizations during therapy sessions. The same format is used throughout: identification of cognitive and behavioral targets, case examples, and suggestions for individual, parent skill-training, and family interventions.

It is hoped that mental-health professionals will find this format and the unified cognitive-behavioral theoretical and practical approach to be a useful and successful aid to improving the psychological and emotional well being of adolescent clients. Perhaps the most valuable aspect of this approach is that it provides a vehicle for teaching adolescent clients techniques for identifying and effectively altering their own self-defeating thought patterns and behaviors—techniques that they may then use over and over again in years to come.

PART I

THEORY AND METHODS

1

A Cognitive-Behavioral Approach with Adolescent Clients

Theoretical, Empirical, and Practical Considerations

The purpose of this book is to present a cognitive-behavioral approach to assessment and therapy specifically adapted for adolescent clients and their families. For pragmatic reasons, adolescence will be defined as the years from 11 through 19, following the onset of puberty. While it may be argued that many adolescent psychological disorders resemble adult disorders, nevertheless, adolescent problems present a distinct set of behavioral and cognitive components, reflecting the adolescent developmental stage.

The terms "cognitive-behavioral therapy," "cognitive learning therapy," or simply "cognitive therapy" have been applied to a variety of procedures, with the common distinguishing feature of simultaneous endorsement of the importance of the role of both cognitive and behavioral processes in shaping and maintaining psychological disorders, and the application of empirically-based cognitive and behavioristic procedures to alter dysfunctional response patterns. Therapy interventions are designed to reduce the frequency of the client's maladaptive responses and to teach new cognitive and behavioral skills until there is a significant decrease in unwanted behaviors and an increase in more adaptive behaviors.

FEATURES AND ASSUMPTIONS OF COGNITIVE-BEHAVIORAL APPROACHES

Cognitive behavioral approaches for adult clients, as outlined by clinicians such as Beck and his colleagues (Beck, 1976; Beck, Rush, et al., 1979; Beck & Emery, 1985). Meichenbaum (1977), Kendall and Hollon (1979), and others rely on two

3

major types of interventions: cognitive-restructuring interventions and behavioral coping-skills interventions. A cognitive-behavioral therapist considers exclusive focusing on only behavior or cognition or affect to be too restrictive, and therefore concentrates on all three areas simultaneously. The therapist focuses on the nature of the client's behavioral repertoire (i.e. competencies and deficits) and on accompanying cognitive processes. The client's cognitions are viewed as part of a complex repertoire of skills, which also includes problem-solving ability and other coping skills, self concept, and interpersonal strategies.

Three important assumptions underlying cogntive-behavioral approaches to psychotherapy have been supported by research over the past decades: (1) that cognitions mediate behavior, (2) that a relationship exists between cognitions and emotional arousal so that the way in which a person labels or evaluates a situation, on the basis of his or her expectancies and assumptions, affects that person's emotional reactions to it, and (3) that particular patterns of maladaptive cognitions are characteristic of specific psychological disorders (Bandura, 1977; Beck, 1976; Ellis, 1962, 1977; Ellis & Grieger, 1977; Goldfried & Davidson, 1976; Goldfried & Goldfried, 1980; Kendall & Hollon, 1979; Mahoney, 1974, 1977; Meichenbaum, 1977).

Cognitive behavioral approaches to family therapy are based on assumptions that family distress stems from a combination of cognitive factors such as family members' distorted or unrealistic appraisals of each other, as well as from dysfunctional interpersonal behavioral exchanges between family members, such as deficits in communication or problem-solving skills (Epstein, Schlessinger & Dryden, 1988).

The cognitive-behavioral clinician seeks to identify the meaning system that the client brings to therapy, which would in turn explain the client's inner dialogue. Cognitions (which include perceptions of reality, beliefs, values, causal attributions, and recurring themes) are elicited and recorded by the therapist, to be used as the raw material in subsequent therapy sessions. A major objective of cognitive therapy is to help clients to gain new perspectives on their problems. Clients are taught how their cognitions can help to explain the etiology and maintenance of their maladaptive emotional and behavioral responses. They are also taught that cognitive change is of central importance in the therapy process. Once clients have grasped these points, they are more likely to be motivated to engage in therapeutic interventions (Meichenbaum, 1976).

The course of therapy alternates between interventions designed to correct faulty cognitions, and interventions designed to increase behavioral competencies. The first of the two major categories of interventions, the cognitive restructuring therapies, are designed to help clients to discover and detect their maladaptive cognitions, to recognize their negative impact, and to supplant them with more appropriate and adaptive thought patterns. Two of the original cognitive restructuring approaches described in the literature are Ellis' Rational Emotive Therapy (Ellis, 1962) and Beck's Cognitive Therapy (Beck, 1976). Ellis viewed the client's internal dialogue as a reflection of irrational belief systems, while Beck viewed the client's thoughts and images as reflections of faulty thinking styles which had to be examined and corrected if the client was to get better.

Coping-skills therapies are a collection of procedures that place their emphasis on helping the client to develop a repertoire of skills that will facilitate adaptation in a variety of stressful situations. An underlying premise is that emotional disorders, such as depression and anxiety, are partially related to a client's failure to develop the necessary skills to cope with what he or she, or others in his or her environment, consider to be routine duties and tasks, or appropriate behaviors. Skill training is designed to foster the client's sense of self adequacy and efficacy.

Coping-skills interventions include procedures such as activity scheduling, assertiveness training, problem-solving training, and self-control skill training. These interventions are comprised of both behavioral and cognitive components, although they tend to be predominantly behavioral in focus. Various forms and components of many of these procedures were originally introduced by behavior therapists.

In cognitive-behavioral approaches, targeted problem behaviors are specified precisely in operational terms, while seminal cognitions related to the problem behaviors are identified, since they function as stimuli in controlling the dysfunctional overt behaviors. Therapists select appropriate techniques and use their own creativity in devising ways of teaching the client more adaptive behaviors to be used in daily life. Therapists use devices such as modeling and behavioral and covert rehearsal during the therapy session to teach the client new coping skills. Principles of operant and classical conditioning, social learning theory, and cognitive mediation are incorporated into therapy interventions to produce changes in targeted dysfunctional behaviors and cognitions, as well as to shape more adaptive behaviors.

Analysis of maladaptive cognitive-behavioral sequences is carried out by therapist and client on an ongoing basis. As the contingencies of reinforcement that maintain unwanted behaviors are identified, therapy techniques are applied in order to alter these contingencies. Cognitive-behavioral psychotherapies are active and goal-oriented, incorporating educational methods such as agenda setting, structure, clarification, feedback, reflection, practice, and homework. The teaching component also involves therapist modelling of new ways of thinking and approaching problems. Continual evaluation of therapy in progress, along with evaluation of results, is also an integral part of the therapy process.

A collaborative and empirical working relationship is established between therapist and client. Clients are encouraged to try out newly learned behaviors in their day-to-day life on the premise that they will be less likely to resist suggestions for change if they can be pursuaded to experiment with new behaviors that will have more rewarding consequences.

The feedback component is crucial to insure that the client has understood the concepts and is sufficiently involved in the therapy process, especially with adolescent clients who may not have initiated the therapy endeavor. This is achieved by direct questioning by the therapist and by careful attention to nonverbal language and affective shifts.

Periodic evaluation of treatment success takes place throughout the course of therapy. Repeated measures, using some of the original assessment instruments or self-monitoring techniques, are employed to determine whether there has been a significant reduction in the frequency and severity of the client's unwanted behaviors, cognitions and emotions. The therapist also seeks to evaluate clients' perceptions of their own progress in terms of daily functioning in various problem areas.

In recent years, cognitive-behavioral approaches have been found to be effective in treating a variety of adolescent disorders, including depression, anxiety disorders, eating disorders, conduct disorders, and disorders of impulse control (Bedrosian, 1981; Block, 1978; Clarke, Lewinsohn & Hops, 1990; DiGiuseppe, 1988; Schrodt & Wright, 1986; Schrodt & Fitzgerald, 1987; Snyder & White, 1979). Characteristics of cognitive-behavioral therapy approaches such as the collaborative and empirical working relationship, the active, goal-oriented, problem-oriented approach, teaching of coping skills, and the emphasis on feedback have been found to be particularly well suited to address problematic aspects of therapy with adolescent clients (Schrodt & Fitzgerald, 1987).

The most effective approaches with adolescents tend to be those which are action-oriented at the start and geared to what the adolescent perceives as "the problem" requiring change. Generally, coping-skills interventions are introduced almost immediately to alter aspects of these perceived problems, so that clients will experience some improvement in symptomatology and therefore be more likely to become involved in their own self-directed programs of behavioral change. However, the therapist will need to strike the appropriate balance between emphasis on self-analytical, cognitive-restructuring techniques and the more action-oriented coping skills techniques. This will differ for each client, based on individual levels of emotional, intellectual, and motivational functioning.

Therapy techniques and homework assignments are simplified for adolescent clients. Interventions are broken down into smaller component steps, and the rationale behind each intervention technique is explained in simple terms. Often, it is helpful for adolescent clients to write down important points during the session, to insure understanding of concepts and procedures being taught.

Essentially, the same basic approach is applied to each symptom, whether cognitive or behavioral (Mahoney & Arnkoff, 1978):

1. The therapist elicits relevant data related to the symptom
2. Underlying assumptions and other cognitions related to the symptom are explored
3. Behavioral- and cognitive-intervention techniques are initiated, the underlying rationale explained, data are authenticated through cognitive techniques, and skills are taught and practiced during the session

4. Homework is assigned. The client is asked to practice or experiment with new behavioral or cognitive responses learned
5. Evaluation of therapy effectiveness

A COGNITIVE SOCIAL-LEARNING THEORY PERSPECTIVE ON ADOLESCENCE

Cognitive-behavioral therapy approaches are consistent with a cognitive social-learning theory conceptualization of both normal and abnormal adolescent development. Social learning theory draws on concepts from a variety of psychological sources, and theoretical concepts are tested empirically. Essential theoretical constructs include the following: that behavior is controlled by its consequences and antecedent discriminitive stimuli, that complex behavior patterns are learned through imitation of observed models, and that learning and performance of behaviors are commonly mediated by cognitive processes.

Application of social learning theory to adolescence has been greatly influenced by the work of Albert Bandura (Bandura & Walters, 1959, 1963; Bandura, 1977). Particular emphasis is placed on the influence of reinforcement contingencies associated with social conditioning shaping different aspects of an adolescent's personality and behavior. Social conditioning is under the influence of the parents' childrearing practices, cultural and social expectations of family and peers, and the child's exposure to influential models, especially parental models initially, and subsequently peer models to an increasing degree as the youngster approaches adolescence. With the onset of adolescence, parents and teachers often decline as important models, while the peer group and selected entertainment heroes become increasingly important as models, especially if parent-adolescent communication breaks down.

Bandura's approach is an outgrowth of earlier behavioral and social-learning models, with some significant new developments. In the early sixties, some behaviorists began to acknowledge the legitimacy of private events as a focus of therapy. Ellis (1962) and Beck (1963) identified the role of irrational beliefs contributing to psychological disorders. Later, Bandura argued that the process of therapy is dependent upon cognitive mechanisms that are effectively activated through behavioral procedures. This initiated a conceptual integration of cognitive and behavioral perspectives.

This "cognitive" social-learning perspective differs from earlier behaviorist models in its interpretation of change processes in psychotherapy, while simultaneously sharing many of the same specific procedures. Whereas earlier behaviorists argued that behavior modification results from the direct effects of the reinforcement contingencies on the response, cognitive social-learning theorists would argue that the reinforcement procedures have not simply strengthened the response, but have produced a cognitive association between the response and its consequences, in the form of the individual's own "rules" for future actions (Mahoney, 1980).

Whereas behavior analysis focuses mainly on overt behavior, and cognitive analysis focuses primarily on the causal role of maladaptive thought patterns associated with psychological disorders, cognitive social-learning theorists have sought to integrate the three regulatory systems of antecedent, consequent, and mediational variables into one theoretical framework (Bandura, 1977; Wilson, 1980). Mechanisms of classical and operant conditioning are presented in more cognitive terms, so that conditioned responses are no longer seen as automatic responses, but as self-activated responses based on learned expectations.

Reinforcements are no longer viewed as automatic strengtheners of behavior, but as sources of information and incentive governing behavior. Internal cognitive processes, which help to determine what is attended to by the individual, how it is initially processed, and whether it will be remembered, are viewed as mediating antecedent and consequent external events that influence behavior. The cognitive social-learning model is similar to phenomenological models of behavior in its emphasis on the role of subjective perceptions, but it differs from phenomenological models in its greater reliance on empirical assessment methods.

According to this perspective, the same principles of learning would be used to explain the development of both normal and abnormal adolescent behavior. The learning process involves cognitive mechanisms that operate through four basic forms of learning: direct associative learning, vicarious learning, symbolic instruction, and symbolic logic, all of which have implications for assessment and therapy (Bandura, 1977).

Direct associative learning (learning under the control of immediate external circumstances) results from parental disciplinary techniques and parental attempts to set down and enforce rules and regulations. Vicarious learning refers to learning acquired through indirect, rather than direct, experiences. Youngsters learn by observing the consequences of the behavior of others, such as parent or peer models. Another form of indirect learning, symbolic instruction, refers to learning through written or spoken language, so that certain beliefs and attitudes may be communicated to the adolescent by parents. Finally, symbolic logic is a form of learning through which a person draws inferences from available information. Reasoning is used to predict consequences or to understand personal experiences. Some of the available information that an adolescent will use in the process of drawing inferences will be in the form of memories acquired from previous experiences. Memories, in the form of either thoughts or images, are continually retrieved and have a strong impact on current feelings and actions.

Bandura emphasized that the maintenance of response patterns does not depend solely on direct external reinforcement, but also on vicarious reinforcement (the positive or negative consequences one observes in others) and on self reinforcement (when people reward themselves for work they consider of good quality). Adolescents learn to set their own level of performance and, when attaining that level, feel satisfied. Successful socialization requires that the adolescent's own judgment of his work, or self-reinforcement, become more important than outside reinforcement.

People labelled "emotionally disturbed" are characterized by the development of variant patterns of experiences due to errors or distortions in perceptions, and by lack of sufficient or appropriate performance skills. Parenting practices and parent role models shape the personality development of the child and adolescent. The family provides the conditions that contribute to effective socialization, including the development of a dependency motive so that the child desires approval and affection from others. The socialization process is viewed by Bandura and Walters (1959, 1963) as the development of habitual response patterns that are acceptable within the society in which the adolescent lives. This process is facilitated by the quality of personal contact parents give the child, and by the witholding of secondary rewards such as approval and attention, while the child is kept in a dependency relationship. If dependency behavior is punished or discouraged by lack of parental affection and nurturance, by parental rejection, or by lack of close dependency ties with the parent, the socialization process and the child's internalization of social values may be disrupted.

The role of families as described by Robin and Foster (1984), is consistent with a social-learning perspective:

> social systems of interacting members, held together by strong bonds of affection, who exercise a mutual control over each other's contingency arrangements. Contingency arrangements regulate the behavior of family members within culturally prescribed norms, or limits. The family's structure or organization defines and constrains patterns of family system regulation. Individual family members have repertoires of interpersonal skills and cognitive sets that both determine and are, in part, determined by their interactions with other members. All family activities occur within a developmental time line. (p. 197)

Since cognitions are conceptualized as learned private events and subject to the same principles as those governing overt behavior, it follows that family members' beliefs, expectations, and attributions, as well as their information-processing styles, will significantly influence family interactions. Maladaptive cognitions held by family members will contribute to parent-adolescent conflict both as mechanisms of processing relationship information (e.g. habitual distortion of reality) and as content variables (e.g. particular dysfunctional self statements and themes).

Social learning theory would consider rebellious, disobedient, and nonconforming behavior as lawfully related to specific social situations and antecedent factors. Pronounced changes in behavior often accompany the onset of adolescence.

Although acknowledging the influence of physiological and hormonal changes on behavior following the onset of puberty, Bandura attributes adolescent behaviors such as rebellion, dependency conflicts, and peer-group conformity primarily to sudden changes in the social training situation, family structure, peer expectations, and other aspects of the youngster's environment (Muuss, 1988). Adolescent aggression is viewed as the consequence of specific antecedent conditions in the child-rearing pattern and the parent-adolescent relationship, such as dependency training, socialization pressure, imitation, and modeling.

NORMAL AND ABNORMAL ADOLESCENT DEVELOPMENT

With the onset of adolescence, the youngster's cognitive development has generally advanced to a stage that gradually allows for deeper levels of analytical and abstract thinking (Inhelder & Piaget, 1958). The youngster no longer accepts the explanations of adults to the same extent as in earlier childhood. The adolescent now begins to generate alternative interpretations and solutions to problems, and to evaluate these alternatives for himself or herself. This is usually accompanied by a new tendency to question authority. Some degree of questioning of rules and regulations, and even of rebellion and refusal to conform to parental or school demands, is viewed as normal development. However, when rebellion seriously compromises future development, for example by impeding school progress or by interfering with development of satisfying pro-social peer relationships, the likelihood of enduring emotional and behavioral disorders is increased.

Developmental psychologists have identified five critical developmental tasks or demands of the adolescent years that must be mastered for a successful transition to adulthood: (1) achievement of independence from parents, (2) adjustment to the physical and psychosexual changes of puberty, (3) development of a system of values and a sense of identity, (4) establishment of effective relationships with peers, and (5) preparation for a vocation or career (Conger, 1977).

Developmental factors are considered by many to be crucial in defining healthy psychological functioning. For example, Achenback (1980) recommends that children be assessed in terms of adaptive progression along one or more dimensions of normal development, such as learning to get along in one's social context by forming friendships, working cooperatively at age appropriate tasks, or obeying rules of society.

Anna Freud (1965) cautioned that many identified childhood and adolescent symptoms are brought about by stresses inherent in the developmental process itself, and are not indicative of a truly pathological process. These symptoms appear during a phase of growth that makes unusually high demands on the youngster's resources. If the situation is not mishandled by the parent, these symptoms will subsequently disappear as adaptation to the developmental level takes place. Since the child's level of functioning normally fluctuates unceasingly, the one aspect of the child's activity that can give an accurate picture of pathology is a serious blockage of the developmental process, namely the child's capacity to move forward in progressive steps until maturation. If this vital process is left intact, mental upsets can be taken as a matter of course.

According to Millon's (1981) perspective, pathologenic learning may arise from: (1) persistent events that create intense anxieties in the child, along with consequently adaptive, self-protective reactions and long-term coping styles and anticipations that diminish anxiety initially, but are maladaptive in the long run, (2) simple conditioning or imitation of maladaptive behaviors, and (3) lack of sufficient experiences necessary for learning adaptive coping behaviors. Examples of the latter include insufficient social experiences, leading to inadequate social skills, or insufficient problem-solving and communication skill training.

Healthy children develop a flexibility in coping strategies and the ability to match appropriate behaviors suited to particular situations. They appraise the situation accurately, apply actions that they have learned were successful in similar situations in the past, or devise novel approaches if the learned strategies are inadequate. At times, if rational task-oriented behaviors do not provide a direct solution to problems, healthy coping may also involve some reliance on distortions to ameliorate discomfort. Traditionally, these patterns of cognitive distortion have been referred to as defense mechanisms, such as rationalization, sublimation, and denial. It is only when the discomforts are too severe or too persistent, that a child's otherwise "healthy" cognitive distortion patterns become pathological. Children and adolescents may learn to expect that the problems and stresses will never subside. Consequently, they may begin to use cognitive distortion patterns indiscriminately as a coping strategy, rather than equipping themselves with more adequate coping behaviors.

Petersen and Hamburg (1986) cite evidence suggesting that adolescents engaging in one behavior that deviates from the norm are more likely to simultaneously or subsequently engage in other abnormal behaviors. Individual adolescents will also tend to manifest problems that overlap two or more of the traditional diagnostic categories. These authors cite further evidence to suggest that about half the psychiatric disorders manifested during adolescence are continuations of problems of earlier childhood.

A significant increase in the frequency of depressive conditions and bipolar affective disorders occurs during the adolescent period as compared to childhood, accompanied by an increase in the frequency of attempted suicide (Rutter, 1986). Other disorders increasing in frequency during adolescence include conduct disorders (Robins, 1979), and anorexia nervosa (Johnson, 1982). The nature of anxiety disorders changes with the onset of adolescence, away from characteristic childhood phobias such as animal phobias toward agoraphobia and social phobias (Marks & Gelder, 1966).

STUDIES OF PARENTING AND FAMILY INTERACTION PATTERNS RELATED TO ADOLESCENT DISORDERS

In the past decades, a great deal of theory and research has focused on the relationship between dysfunctional child-management techniques and family-interaction patterns and adolescent emotional and behavioral disorders. These studies provide support for a cognitive social-learning perspective on abnormal adolescent development.

Dysfunctional Parenting Behaviors Linked to Adolescent Disorders

Clinicians have repeatedly identified links between various child-management styles and corresponding child, adolescent, and adult disorders. For example, Missildine (1963), drawing on his clinical work with children and their parents, outlined seven categories of dysfunctional parental childrearing styles and corresponding categories of maladaptive response patterns manifested by the child. These categories included: punitive parent, rejecting parent, overcoercive parent, overindulgent parent, oversubmissive parent, neglectful parent, and perfectionistic parent. Categories of characteristic maladaptive adolescent response patterns, corresponding to each dysfunctional parenting style identified by Missildine, are shown in Appendix C.

Numerous research studies have sought to demonstrate links between inadequate parenting and adolescent emotional and behavioral disorders that undermine successful coping in the family, peer, and school environments. For example, parental punitiveness, characterized by verbal and physical aggression, has been linked to adolescent aggression, and other conduct disorders (Bandura & Walters, 1963; Herbert, 1980; Nichols, 1984; Sears, 1961). Several parent factors have been found to be related to episodes of child abuse, including deficits in childrearing and social skills, extreme sensitivity to stress, impulsivity, and cognitive distortions and misattributions (Morton, Twentyman & Azar, 1988).

Parental rejection and hostility have been linked to subsequent social withdrawal, low self esteem, antisocial behavior, and depression in adolescence and adulthood (Becker, 1964; Crook, Raskin & Eliot, 1981; Herbert, 1980). Severe parental emotional neglect of the child has been linked to extreme depression, hopelessness, and diffuse anger (DiGiuseppe, 1988).

Authoritarian parenting, which relies on excessive use of coercion, has been linked to dysfunctional adolescent dependence on the parent, undermining the adolescent's ability to function independently from parents. Independence is seen as a necessary prerequisite for successful adjustment to physical and psychosexual changes of puberty, development of a system of values and a sense of identity, establishment of effective peer relationships, and preparation for a vocation or career (Bloom, 1980; Conger, 1977).

Lax, or inconsistent discipline is another dysfunctional parenting style, characterized by parental failure to administer consistent sanctions for adolescent misdemeanors, parental threats which are not followed up, mild, ineffective punishments, failure to establish explicit rules, and parental submission to adolescent coercion. Lax, inconsistent approaches to discipline have been linked to components of adolescent conduct disorders, including poor impulse control, lack of empathy, and deficits in internal rule formation (DiGiuseppe, 1988; Herbert, 1980; Nichols, 1984; Patterson, 1975; Wright, 1971).

Absence of Effective Parenting Behaviors

Parents of adolescents with psychological disorders are also characterized by failure to manifest certain *positive* parenting behaviors linked to healthy adolescent development. In terms of child-management techniques, they are characterized by failure to reward good behavior, failure to use positive reinforcement in the form of praise, failure to reward and condition prosocial behaviors such as honesty, self control, helpfulness, and problem-solving skills, and failure to use "psychological" discipline techniques, such as threatened withdrawal of approval and love following misdeameanors, and reasoning and explanation to back up their decisions (Nichols, 1984; Wright, 1971). They are also characterized by failure to provide explicit rules, failure to make firm moral demands, and failure to provide adequate supervision, which often stems from family disadvantage and disorganization (Herbert, 1980).

Failure to exhibit behaviors consistent with family cohesiveness is also cited. Orford (1980) outlines what he considers to be the chief characteristics of a cohesive family, on the basis of clinical studies. Family cohesion is defined as the extent to which family members are considered to be commited, helpful, and supportive to each other. Cohesive families are characterized by (1) time spent in shared activities, (2) relatively low rates of withdrawal, avoidance, and segregated activities, (3) a high rate of warm interactions, versus critical hostile interactions, (4) fuller communication between members, (5) generally favorable, versus critical, evaluation of family members, (6) perceived affection between family members, and (7) satisfaction with the family group and optimism about its future stability.

Factors Related to Excessive Parental-Adolescent Conflict

Robin and his colleagues have carried out extensive work in the area of parent-adolescent conflict (Robin & Foster, 1984, 1989). When developmental changes of adolescence disrupt existing patterns, the way in which the family members go about finding new patterns to accommodate the maturing adolescent determines whether normal levels of parent-adolescent conflict will escalate to clinical proportions. These authors identify the following family factors that predispose family members to excessive conflict: (1) poor problem-solving skills interfering with conflict resolution, (2) poor communication skills, (3) distorted cognitions held by both adolescent clients and their parents, and (4) structural family problems, such as too much or too little adolescent autonomy and dysfunctional cross-generational coalitions that undermine effective parental control. In addition, parents and adolescents involved in family therapy frequently lack assertiveness skills, so that they are deficient in the ability to make requests of other family members, to refuse others' requests, and to give and receive positive compliments (Epstein, Schlesinger & Dryden, 1988).

Too little adolescent autonomy may result in parental loss of affectionate reinforcers, or in guilt and anxiety experienced by adolescents stemming from perceived disloyalty to the family following rebellious independent behaviors. Too much adolescent autonomy is problematic when the teenager lacks sufficient judgment to make mature, self-enhancing choices. Dysfunctional cross-generational coalitions may occur when one parent sides with the adolescent against the other parent, thereby undermining disciplinary effectiveness.

Robin and his colleagues have identified characteristic components of dysfunctional communication styles in families referred for therapy, such as defensiveness, commands, ignoring, "putdowns," and overall negative styles. In comparison, control families are characterized by higher rates of positive and supportive communication, and by higher rates of agreements, evaluations, humor, problem specification, and solution proposal (Robin & Foster, 1984; Robin & Weiss, 1980).

Family Factors Associated with Adolescent Conduct Disorders

The following factors have been found to characterize families of youngsters with persistent conduct disorders: (1) discord and quarreling, (2) lack of affection, (3) discipline that is inconsistent, ineffective, and either too severe or lax, (4) divorce or separation of parents, (5) parents, especially fathers, with high rates of psychological problems, particularly excessive aggression, and (6) parents showing excessive rejecting, hostile, or critical behavior toward children (Herbert, 1980). Delinquents also tend to be poorly supervised by parents, with poor supervision in turn related to family disadvantage and disorganization. There is a greater tendency for working-class children to move out of normal adult control and supervision at an earlier age than their middle-class counterparts, which may help to explain the frequently-cited higher incidence of delinquency among working-class youth.

Herbert suggests that many conduct disorders take root because of the inability of parents to confront their youngster's coercive behavior at an important developmental stage. It is crucial that parents take control of the son's or daughter's behavior in a manner that will shape empathy and impulse control in the child—prerequisites for the child's socialization and moral development. Parents of adolescents manifesting conduct disorders have been found to unwittingly provide positive reinforcement for deviant adolescent behavior, including coercive behaviors (DiGiuseppe, 1988; Patterson, 1975). DiGiuseppe reviews research suggesting that parents of conduct disorder children are less effective in stopping their children's deviant behavior, more vague in giving commands, more likely to be involved in long sequences of coercive behavior with their children, less likely to perceive deviant behavior, and more likely to provide attention and positive consequences for deviant behavior, more punitive, and more likely to issue commands.

Additional parent behaviors interfering with effective child management include severe marital discord, divorce, separation, family violence, parental psychiatric problems, and parental alcoholism (Herbert, 1980; Petersen & Hamberg, 1986; Steinglass et al., 1987). What is probably crucial in the upbringing of conduct-disorder adolescents is that early maladaptive learning was continually reinforced, while pro-social actions were not encouraged so as to persist over time to counteract, compete with, and replace maladaptive patterns.

Fostering of pro-social behavior is as much a part of effective parental discipline as suppression of the child's unacceptable behaviors, so that praise and encouragement are as important as punishment. Some pro-social behaviors that must be rewarded and shaped in the home include honesty, helpfulness, and self control (so that the youngster learns to produce changes in his own behavior in order to conform to specific standards). Honesty, helpfulness, and self-control must be both rewarded and modeled by parents, so that it would be expected that parents who are low on these qualities themselves, and who refrain from praising their children for displaying these behaviors, would be those parents who have children who are also deficient in these qualities.

Problems occur when important conditions in a parent's approach to childrearing, known to foster internalized rule formation in the child, are lacking (Wright, 1971). These include lack of firm moral demands made on the youngster, lack of consistent use of sanctions administered for misconduct, and lack of effective psychological disciplinary techniques (such as threatened withdrawal of approval and love following misdemeanors, and reasoning and explanations to back up parental decisions).

Patterson (1975, 1982) lists possible reasons for a youngster's failure to replace primitive coercive behaviors with more mature adaptive behaviors. These include (1) the parent's failure to condition pro-social skills such as the use of language for problem-solving and other self-help skills, (2) the parent's provision of rich schedules of positive reinforcement for coercive behaviors, (3) parental inconsistent or lax use of punishment following a youngster's display of coercive behaviors, and (4) parental use of weak conditioned punishers as consequences for coercion. According to Patterson's coercion theory, the consistent application of effective punishment such as time out and loss of privileges is necessary for long-term reduction in rates of children's antisocial behavior. Patterson and Stouthamer-Loeber's (1984) findings suggest the importance of parental monitoring and discipline. Parents of delinquent adolescents were found to be indifferent trackers of their sons' whereabouts, the kind of companions their sons kept, or the type of activities in which the sons engaged.

Dysfunctional Cognitions Characterizing Families of Disturbed Adolescents

A body of research in recent years has grown out of attempts to identify categories of cognitions characteristic of families of problem adolescents. For example, Roehling and Robin (1986) identified unrealistic beliefs that differentiated distressed families of adolescents with adjustment, conduct, or relationship problems from normal families. Parents and adolescents from problem families were found to adhere more rigidly to a number of unrealistic beliefs that tended to elicit angry affect, impede problem-solving, and increase reciprocal negative communication. Fathers from problem families were found to have a higher frequency of beliefs characterized by themes of (1) ruination (the belief that with too much freedom teenagers will ruin their futures), (2) obedience (the belief that parents deserve absolute respect and obedience), (3) perfectionism (the belief that teenagers should instinctively behave in a flawless manner), and (4) malicious intent (the belief that adolescents intentionally misbehave to hurt their parents).

Problem adolescents displayed more unreasonable beliefs than normal controls concerning (1) ruination (the belief that parental rules and regulations will ruin the teenage years), (2) unfairness (the belief that it is catastrophic when parents treat teenagers unfairly), and (3) autonomy (the belief that parents should give adolescents complete freedom to make decisions concerning rules and regulations).

Maladaptive beliefs held by parents experiencing excessive parent-adolescent conflict include parental self-blame (a belief that the parent is at fault for the adolescent's misbehavior), and parental fear of the adolescent's disapproval of childrearing actions (Robin & Foster, 1984). Additional dysfunctional cognitive patterns observed in families with excessive parent-adolescent conflict include inflexible beliefs precluding democratic decision-making and negative interpretations of relationship events related to corresponding hostile affect (Robin & Foster, 1989).

DiGiuseppe (1988) found families of children with conduct disorders to be characterized by dysfunctional parental beliefs about childrearing underlying negative parental emotional reactions such a guilt, anger, and discomfort anxiety For example, attributions of self-blame interfering with implementation of disciplinary measures were found to be characteristic of parents who believed that they were somehow responsible for having caused the youngster's problem or for failing to prevent the problem.

Epstein et al. (1988) recommend paying particular attention to three categories of inaccurate or distorted cognitions held by family members: (1) beliefs about the nature of family relationships (including unrealistic beliefs about loyalty expectations and other qualities that constitute "good" family interactions, and beliefs about family rules and structure, especially if these beliefs are not shared by both parents), (2) attributions about the causes of family problems, and (3) expectancies about the likelihood that certain events will occur in the future.

Cognitive distortions characteristic of abusive parents include (1) unrealistic expectations about what a child or adolescent should be doing at any given age, and (2) parental misattributions of deliberately antagonistic behavior or negative personality traits, such as "bad" or "evil," to the child (Morton et. al., 1988).

Characteristic Cognitions of Adolescent Clients

Investigations of typical cognitive themes, distortions, and cognitive response styles of adolescent clients have yielded useful data for the practitioner. Cognitive distortions of adolescent therapy clients tend to revolve around concerns about physical appearance and physical changes accompanying the onset of puberty, sexual identity and sexuality (including dysfunctional ideas accompanying masturbation, gender confusion, and homosexual urges and behaviors), competency in school, peer relationships, athletics, and concerns about autonomy and control in relationships with parents and school authorities (Bedrosian, 1981).

In a study comparing cognitions of normal controls with adolescent girls referred for therapy because of dysfunctional interpersonal coping styles, referred clients reported a higher frequency of negative descriptors when asked how their parents and their classmates would describe them (Zarb, 1990). In contrast to neutral and positive descriptors reported by controls, referred subjects reported that their parents would describe them with negative discriptors categorized as "promiscuous," "psychologically abnormal," "worthless," and "cruel." They reported that classmates would describe them with negative descriptors falling into categories of "inadequate academic performance," "psychopathology," and "conduct disorder."

The referred subjects also differed from controls in their typical interpersonal coping styles during stressful interactions with parents and peers. When asked to report their typical responses in stressful situations with parents, the referred subjects, unlike the controls, tended to report responses categorized as "active defiance," "passive defiance," and "passive helplessness." In stressful situations involving peers, referred subjects tended to report responses categorized as "verbal abuse," "physical abuse," and "withdraw-internalize," In contrast, controls tended to report responses categorized as "talk-it-over" and "defer."

Troubled adolescents have also been found to be deficient in interpersonal problem-solving skills and in the ability to take the perspective of others. Research suggests that maladjusted adolescents are less able than normals to conceptualize a step-by-step plan that incorporates details of action and consideration of potential obstacles (means-ends thinking). Maladjusted adolescents also tended to conceptualize a narrower range of solutions to everyday problems (alternative thinking) and are less proficient at perspective-taking (the appreciation of the perspective of others involved in a particular situation) (Spivak, Platt & Shure, 1976).

PSYCHOTHERAPY WITH ADOLESCENT CLIENTS

Theory and research reviewed thus far suggest the need for a therapy approach that takes into account significant normative changes that occur during adolescence, both within and outside of the individual, that produce challenge, if not stress, for the "average" adolescent. (Petersen & Hamburg, 1986). Changes in aspects of individual maturation during adolescence include biological changes in physical appearance and size with the onset of puberty, changes in cognitive capacity (e.g. development of a capacity for abstract thinking), changes in psychological development (e.g. greater capacity for self awareness and moral reasoning), and changes in social development (e.g. increased emphasis on intimacy with peers, conformity to peer group, and greater anxiety about friendships). Aspects of maturation occur at different rates for different individuals, so there will be substantial variation among adolescents in behavioral and cognitive abilities and skills mastered at any given age.

Therapy approaches with adolescent clients will also need to take into account contextual changes during the teenage years, affecting family, peer group, and school functioning. In the family, important functional changes occur in family interactions and in the parent-adolescent relationship. These typically stem from parents' attempts to resist the adolescent's demands for greater autonomy. Family patterns of communication in family decision-making situations may also be altered, accompanying the youngster's gradual development of mature, adult-like behaviors.

In the peer context, the adolescent will generally have an opportunity for contact with a greater variety of peers, in a variety of settings. Romantic involvements are also likely to develop during middle adolescence. Within the school context, there is a transition from a protected elementary-school environment to a more complex intermediate- or secondary-school setting, accompanied by a transition from single to multiple classrooms, teachers, and sets of classmates.

For most adolescents, these normative changes actually appear to create resources and opportunity for growth, resulting in increased capacities and competence, such as increased responsibility for ones own behavior. However, some adolescents experience unusual stresses and fail to adapt to these normative changes. Maladaptive patterns of coping with these maturational or contextual demands may significantly jeopardize adaptive coping in subsequent phases of development, resulting in chronic dysfunctional behavior styles characteristic of adolescent psychopathology. For example, an adolescent who is overwhelmed by the challenges of transition to the more complex structure of secondary school, may experience severe depression, followed by social withdrawal, avoidance of school leading to academic failure, increased parent-adolescent conflict, and eventual withdrawal from school, affecting potential for future development.

The comprehensive cognitive-behavioral approach to psychotherapy with adolescent clients espoused in this book endeavors to meet the needs of adolescent clients through a combination of individual sessions with the adolescent client, family sessions, parent-training sessions, and school-based interventions. Involvement of parents in assessment and therapy is important since parents, as the primary socializing agents, and family interaction patterns still significantly influence emotional and behavioral functioning of adolescent children.

Family sessions are often used as a device for securing the involvement of unmotivated adolescent clients (and parents) in the therapy endeavor, since it is important that both are actively involved in their own self-directed program of behavior change. Family sessions allow adolescent clients to negotiate for some of the things they want in exchange for altering some of their own behaviors. They also provide a mileau for changing dysfunctional family interaction patterns and cognitions maintaining adolescent disorders and for teaching communication, problem solving, and negotiation skills lacking in problem families.

Parent skill-training sessions are the outgrowth of research linking dysfunctional parenting to adolescent disorders. Incorporation of cognitive interventions into behaviorally-oriented, parent skill-training is important, given research demonstrating that dysfunctional parent cognitions interfere with implementation of effective child-management and disciplinary measures.

The adolescent developmental literature also suggests that cognitive restructuring interventions would be appropriate for teenage clients, in addition to more behaviorally-oriented techniques, since with the onset of adolescence the young person is capable of introspection. The emergence of new conceptual abilities accompanying the evolution of formal operational thinking described by Piaget frees the adolescent from the narrow, constricted conceptualization of self and the world accessible to the child and facilitates an ability to form alternative explanations and consider different perspectives—necessary prerequisites for cognitive-restructuring strategies. These new cognitive abilities would also be expected to facilitate the learning of problem-solving skills.

Therapists working with adolescent clients will encounter a number of problems reflecting the adolescent developmental stage, many of which are well documented in the literature. These include problems of time distortion, exaggerated sense of peer loyalties, mistrust of adults, extreme self consciousness, and periodic suspension of logic (Schrodt & Fitzgerald, 1987). Insufficient motivation for change is another common problem. Many adolescent clients are cajoled into becoming involved in psychotherapy by parents, teachers, or others, even though they themselves see no need for change. Unlike adult clients, they are unable to look back and see the chronic nature of their problem behaviors. Adolescents often mistakenly believe that their problems will suddenly disappear without effort on their part. For example, adolescents who are chronic school failures and truants will frequently state that they will have no problem passing courses next term, or whenever it is that they decide to apply themselves, even though school records indicate a long history of poor work habits and academic achievement levels far below grade level that will take a great deal of effort to change.

Client motivation is also affected when behaviors targeted for change, such as truancy or substance abuse, are under the conflicting influence of positive short-term consequences and aversive long-term consequences. Lacking a long-range perspective, adolescent clients are frequently reluctant to give up daring or reckless behaviors that gain the respect of peers and are highly rewarding in the short term.

One problem encountered periodically with adolescent clients is the young person's refusal to talk during individual therapy sessions. Adolescent clients are often shy, and uncomfortable when faced with the prospect of discussing their problems with adults. This type of situation calls for a directive approach, with considerable reliance on structured interview techniques, in order to reduce long awkward silences which could easily jeopardize the therapeutic endeavor. At other times, adolescent clients will use their silence as a manipulative ploy to force termination of therapy. The therapist may then have to rely exclusively on family sessions, where provocative comments from family members are more likely to elicit some response from the client.

Therapists must be aware of the way in which adolescent clients perceive them. They may be perceived initially as the parents' or teacher's advocate, embodying qualities that the teenager is rebelling against. It is important for the therapist to find out early on what the adolescent client wants, his or her goals for change, if any, and to convey the sense of commitment to helping clients solve what *they* perceive to be "the problem." Clients are assured that they can be taught skills that will lead to increased control over unwanted conditions, such as anxious or depressive feelings, unsuccessful relationships with parents or peers, or unpleasant school experiences.

In addition to poor motivation, therapists must also be prepared to deal with other challenging characteristics of adolescent clients, including lack of persistence, difficulty verbalizing problems and concerns, and poorly developed abstract reasoning skills. Therapy homework assignments are often not carried out, so that the majority of work with adolescent clients will often have to be accomplished during the session. Irregular attendance at therapy sessions is often a difficulty. A common frustration with adolescent clients is that when they perceive a slight improvement in their situation, they discontinue attending therapy sessions and do not reappear until they are again in a serious crisis. Although stressing the importance of regular attendance in order to ensure positive change, and in spite of having established some form of contract for attendance with the client, the therapist will still need to be flexible when clients do not show up or when they show up unexpectedly at unscheduled times.

The cognitive-behavioral approach and social learning contributions to the understanding of adolescence, and related research reviewed in this chapter have formed the basis for selection of assessment methods and instruments. These will be outlined in the next chapter.

2

The Assessment Approach and Data Collection Methods

The literature on factors related to adolescent psychopathology reviewed in the previous chapter suggests the need for a multidimensional assessment approach tapping a variety of family, peer, and school variables. This literature and the cognitive-social learning conceptualization of normal and abnormal adolescent development influenced the selection of variables for the assessment approach outlined in this chapter. The design of specific assessment procedures and techniques was influenced by the cognitive-behavioral therapy orientation.

The therapist carries out a functional analysis of behavior by first breaking down the complex behaviors or behavior chains of vaguely-defined presenting problems such as "truancy" or "family conflict" into the various behavioral components of each problem. These are designated as target behaviors.

The therapist then endeavors to collect quantifiable and replicable measures of three types of behavior: overt motor behaviors, emotional behaviors, and cognitive verbal behaviors. Attempts are made to quantify behavioral responses associated with each presenting problem in terms of frequency, intensity, and duration, and to identify dysfunctional behavioral excesses or deficits. Cognitions accompanying targeted dysfunctional behaviors are elicited and recorded.

The next step involves a detailed analysis of contingency arrangements influencing and controlling the occurrence of each of these target behaviors. Antecedents and consequences of dysfunctional behaviors are identified and recorded. These will include factors in the family, peer, and school environment, such as the actions of significant others (family members, peers, school personnel) that function as reinforcers maintaining problem behaviors. With this knowledge of contingencies, the therapist is in a position to plan interventions to alter environmental stimuli maintaining the unwanted behavior. The therapist will also teach the client new, more adaptive coping skills to modify dysfunctional deficits and excesses, thereby decreasing the frequency and intensity of unwanted problematic behaviors.

Constructs from social-learning theory and applied behavior analysis are useful in determining how a particular pattern of behavior "functions" for the adolescent client or for the family. Terms such as positive reinforcement, negative reinforcement, punishment, and avoidance are useful in explaining reported or observed behavioral sequences.

Cognitive data that are immediately accessible only to the individual must be inferred from verbal self reports of the adolescent client or the parent. Accuracy of measurement is problematic here; the assessor must keep in mind that verbal and cognitive behaviors may not always correspond.

THE ASSESSMENT APPROACH

This approach was primarily influenced by Kanfer and Saslow's (1965) guidelines for a functional behavioral analysis, Mischel's (1984) suggestions for cognitive-behavioral assessment and cognitive-assessment techniques of Beck and his colleagues, and other clinicians (Beck, 1976; Beck et al., 1979; Beck et al., 1985; Guidano & Liotti, 1983; Kendall & Korgeski, 1979; Meichenbaum, 1977; Clarke et al., 1990). Family assessment procedures were influenced by Robin and Foster (1984, 1989) and Missildine (1963).

The assessment approach and data collection instruments have been designed to insure a comprehensive assessment of major areas of the adolescent's functioning. Specifically, methods and procedures have been designed for an initial functional behavioral analysis of presenting problems, and for the assessment of cognitive variables, family variables, peer-relationship variables, and school performance variables. Procedures are also suggested for assessment of the client's coping style during preadolescent years.

Data related to the above areas will be collected from a variety of sources: the adolescent client, parents, school personnel, and the therapist's own observations of the adolescent interacting with family members, and possibly with school personnel. Four methods of assessment will be used:

1. structured clinical interviews with adolescent client and parents
2. behavioral observations during family sessions
3. repeated self report measures
4. school behavior report forms

Six major areas will be assessed, using specifically-designed data collection and data analysis instruments, as shown in Table 2.1. The objective is to provide a systematic and comprehensive probe of critical areas of the adolescent's functioning, consistent with underlying cognitive-social-learning theory and related adolescent research. This will insure sufficient information for accurate identification of major components of the youngster's problems. It will also provide the necessary background for generating accurate hypotheses about reinforcement contingencies and

TABLE 2.1
Assessment Methods

Assessment Areas	Data Collection Instruments	Data Summary Instruments
Presenting Problem Assessment	• Initial Presenting Problems Interview	• Presenting Problem Initial Treatment Plan
Cognitive Assessment	• Thoughts and Behavior Diary	• Cognitive Data Summary Form
Family Assessment	• Family-Peer-School Performance Interview Parts A-D • Family Communication Patterns Checklist • Family Problem-Solving Patterns Checklist • Family Structural and External Problems Checklist • Dysfunctional Childrearing Styles Checklist	• Functional Analysis of Interpersonal Interactions
Peer Relations Assessment	• Family-Peer-School Performance Interview Parts A-D	
School Performance Assessment	• Family-Peer-School Performance Interview Parts A-E • Teacher Report Form • Past School Record Form	• School Data Summary Form
Preadolescent Behavior Assessment	• Family-Peer-School Performance Interview Part D • Past School Record Form	

influential models that have shaped, and are currently maintaining, the adolescent's dysfunctional behaviors. Involvement of parents in the assessment process is important, and it is also helpful to secure involvement of school personnel, whenever appropriate and feasible.

It may not always be possible to use every assessment technique with every client, due to time constraints, and to the problem of unavailable or uncooperative parents or teachers. However, attempts should be made to secure data from as many sources as possible.

Most of the assessment procedures have been designed for use during initial sessions, although this may not be the most feasible arrangement in some cases. An important consideration is the necessity of demonstrating the benefits of the therapy to the adolescent or to the family early on, and this often necessitates introduction of therapy interventions during initial sessions. In any case, the assessment is meant to be ongoing, so that fresh information about the client's habitual thought and behavioral patterns, and the consequences of the client's adaptive and maladaptive behaviors in home, peer, and school environments will be evaluated repeatedly throughout the duration of therapy.

In addition to the data collection instruments listed in Table 2.1, data analysis instruments have also been designed to be used as tools by the therapist in organizing and making sense of information collected, and for planning treatment interventions. Therapy strategies and outcome criteria for determining therapy effectiveness are meant to be a direct outgrowth of the proposed assessment procedures. As shown in Table 2.1, the data collection instruments include:

I. Structured Clinical Interviews
    Initial Presenting Problems Interview (Appendix A)
    Family-Peer-School Performance Interview (Appendix B) (Client and
        Parent Forms)
II. Family Behavior Checklists (Appendix C)
    Family Communication Patterns Checklist
    Family Problem-Solving Patterns Checklist
    Family Structural and External Problems Checklist
    Dysfunctional Childrearing Styles Checklist
III. Repeated Self Report Measures
    The Thoughts and Behavior Diary (Table 2.4)
    Self Evaluation of Family-Peer-School Coping (Table 2.11)
IV. School Data Forms
    Teacher Report Form (Table 2.8)
    Past School Record Form (Table 2.9)

The two structured clinical interviews, the Presenting Problems Interview and the Family-Peer-School Performance Interview, were designed to be used during individual interviews with the adolescent client and with parents. (A corresponding form of the Family-Peer-School Performance Interview has been specifically designed for parents.) Basically, the adolescent is asked to provide information about his or her major complaints and problems, and to describe his or her own behavioral interactions with significant others, as well as his or her performance in home, peer, and school environments. Parents are asked to present their views of the adolescent's problems, their views and approach to discipline with the adolescent, and their description of their son's or daughter's typical daily activities, school behavior, and preadolescent coping styles.

The four family behavior checklists are useful references to help the therapist to identify both maladaptive and adaptive interpersonal response styles, along with family skill deficits for therapy intervention.

Two instruments have been designed to be used as repeated self-report measures with the adolescent client: The Thoughts and Behavior Diary and the Self Evaluation of Family-Peer-School Coping form. The first is used to encourage the adolescent to record behavioral and cognitive responses to upsetting or stressful situations that occur during the week, between therapy sessions. This generates data for an ongoing functional analysis of the client's thought and behavior patterns related to identified problems. The latter is a useful technique for ongoing evaluation of therapy effectiveness.

Additional data collection forms include (1) the Teacher Report Form and (2) Past School Record Form. The first was designed to tap teachers' perceptions of the client's current school performance. The second provides a format for collecting information from the client's ongoing school record file.

One of the structured interviews, the Family-Peer-School Behavior Interview, has been designed to elicit information relevant to all of the major assessment areas. Therefore it will be discussed at this time before going on to address each area separately.

The Family-Peer-School Behavior Interviews

The Adolescent Client Form and the Parent Form of the Family-Peer-School Behavior Interview are shown in Appendix B. They have been designed to elicit information about the client's functioning in his or her home, peer, and school environments, tapping information about parent and peer models to which the client has been exposed, parenting practices that have shaped the client's development and the client's corresponding patterns of responding to these practices, the adolescent's characteristic response styles in stressful situations involving interactions with parents, peers, and teachers, and the adolescent's self-perceptions and beliefs about the way significant others evaluate him or her. It also taps information about the client's daily activities, past and present school performance, styles of coping with stress during childhood years, coping-skill strengths and deficits, and types of experiences and events that the adolescent finds positively and negatively reinforcing.

In some sections of the interview, information is obtained from both the adolescent, using the Adolescent Client Form, and from the parents, using a corresponding Parent Form. It is important to keep in mind that self-report data may not always reflect actual behavior and events, but rather the individual's *perception* of these behaviors and events. For example, discrepancies are greater between parent and adolescent reports of dyadic communication patterns in distressed, as compared to nondistressed, families (Robin & Foster, 1984). Therefore, important information is contained in discrepancies between the parents' and the adolescent's answers to corresponding questionnaire items.

The interview items have been designed to be as open-ended as possible. Most items function as a rich source of cognitive data, providing information about the adolescent's (and the parents') perceptions, causal attributions, and beliefs with respect to the client's peers, teachers, classmates, family members, and family structure and functioning.

There are five parts to the Adolescent Client Form of this interview:

Part A. Influence of Significant Others
Part B. Adolescent's Characteristic Stress-Interaction Patterns with
         Significant Others
Part C. Typical Activities of Daily Living
Part D. Preadolescent Behavior
Part E. Client's Perception of School Behavior

Part A of the interview has been designed to collect information about influential family, peer, and school role models. It also taps the adolescent's perceptions of how he or she is evaluated by significant others. The youngster is first asked to describe family members, friends, classmates, and teachers, and then he or she is asked how each would describe him or her.

The client's descriptions of his or her parents often contain information about maladaptive parental coping styles or a destructive marital relationship. For example, a father may be described as a heavy drinker or as a man with a violent temper. Similarly, descriptions of siblings and friends may reveal pertinent information about peer role models who share maladaptive coping styles. The youngster's perception of how parents, and other important people in his or her life would describe *him* or *her* provides information about the client's self concept.

The items in Part B of the interview have been designed to elicit information about the adolescent's typical response styles in stressful situations involving significant others. First, the youngster is asked to give examples of recent upsetting situations involving each parent. This provides insight into the types of situations that are upsetting for the adolescent, typical parental response styles, and the client's typical way of handling these situations, as well as his or her thoughts and feelings at the time. The same questions will also be asked with respect to peers and teachers.

The youngster is also asked directly about parental disciplinary styles, about his or her own characteristic responses to parental disciplinary actions, and about the final consequences of these actions. This will provide insight into the effectiveness of the parents' disciplinary attempts. The youngster should be encouraged to expand upon his or her answers to these questions so as to provide enough information to allow the therapist to generate hypotheses about relationships between maladaptive parenting styles and dysfunctional response styles manifested by the adolescent. For example, if a mother takes excessive responsibility for helping her son complete homework tasks, or actually completes homework assignments for him, she may be failing to set adequate age-appropriate expectations for the son, who would have learned a general pattern of abdication of responsibility.

The items on Parts A and B of the Adolescent Client Form have been found to significantly differentiate on several variables between normal and referred adolescent girls with family-related problems. These include categories of themes characterizing perceived parental and peer evaluation, parental models, parental disciplinary practices, types of interactions with parents and peers perceived to be stressful by the adolescent, and typical adolescent response styles in stressful interactions with parents and peers (Zarb, 1990).

Part C of the interview is designed to elicit information about the client's typical patterns of daily living. The client is asked to describe a recent typical week day, and a typical day on the weekend. This information will help the therapist to detect self-defeating patterns such as excessive amounts of sleep or T.V. viewing, or extreme family disorganization. It will provide information about amount and type of activities the client engages in with peers, and about dysfunctional patterns such as long hours of loitering, or staying out all night. It also provides some indication of time spent with parents, time spent doing homework, and time spent working at part-time jobs.

Part D of the interview is designed to collect information about major stressful events or ongoing sources of stress experienced by the youngster during preadolescent years. Information about the client's strategies for coping with these events will also be collected. The second half of this section taps the client's perception of the way in which he or she was evaluated by significant people in his or her early life.

Part E of the interview is designed to elicit information about the youngster's view of his or her own academic performance, as well as his or her view of the quality of his or her relationships with significant people in the school environment. This is of particular importance for adolescents with school-related problems, but it is also crucial information for most clients since adequate school performance tends to be correlated with positive self concept.

MAJOR ASSESSMENT AREAS

Following a brief overview of the assessment process, each of the assessment areas will be discussed separately, with the corresponding data collection and analysis instruments designed for each area. The first few sessions will be geared toward obtaining sufficient information for an accurate functional analysis of behavioral and cognitive components of presenting problems and additional disorders.

An important goal of the initial interview is to establish rapport with the client and to convey the impression that identified problems are not insolvable and that the client can in fact be helped by the counselling relationship.

It is crucial that clients be given the chance to vent their feelings, concerns, and complaints during the initial session, with minimal interruption, since clients often rehearse what they plan to say before arriving at the therapist's office. This is particularly important when the client is not self-referred, but has been referred for therapy by parents or teachers. While listening to this initial outpouring, the therapist seeks to convey understanding and support.

Initially, the adolescent is encouraged to talk freely without interruption or specific directives from the therapist. This will yield crucial information about clients' major complaints, what they perceive to be the primary problems, and what worries, frightens, or depresses them most. At the same time, the therapist may begin to clarify definitions of problem areas by asking the client to give specific examples from daily life to illustrate a particular problem. As the client talks about major complaints or problems, the therapist may simply jot down key statements verbatim, particularly statements reflecting attitudes, assumptions, beliefs, and statements with high emotional content.

Periods of unstructured interview time will also yield information about what the client does and does not consider problematic. Clients may not want to acknowledge that certain of their behaviors are problematic because they do not wish to alter the status quo. It is important to pay attention to topics that clients repeatedly introduce, and to other topics that clients would be expected to introduce, but do not. Gradually, the therapist will introduce items from the Initial Presenting Problems Interview, to be followed in later sessions by introduction of data collection techniques designed for the remaining assessment areas.

The importance of individual interviews with the parents, plus at least one family assessment session, cannot be overemphasized, except in those cases where it would seriously jeopardize the therapist-client relationship or the therapy endeavor. These provide the therapist with direct exposure to parental viewpoints on the nature and cause of the adolescent's problems, the quality and characteristics of the marital relationship, each parent's evaluation of the adolescent, parental attitudes and beliefs, and pathological coping styles of family members. In addition, it gives the therapist an opportunity to assess the appropriateness and feasibility of subsequent family interventions. If the parent is unable or unwilling to attend an interview session, alternative arrangements may be possible, such as administering the "Parent Form" of the Family-School-Peer Behavior Interview over the phone.

During family sessions, the atmosphere is often emotionally charged, so that the therapist has the opportunity to witness the response styles of individual family members under stress. The therapist may use a problem-oriented format for eliciting crucial information on family functioning. Topics of family disagreement or conflict are introduced by the therapist, who then observes the behavior of various family members as they discuss or attempt to solve problems. The therapist may ask individual family members for their perceptions of the problems, and then note who tends to take the adolescent's side, if anyone, whether there is general agreement between the parents, or whether marital disagreement on issues is problematic.

Family members may be encouraged to introduce topics they perceive to be important and problematic. At times, the therapist may allow family discussions to continue unimpeded for some time. At other times, the therapist may choose to intervene, in order to elicit viewpoints and participation from various family members. The direction and content of family discussions may be controlled by therapist interjections. Examples of simple interjections include: "What are your feelings about that?" "Let's hear John's view on this point." "Can you explain to your mother why you behaved in that way?" "What was your reaction to that?"

Interviews with school personnel, when appropriate, are also highly recommended. With additional information from parent and teacher interviews and family sessions, the therapist will have a more comprehensive view of the youngster's functioning at home, with peers, and at school. Adolescent clients very often perceive themselves as blameless, and perceive their parents or teachers as the sole cause of their problems. Comparison of several viewpoints enhances accuracy of interpretation and diagnosis.

PRESENTING-PROBLEM ASSESSMENT

Clients (and those referring clients for therapy) are initially encouraged to speak freely about the problems and concerns. The therapist will gradually begin to identify major components of the presenting problems, as well as dysfunctional behaviors and cognitions, which will subsequently become targets for therapy. Data collection is aided by the structure of the Initial Presenting-Problems Interview, which was designed to be used separately with adolescent clients and with parents (and other referring agents, if applicable).

The Initial Presenting-Problems Interview

This interview, shown in Appendix A, is used to elicit detailed descriptions of presenting problem behaviors and their consequences from the point of view of both the adolescent client and the parents. The interview consists of two parts:

Part A. Problem Definition
Part B. Reinforcement Contingencies of Identified Problems

Part A directs the therapist to encourage adolescent clients to state their major complaints, their perceptions of the "problem," and reasons for seeking psychotherapy if self referred. The therapist guides the client by asking for specific examples to illustrate the complaints or problems. The therapist will also ask for information about the frequency, intensity, and duration of the specified problems, to be verified later with other data from parents, school personnel, or others. Finally, as the client talks about a particular problem and gives examples to illustrate the problem, the therapist will ask for the client's views about the cause of the problem. Clients will also be asked to report the thoughts that go through their heads when specified problems occur or when they ruminate about the problems.

Once the components of the presenting problems have been identified, the therapist is then ready to move on to Part B of this interview, which is concerned with a preliminary identification of contingencies responsible for shaping and maintaining the unwanted behavior. The therapist systematically inquires about antecedents of the problem behavior, about the reaction of significant others to the client's problems, and about other negative or positive consequences or events associated with the problem. Finally, clients are asked about their emotional responses to presenting problems (e.g. "How do you *feel* when this happens?").

Data collection using the Initial Presenting-Problems Interview" with an adolescent client is illustrated in Table 2.2. In this case, a 17-year-old boy was referred to a therapist because of chronic truancy and drug abuse in the company of peers. He had received failure grades in six out of eight courses on his March report card, in a school noted for its high academic standards. There were only two months of school left before final exams, and the boy's truancy and drug abuse had increased significantly in recent weeks. This same pattern had also occurred the previous two years.

Components of the presenting problems of academic failure, truancy, and drug abuse for this boy included: (1) the boy's sense of hopelessness, and his belief that it would be impossible to pass any of his courses, causing him to give up, (2) a habitual pattern of failure to initiate and carry through academic tasks, (3) the boy's extreme need for peer recognition and acceptance, which he was unable to achieve with pro-social peers, but *was* able to achieve with a truant peer group, and (4) insufficient academic and study skills to cope with the high standards of his school. (His achievement-test levels in math and English were far below minimal requirements for success at that particular school.)

Information was also obtained independently from the boy's father by using the same form of the Initial Presenting-Problems Interview. It became clear that the parents abdicated responsibility by failing to attempt to work through this problem with their son. Instead, they blamed their son's truant peers and irresponsible school authorities, who the parents felt were supposed to force youngsters to attend class. The parents also failed to set and enforce appropriate limits on other unacceptable behaviors, such as staying out all night. Instead, the frustrated father repeatedly

TABLE 2.2
Case Study Demonstrating Initial Presenting-Problems Interview

PART A. PROBLEM DEFINITION

Description of Presenting Problems	*Frequency, Intensity, Duration*	*Related Cognitions*
1. ACADEMIC FAILURE		
• "Don't know why I'm failing"	• 6 courses	• "Classmates think I'm dumb"
• "Can't concentrate in class"	• 2 years duration	• "Next year I'll change (pass)"
2. TRUANCY & DRUG ABUSE		
• "Don't want to skip but kids persuade me"	• daily	• "If I refuse to join the other (truant) kids, I'll be friendless"
• "Skipping is fun; school is boring"	• 6 months duration	
3. PARENT-ADOLESCENT CONFLICT		
• "Parents hate me, and want to break up my friendships"	• 4 years duration	• "Dad has no right to tell me what to do"
		• "Dad thinks I'm worthless, and he's probably right"

PART B. REINFORCEMENT CONTINGENCIES OF PRESENTING PROBLEMS

Target Behaviors	*Antecedents*	*Consequences*
1. ACADEMIC FAILURE	• client: "It's hopeless; no use trying" • poor study skills • poor academic skills	• avoidance (truancy) • parents angry; abdicate responsibility
2. TRUANCY & DRUG ABUSE	• peers suggest skipping; drugs	• temporary relief • peer approval • academic failure • school suspension
3. PARENT/ ADOLESCENT CONFLICT	• school phones parents regarding truancy	• parental anger, threats • client rebels; stays out all night

accused the son of being lazy and worthless, and threatened to expel him from the family home.

The boy's sense of hopelessness and his decision to give up was reinforced by the school's all-or-none policy, which stipulated that a student continue to attend all eight courses consistently, including those which he no longer had any chance of passing, or risk suspension from school.

TABLE 2.3
Presenting-Problems Summary and Initial Treatment Plan: Case Illustration

Targets	*Possible interventions*
1. *Academic failure* • task impersistence • study-skills deficit • academic skills deficit • "hopelessness" theme	*School Interventions:* • negotiate reduced course load • explore transfer to easier school *Individual Therapy* • study-skills training • self-monitoring training • cognitive restructuring
2. *Truancy* • truant peer associations • impulsivity	*School Interventions:* • negotiate close school-parent attendance monitoring • facilitate involvement in pro-social peer activities *Individual Therapy:* • self-monitoring training • pro-social skills training
3. *Parent/adolescent conflict* • parental abdication of responsibility • poor family communication • poor family problem solving • inadequate parental expectations • inadequate parental control	*Family Interventions:* • communication-skills training • problem-solving skills training • behavioral contracting

After information was collected from the boy and his father, the Presenting-Problems Summary and Initial Treatment Plan format (Table 2.3) was used to designate components of the presenting problems as "target behaviors." Possible therapy intervention strategies corresponding to each of the target behaviors were noted at that time.

The Presenting-Problems Summary and Initial Treatment Plan

This data analysis form was designed to aid the therapist in recording and organizing data related to presenting problems. Although all the components of the presenting problems will not not be completely clear to the therapist after the first sessions, it is still useful to use this form from the start to record and organize data.

First, the major problems are identified. The therapist then identifies components of the problem to be designated as possible target behaviors for intervention. Possible therapy interventions are also noted from the start, corresponding to each of the target behaviors or cognitions identified. The client's and family's strengths, as well as weaknesses, are also taken into account when designing therapy interventions.

The information on this form will be updated, revised, and refined each week, as part of the ongoing data collection, data analysis, and design of treatment interventions.

The use of this form with the above case history is illustrated in Table 2.3. With respect to the problem of ongoing academic failure, school interventions might involve setting up a meeting with school personnel to explore the possibility of a reduced course load, allowing the boy to drop those courses he had no chance of passing in order to increase his chances of passing the two courses in which he was still receiving borderline marks. Another intervention might be exploration of a more appropriate school for the boy for the following academic year, consistent with his current academic achievement levels, thereby increasing chances for future academic success. A meeting between family and school personnel might also be arranged in order to plan a system for closer cooperation between school and parents for monitoring the boy's attendance. Finally, the school might be asked to facilitate the boy's involvement with peers in pro-social extracurricular activities.

In terms of individual therapy, interventions were needed to alter the boy's long-standing deficits in study skills and task persistence. These might include study-skills counselling to teach the boy how to keep a record of assignments, to plan study periods, to choose an appropriate study environment, and to keep to a study schedule. Study-skills counselling and self-monitoring training would be appropriate interventions. Furthermore, in order to improve the boy's chances of forming satisfying associations with non-truant peers, social-skills training would be appropriate.

Family therapy interventions would be directed toward altering the parents' lack of effective disciplinary skills and toward their abdication of responsibility manifested in their failure to deal with their son's truancy and his disregard of parental curfews. Parental failure to establish appropriate academic expectations for their son would be another target, as well as poor communication and family problem-solving skills. Possible interventions noted were family communication skills training, problem-solving skills training, and behavior contracting.

COGNITIVE ASSESSMENT METHODS

Methods and guidelines discussed in this section are useful for initial and ongoing identification of both the adolescent client's and the parents' cognitive distortions and negative maladaptive cognitions contributing to dysfunctional behavioral and emotional patterns. They will subsequently be made aware of the part played by these cognitions in maintaining unwanted emotional and behavioral responses, and cognitive therapy interventions will then be used to alter identified dysfunctional cognitions.

What Cognitive Phenomena to Assess

With respect to types of cognitive phenomena to focus on during the ongoing assesssment, cognitive therapy research suggests the importance of self-statements, beliefs, attitudes, attributions, and self-efficacy expectations accompanying stressful situations and conditions (Kendall & Korgeski, 1979).

Important cognitive data are often contained in client reports of emotional responses, evaluations, plans, and personal historical facts (Meichenbaum, 1976, 1977). Kendall and Korgeski (1979) suggest assessment of *both* functional and dysfunctional cognitions as a prerequisite to investigating the role played by dysfunctional cognitions in the development of particular psychological disorders.

Categories of distorted thinking styles characteristic of adult patients suffering from depression and anxiety disorders identified by Beck and his colleagues (Beck, 1976; Beck et al., 1979) provide a useful reference for cognitive assessment of adolescent clients as well as adult clients. Research suggests that central symptoms of adolescent depression are similar, if not identical, to those of adult affective disorders (Clarke et al., 1990) and that cognitive distortions, automatic thoughts, and schemata of adolescent clients are quite similar to those observed in adult clients (Schrodt & Fitzgerald, 1987).

During both the initial assessment and ongoing therapy sessions, the therapist pays particular attention to statements made by the client that seem to reflect distorted or negative cognitions. Clients' "automatic thoughts" accompanying reports of stressful situations or conditions are an important source of cognitive data. Clients' automatic thoughts (directly accessible thoughts or cognitions that occur instantaneously and are habitual and plausible to the individual) will be found to contain data about their present perceptions of situations, past memories, affective responses, and deeper beliefs. In addition, automatic thoughts often contain self evaluations, and elements of this self-evaluation process in turn encompass past memories, present perceptions, and related affect.

Definitions of five types of interrelated cognitive phenomena identified by Baucom and Epstein (1990) provide the therapist with useful guidelines or cues as to what types of client statements to pay attention to:

perceptions: about what events occur;
attributions: about why events occur;
expectancies: predictions of what will occur;
assumptions: about the nature of the world and correlations among events;
beliefs: about what "should" be.

Although these cognitive phenomena are all aspects of normal information processing, they are also susceptible to distortion. Cognitive distortions are defined as errors in the process of collecting and using information independent of the particular content of that information. Baucom and Epstein (1990) suggest evaluation of the appropriateness of a cognition in terms of two criteria: how valid it is as a representation of objective reality, and how reasonable it is as a standard or as an explanation for relationship events when there are no clear objective criteria available for determining reality. These authors also suggest that an individual's beliefs (or standards) tend to be dysfunctional when they are inflexible, unattainable, or so extreme that meeting them takes a significant toll on the person. However, they caution that information-processing errors present in cognitive distortions are not instances of "pathological thinking" in themselves, since research on social cognition indicates that they also occur in non-clinical groups and that it is the frequency with which they occur or the degree to which individuals test the validity of such cognitions that differentiates non-clinical from clinical groups.

Distorted information processing styles identified by Beck and his colleagues are listed below. Although Beck was able to identify particular types of thought content specific for different types of disorders, he found that the formal characteristics and processes of distortion were similar for several nosological categories. He identified the following processes involved in the conceptual errors and distortions characterizing the thematic content of the verbalizations of patients with depression, anxiety disorders, and other diagnostic labels (Beck, 1963; Beck et al., 1979; Beck et al., 1985):

- Arbitrary Inference—The process of forming an interpretation of situations, events, or experiences where there is no factual evidence to support the conclusion, or the conclusion is contrary to the evidence.
- Selective Abstraction (or Loss of Perspective)—The process of focusing on a detail taken out of context, ignoring other more salient features of the situation.
- Overgeneralization—The process of drawing a general conclusion on the basis of a single incident.
- Minimization and Magnification—The process of gross underestimation of events (such as one's performance, achievement, or ability), or gross exaggeration (usually of an event perceived as traumatic) in which the person dwells on the worst possible outcome of a situation.
- Dichotomous Thinking—A tendency to interpret things in absolute, black-or-white terms, with little or no tolerance for uncertainty or ambiguity.
- Personalization—The unsupported perception that an event reflects upon oneself.
- Emotional Reasoning—Equating subjective affective data with fact.

The above distorted information processing styles may be suggested by the statements of both adolescent clients and their parents. In addition to Beck's categories of distorted thinking styles, the following fallacies summarized by McKay, Davis and Fanning (1981) have also been found by the author to occur frequently with adolescent clients, and are useful guidelines for cognitive assessment:

- Control Fallacies—The external control fallacy is a belief that others are responsible for one's own problems. The flip side of this is another control fallacy, a person's belief that he or she is responsible for other people's problems.
- The Fallacy of Fairness—The belief that what one wants is the only thing that is "fair."
- The Fallacy of Change—The belief that another person must be (or can be) pressured to change so that one can be happy.
- "Shoulds" fallacies—Inflexible personal rules and expectations held by a person, usually believed by the person to be absolute in all situations and which include the words "should," "ought," or "must."

Beck and his colleagues have also identified several themes characterizing self statements of depressed and anxious patients (Beck, 1963, 1976; Beck et al., 1979; Beck et al., 1985). These provide a useful reference for cognitive assessment of adolescent clients:

Depression Themes
- low self esteem,
- self criticism and self blame,
- negative interpretation of events,
- negative expectations for the future,
- perception of responsibilities as overwhelming,
- hopelessness, lack of gratification,
- anger and blame against person or agency.

Anxiety Themes
- personal danger,
- loss of control,
- exaggerated description of external demands and pressures.

Although cognitive distortions are of major interest, it is also important for the therapist to note negative client cognitions that appear to be accurate, but which seem to be contributing to dysfunctional behavioral or affective responses. Attempts will not be made to modify *realistic* cognitions; instead, cognitive-behavioral interventions will be used to alter the aspects of the problematic situation fostering the negative cognitions.

Common themes in psychotherapy with adolescents identified by Schrodt and Fitzgerald (1987) provide futher guidelines:

- concerns about physical appearance,
- concerns about autonomy and control,
- concerns about competency,
- concerns about peer status,
- concerns about sexuality and sexual identity.

In addition, the following list of cognitive themes characteristic of parents and adolescents in conflict with each other have been identified by Robin and his colleagues, and are useful for the identification of significant cognitions contributing to dysfunctional parent-adolescent interactions (Roehling & Robin, 1986; Robin & Foster, 1984, 1989):

- perfectionism,
- ruination,
- fairness,
- love/approval,
- self blame,
- malicious intent,
- autonomy.

Categories of cognitive distortions and themes characterizing disturbed families, reviewed in Chapter One, provide the therapist with further guidelines:

- bad or evil child themes,
- child purposely causing harm to parents themes,
- beliefs about family rules,
- beliefs about child rearing approaches,
- beliefs about distribution of power in families,
- beliefs about qualities of good family interactions,
- attributions about the cause of family problems,
- parental attributions of self-blame for children's problems
- expectancies about negative future family occurrences,
- parental expectations about how children should behave,
- loyalty expectations.

Assessment of Cognitions Accompanying Intense Emotional Reactions

Cognitive-behavioral therapists view emotions as being mediated by cognitions, and also as mediators of cognitive processes. Therefore, emotional reactions such as tears, anger, or elation during family or individual sessions should be followed by the therapist's probe of cognitions accompanying emotional outbursts of adolescents or parents. The emotional reaction provides a cue for the therapist to ask questions such as: "What is going through your head right now?" "What are you feeling right now?"

Parental emotions of guilt, anger, and discomfort anxiety are characteristic of parents who have difficulties handling their children. It is therefore necessary to uncover irrational beliefs underlying these emotional reactions, such as parental attributions of self-blame.

Collection of Cognitive Data

The proposed assessment format relies on several methods for collection of cognitive data. These include:

1. items on the structured clinical interviews,
2. assessment during sessions.

STRUCTURED INTERVIEW DATA

Items on the structured clinical interviews have been designed to elicit adolescents' and parents' reports of automatic thoughts, attitudes, attributions, expectations, assumptions, and beliefs. Examples of items designed for this purpose on the Initial Presenting-Problems Interview include: "What do you see as the major problem?" "What causes the problem?" "Why does the problem occur?" "What goes through your head when the problem occurs?"

Similarly, several items on the Family-Peer-School Behavior Interview have been designed to elicit statements reflecting significant perceptions, attributions, beliefs, and other cognitions: "How would this person (e.g. mother, father, classmate) describe you?" "What thoughts were going through your head at the time?" "What was the cause of each (upsetting or stressful situation)?" "What was your way of coping with these situations?"

THERAPIST PROBES DURING SESSIONS

During the therapy sessions, the therapist pays attention to spontaneous statements made by clients and probes for more information during discussion of problems and emotionally-charged issues. Spontaneous statements made by clients during the session will often contain significant cognitions. The therapist makes a note of cognitive distortions, to be addressed later using cognitive restructuring interventions.

In addition, when the client is discussing problem areas or emotionally-charged issues, this may be a cue to the therapist to probe deeper. The therapist uses a similar approach during both individual and family sessions when clients are discussing upsetting experiences, as suggested by Beck et al. (1979). The therapist asks for a precise description of what behavioral interactions took place, accompanying emo-

TABLE 2.4
Thoughts and Behavior Diary

When you feel upset, write a short description of the situation and record the "automatic thoughts" that are going throught your head at the time. Or, at other times, if you become aware that you are thinking negative thoughts, try to identify and write a short description of the situation or "activating event" causing those negative automatic thoughts.

Upsetting Situations Rate and Describe the Situation	*Automatic Thoughts* Record your automatic thoughts accompanying this situation

not   very
upsetting   upsetting

0   1   2   3   4   5

tional reactions, and a verbatim account of stream-of-consciousness thinking and automatic thoughts accompanying the situation.

The therapist goes on to probe for attributions, expectancies, and beliefs by asking questions such as: "What was the cause of that?" "Why did the person react in that way?" "What might happen?" "What do you think that means?"

THE THOUGHTS AND BEHAVIOR DIARY

The Thoughts and Behavior Diary (Table 2.4) functions as a guide for client recording of thoughts accompanying upsetting situations that occur between sessions. It is used to teach clients to identify their own dysfunctional cognitions related to their maladaptive behavioral and emotional responses. It also provides a repeated measure of the frequency, intensity, and duration of dysfunctional automatic thoughts accompanying situations upsetting to the client, to be used throughout the course of therapy as one indicator of therapy effectiveness.

The simple format of this instrument makes it appropriate for use with adolescents. As part of a weekly homework assignment, the client is asked to record upsetting situations as they occur throughout the week, to rate each in terms of severity, and to record automatic thoughts accompanying the stressful situation. The "upsetting situations" referred to in column one usually involve interactions with significant others, but may also include solitary activities, or ruminations on past or ongoing problems, or stressful events such a poor exam result.

If the client fails to carry out this "homework" assignment, therapist and client may work on it together during the session. The client is asked to recall any upsetting

TABLE 2.5
Cognitive Data Summary Form: Case Illustration

Dysfunctional Cognitions (self statements, themes, beliefs attitudes, distorted thinking styles)	*Consequences*
ADOLESCENT CLIENT	
• "I'm stupid at school"	• give up trying; truancy
• "Either I skip with the kids or I'll have no friends"	• truancy; drug abuse school failure; parent angry
	• peer approval
• "Dad thinks I'm worthless"	• depression
• "Parents have no right to tell me what to do"	• defy parental rules
PARENT	
• "If my son respected me, he'd give up his friends, and stay home every night"	• inappropriate parental demands ignored by the son; ongoing parent-adolescent conflict
• "My son has ruined his life, I can't help him"	• abdication of parental responsibility to help son problem-solve; failure to set and enforce appropriate limits

situations that took place during the past week, to rate and report the details of each situation, and to recall accompanying thoughts.

Cognitive material collected by any of the above methods may be summarized and organized on the Cognitive Data Summary Form as shown in Table 2.5. Meichenbaum's suggestions for a functional cognitive analysis include (1) the organization of the basic data into reconstruction of the kind of information processing taking place, (2) the identification of general themes, and (3) identification of the client's causal theories, irrational beliefs, and basic assumptions (Meichenbaum, 1977).

FAMILY ASSESSMENT METHODS

The selection of family variables for assessment is based on empirical findings linking various family factors to adolescent psychological disorders. Major problem areas are different for each family, necessitating comprehensive assessment. Robin and Foster's (1984, 1989) suggestions for systematic and precise assessment of family behavior patterns characterizing parent-adolescent conflict have influenced the overall family assessment scheme. They recommended three major areas of family

TABLE 2.6
Family Assessment Methods

Variables	Assessment Methods
I. PROBLEMS OF FAMILY FUNCTION	
A. *Dysfunctional Interpersonal Interaction Patterns*	• Initial Presenting-Problems Interview • Family-Peer-School Performance Interview (parts) • Behavior Checklists (family sessions) • Informal Observation (family) • Functional Analysis of Interpersonal Interactions
B. *Family Skill-Deficit Areas* 1) Family Communication Skills	• Family Communication Patterns Checklist
2) Family Problem-Solving Skills	• Family Problem-Solving Patterns Checklist
3) Parental Childrearing Styles	• Dysfunctional Childrearing Styles Checklist
II. PROBLEMS OF FAMILY STRUCTURE	• Structured Clinical Interviews • Family Structural and External Problems Checklist
III. FAMILY PROBLEMS EXTERNAL TO PARENT-ADOLESCENT RELATIONSHIP	• Structured Clinical Interviews • Informal Observation and Interview • Family Structural and External Problems Checklist

assessment: family function, family structure, and major areas of chronic family stress, external to the parent/adolescent relationship.

Assessment of family function includes analysis of family skill areas, such as family communication and problem-solving skills, as well as parental childrearing skills. Assessment of family structure is concerned with broader family patterns, such as power hierarchies and dysfunctional family alignments. The final category, major areas of chronic family stress, is concerned with identification of pathological family situations frequently cited in the literature as characteristic of families with problem adolescents, such as parental alcohol abuse, marital conflict and separation, and parent psychopathology.

Since there is a great deal of overlap between the major areas of family assessment, they will be assessed concurrently, using sections of the structured clinical interviews, observational techniques, and cognitive assessment methods during individual and family sessions.

Assessment methods for each problem area are shown in Table 2.6.

TABLE 2.7
Functional Analysis of Interpersonal
Interactions: Case Illustration

Interaction Sequence	Consequences (Reinforcement Contingencies)
(ANTECEDENT: Mother denies daughter's request)	
• Daughter calls mother "stupid"	
• Mother retaliates against daughter	• Daughter gets parents to argue with each other and father to side with her
• Father defends daughter	
• Mother blames father for causing daughter's problems by always taking her side	• Mother gets to accuse father, thereby relieving own guilt
• Father blames mother for being insensitive to daughter	• Father gets back at mother by refusing to support her against daughter

Assessing Family Functioning

Assessment of family functioning in the proposed format will include: (1) a functional analysis of interaction patterns between dyads and triads of family members, especially parent-adolescent dyads, (2) an assessment of family skills in the areas of family communication, family problem-solving, and parental child-rearing styles.

FUNCTIONAL ANALYSIS OF FAMILY INTERACTION STYLES

While observing interactions during family sessions, or when analyzing interview data, the therapist will become aware of dysfunctional parent-adolescent interaction sequences. Details of the interaction and hypothesized reinforcement contingencies may be summarized on the Functional Analysis of Interpersonal Interactions form, as illustrated in Table 2.7. Analysis of interlocking contingencies may be aided by determining the "payoffs" for individual family members that serve to maintain the dysfunctional patterns. The therapist should especially note interactions contributing to patterns of coercion, inappropriate negative (or positive) reinforcement, punishment, and avoidance.

IDENTIFICATION OF FAMILY SKILL DEFICITS

Four family behavior checklists have been designed to aid the therapist in identifying dysfunctional family interaction styles and skill deficits that will subsequently become targets for intervention:

1. Family Communication Patterns Checklist,
2. Family Problem Solving-Patterns Checklist,

3. Family Structural and External Problems Checklist,
4. Dysfunctional Childrearing Styles Checklist.

These checklists (shown in Appendix C) are particularly useful for recording behaviors observed during family sessions (although they may also be used as tools for summarizing data from structured interviews and other sources).

During family sessions, while family members are discussing or attempting to solve identified problems, the therapist has an opportunity to observe behavioral interactions of family members. The behavioral checklists help to focus the therapist's attention on particular behaviors and interaction styles identified in the literature as characteristic of families of problem children and adolescents.

These checklists provide an alternative to the more formal behavioral-observation coding systems used in research investigations, which are impractical for routine clinical use. The construction of the first three checklists was influenced by Robin and Foster (1984, 1989), who defined crucial family variables for assessment, based on empirical findings identifying specific dysfunctional family interaction patterns that predispose family members to excessive conflict. The Family Communication Patterns Checklist and the Family Problem-Solving Patterns Checklist are designed to allow for recordings of direct observations and frequencies of behavioral responses during the family session, if this is feasible. Alternatively, therapists may use all four of the checklists between sessions as references for recording their observations about family skill deficits. These will not be direct behavioral observations, strictly speaking, but will involve therapist inferences and hypotheses about behaviors observed.

The work of Missildine (1963), reviewed in Chapter One, provided a basis for development of the fourth checklist, the Dysfunctional Childrearing Styles Checklist. This was designed to aid the therapist in identification of broader maladaptive parenting styles and corresponding adolescent dysfunctional response styles, which are encountered repeatedly in referred families. In addition to providing a useful tool for facilitating observation during family sessions, it was also designed to be used by the therapist in organizing and analyzing data pertaining to parental child-management techniques and their consequences. This would include both interview and observational data.

Parenting practices have had the longest and most consistent influence in the adolescent's life. Most adolescents are still living in the parental home and thus are subject to direct daily parental influences. Therefore, information about parental models to which the youngster has been exposed, and the adolescent's typical response to particular parental discipline techniques will help the clinician to generate plausible hypotheses about conditions maintaining current problematic adolescent behaviors. The accuracy of these hypotheses will depend on the therapist's clinical expertise and knowledge of family interaction and child-development literature.

IDENTIFYING ASPECTS OF HEALTHY FAMILY FUNCTIONING

When assessing family communication and problem-solving styles, attention should be paid to positive, as well as negative patterns. For example, positive communication behaviors include agreement, evaluation, humor, and solution proposals.

Attention should also be paid to other aspects of healthy family functioning demonstrated during family sessions, such as behaviors suggesting family cohesion and reciprocal affection. These constructs, while difficult to operationalize, are nevertheless important to assess in some form. In the proposed format, data from structured clinical interviews, along with behavioral observations, will provide a good indication of the presence or absence of those behaviors associated in the literature with family cohesion and reciprocal affection. As summarized by Orford (1980), these behaviors include time spent in shared activities, relatively low rates of withdrawal, avoidance, and segregated activities, a high rate of warm interactions versus critical hostile interactions, fuller communication between members, generally favorable versus critical evaluation of family members, perceived affection between family members, and satisfaction with the family group and optimism about its future stability.

Assessing Family Structure and Areas of External Family Stress

Assessment of family structure is necessary in order to identify dysfunctional family power or alignment problems interfering with effective parenting. Structural problems related to increased family conflict identified in the literature include: too much or too little adolescent autonomy, along with cross-generational alignments, coalitions, and triangulations that may be undermining successful child management (Minuchin, 1974). Guidelines for assessing family structure are provided in parts I and II of the Family Structural and External Problems Checklist. Additional information about family structure may be elicited using the structured clinical interviews with the adolescent client and his parents.

Section III of the same checklist facilitates identification of family problems external to the parent-adolescent relationship that may be undermining the parent's effectiveness in handling the adolescent. Problems in this category would include parental alcoholism, marital conflict and divorce, parent psychopathology, sibling's problematic behavior, and sickness or death of a family member. Although these problems may have originally developed independently, they will eventually affect the quality of the parent-adolescent relationship.

PEER RELATIONS ASSESSMENT

Failure to successfully resolve the crucial developmental task of forming satisfying peer relationships usually has long-lasting negative effects. The youngster is deprived of an important source of positive reinforcement, eventually becoming anxious or depressed. Several factors may interfere with formation of satisfying peer relationships, including failure to acquire adequate social skills, embarrassment about poor academic performance, physical deformities or unattractiveness eliciting peer ridicule, and parental discouragement of friendships. Dysfuntional family interactions are often related to peer-relationship problems. For example, clients may be embarrassed about their families—for example, because of parental alcohol abuse or mental health problems—and therefore fail to form close peer relationships for fear that outsiders will learn about the shameful home environment.

In the proposed assessment format, information about the client's peer relationships is collected using parts of the Family-Peer-School Performance Interview. The client is asked to describe his or her best friend, the teenager he or she admires most, and classmates. He or she is also asked to predict how they would describe him or her. This provides information about peer models, and self concept related to age mates. In addition, information about the number and type of activities engaged in with peers is elicited by a request that the client describe a typical day. This will also shed light on the presence of antisocial, or asocial patterns. Additional questionnaire items have been designed to elicit information about peer relationships in the past. Other sources of peer-relations data are the parents (using the Parent Form of the Family-Peer-School Performance Interview), school personnel, and school records.

SCHOOL PERFORMANCE ASSESSMENT METHODS

Several areas of current school behavior will be assessed, including academic performance, school attendance, and interpersonal behavior in the school setting. Attempts will also be made to collect information about the adolescent's past school performance.

Sections of the Family-Peer-School Performance Interview were designed for collection of data from all of the above areas. Part E of this interview, Client's Perception of School Behavior, utilizes open-ended questions to encourage the client to identify and describe areas of school functioning viewed as problematic. Self-ratings of current academic performance, attendance, and relationships with classmates and teachers are also elicited. Following this, clients are asked for systematic accounts of their marks and attendance in each of their current subjects, and the major reasons for failure in any subjects in which marks fall within the D or F ranges. Other sections of the Family-Peer-School Performance Interview were designed to provide descriptive information about the quality of clients' typical interpersonal interactions with classmates and teachers, as well as their perceptions of classmate and teacher-evaluations of them.

Teachers' reports provide another important source of school performance data.

TABLE 2.8
Teacher Report Form

STUDENT'S NAME:

SUBJECT:

REPORT OR TEST MARKS TO DATE:

Please check the rating you would give this student in each of the following areas:

PERFORMANCE AREAS	ABOVE AVERAGE	AVERAGE	BELOW AVERAGE
1. Academic Skills			
2. Application			
3. Attendance			
4. Conduct			

Please Comment: _____

_____

_____

The Teacher Report Form, and the Past School Record Form have been designed for this purpose (See Tables 2.8 and 2.9). The therapist may request that the client's school counsellor or principal distribute the Teacher Report Form to the client's teachers so as to collect the necessary information. School personnel may also be requested to record information from the adolescent's past school record file on the Past School Record Form. (The therapists may be able to collect this information if they have access to school records.)

In addition, the therapist may be able to obtain further information through informal observation of the adolescent clients as they interact with school personnel during meetings at the school. The Functional Analysis of Interpersonal Interactions, already shown in Table 2.7, is again useful for recording descriptions of observed interactions and their consequences.

The School Data Summary Form (Table 2.10) is a data analysis instrument designed to aid the therapist in organizing and analyzing information obtained from

TABLE 2.9
Past School Record Form

STUDENT'S NAME:
CURRENT GRADE:

Please record all instances of significant school problems recorded in the student's ongoing school record.

SCHOOL GRADE	PROBLEMS RECORDED	Skills	REASONS FOR SCHOOL FAILURE		
			Appli-cation	Atten-dance	Conduct

(1) structured clinical interviews with the client and parent, (2) teachers and other school personnel currently involved with the client, and (3) past school records.

PREADOLESCENT BEHAVIOR ASSESSMENT METHODS

In addition to current influences in the family, peer, and school environment, factors that influenced the adolescent's functioning in these areas in the past may still have a significant effect on current functioning. According to a cognitive social-learning perspective, memories are continually retrieved by the individual and may surface in the form of private speech, beliefs, attitudes, images, or emotional reactions. In addition, current coping styles may be a carryover from earlier attempts to deal with sources of environmental stress. For this reason, information about past thought and behavior styles is helpful in understanding current functioning.

Assessment methods in this area are designed to elicit information about major stressful events, ongoing situations, or upheavals during earlier years that the client

TABLE 2.10
School Data Summary Form: Case Illustration

CURRENT SCHOOL PERFORMANCE

SUBJECTS	MARK	ATTENDANCE	REPORTED REASON FOR FAILURE	
			Client	Teacher
English	45%	good	• don't understand	• poor skills
History	45%	good	• too hard	• poor skills
Math	38%	poor	• always poor at math	• poor skills and application
Typing	30%	poor	• no friends in that class	• truant
French	40%	poor	• classmates dislike me	• poor skills and attendance

A. COMPONENTS OF STUDENT'S ACADEMIC SKILLS PROBLEMS

• client's perception: failure due to insufficient abilities

• teachers' perceptions: failure due to poor application and attendance

B. COMPONENTS OF STUDENT'S SCHOOL ATTENDANCE PROBLEMS

• social anxiety: client truant to avoid perceived peer rejection and teacher ridicule

C. COMPONENTS OF STUDENT'S CLASSMATE/TEACHER RELATIONSHIP PROBLEMS
• client's perception of classmates as rejecting

• client's fear of being publicly criticized by teacher
• past history of "school phobia"

perceived as particularly upsetting. These may have interfered to a significant degree with successful coping with developmental tasks. Information is also elicited about the client's characteristic style of coping with these sources of stress. More specifically, information is collected pertaining to persistent (or acute) events that created anxiety, depression, or other severe, chronic emotional reactions in the past, and information pertaining to maladaptive coping patterns developed by the child in response to these events. The preadolescent behavior analysis will help to clarify how parenting practices, family disruptions, negative peer relationships and school experiences, and other events have shaped and maintained the client's maladaptive coping patterns over the years.

Data are collected utilizing Part D of the Family-Peer-School Performance Interview with both the client and parents. The client is first encouraged to talk

TABLE 2.11
Self Evaluation of Family-Peer-School Coping (Repeated Measure)

How well are you coping at the present time in each of the following areas?

Area	Rating 1-poor; 2-fair; 3-very good	Explain
FAMILY RELATIONSHIPS		
PEER RELATIONSHIPS		
SCHOOL PERFORMANCE AND RELATIONSHIPS		

about incidents which had a negative emotional impact in previous years. This non-directive approach is useful because it allows clients to identify situations that were important for them, some of which may come as a surprise to the therapist. Following this, a more structured exploration of areas of past functioning is initiated, covering relationships with significant others and past school performance. The client is asked how he thinks significant others would have described (evaluated) him during his elementary and junior high school years. Additional preadolescent information may also be obtained from the client's ongoing school records, and subsequently summarized on the Past School Record Form.

ASSESSING CHANGE

Finally, the Self Evaluation of Family-Peer-School coping form (Table 2.11) is used to monitor the client's perceptions of his or her current progress in three major areas of daily functioning. These areas correspond to the major assessment areas covered by the data collection instruments, as well as broad areas of therapy intervention with adolescent clients. This instrument provides an ongoing measure of the accuracy of the client's perceptions, and additional information about aspects of change, or lack of change, that the client considers to be important. It may also be used as an indication of therapy effectiveness.

3

Cognitive-Behavioral Coping-Skills Interventions

Several Cognitive-Behavioral Coping Skills Interventions found to be appropriate and effective with adolescent clients are described in this chapter. Some of the techniques were originally designed by behavior therapists to bring about changes in overt behavior patterns. However, with growing emphasis over the years on the importance of altering maladaptive cognitions feeding into dysfunctional behavior patterns, many therapists have added cognitive assessment and change components, and this has led to a change in terminology from behavioral to cognitive-behavioral coping-skills interventions.

Most of the techniques described here have been simplified and adapted to some extent for use with adolescent clients. References are provided for readers who wish more detailed information. The techniques are arranged in alphabetical order, for easy reference:

Activity Scheduling
Assertiveness Training
Behavior-Analysis (A-B-C) Skill Training
Contingency-Awareness Training
Conversation-Skills Training
Goal Planning
Graded-Task Assignment
Interpersonal Coping-Skills Training
Problem-Solving Training
Relaxation Training
Self-Monitoring and Self-Control Skills Training
Time-Management Training

ACTIVITY SCHEDULING

The purpose of this technique, based on Lewinsohn (1972, 1976) is to help clients to structure and plan daily activities and routines and to set goals that will enable

51

them to increase their activity levels and function in a more normal and effective way on a day-to-day basis. This technique has been found to be particularly effective with depressed clients who suffer from problems of inactivity, lack of motivation, and lack of pleasurable experiences.

First, clients are asked to provide baseline information about their current activities, from the time they get up in the morning until going to bed at night. A simple explanation of the rationale for collecting baseline data may be given at this time. For example, clients may be told that in order to alter unwanted behavior patterns, it is first necessary to carefully observe these patterns by keeping a record of how frequently specified behaviors occur.

Next, the relationship between positive mood and pleasant activities is discussed. Clients are asked to rate and record their mood on the same sheet with his activities, each morning, afternoon and evening, on a six-point scale ranging from "unhappy/very upset" to "very happy/not upset." See the Daily Activity Sheet (Appendix D).

This exercise will provide the therapist with crucial information about the client's functioning in several areas. For example, the therapist may learn that the adolescent is spending an excessive amount of time sleeping or watching T.V. Information will also be provided about type and frequency of peer activities, and patterns of school attendance. The client and therapist may jointly utilize this information during the session to analyze the relationship between mood and various activities. Clients may also be asked what goes through their heads while engaging in various activities, so that relevant cognitive data may be addressed as part of this intervention.

The client is next instructed to schedule activities for specific times each day for the following week, to check off each activity engaged in, and to bring this information to the next session. The therapist asssists the client with suggestions designed to increase the frequency of pleasant, self-fulfilling activities.

Scheduling of activities selected to promote pleasure and mastery has been found to be effective with depressed adult clients (Lewinsohn, 1976; Beck et al., 1979). In order that clients become more aware of potentially satisfying events, they may be asked to recall formerly pleasurable events and to list new, potentially pleasurable activities. Often, depressed adolescent clients are unable to generate a list of pleasurable activities, so that the therapist may need to mention several activities and have the client rate the degree of pleasure associated with each.

The client is asked to schedule and engage in activities identified as pleasurable for a certain amount of time each day. Clients are also asked to rate the degree of pleasure and mastery associated with performance of each activity, in order to become aware of changes in mood when certain activities are being pursued. It is also useful to have clients record their cognitions associated with various activities, in order to get a better idea as to why certain tasks may or may not elicit feelings of pleasure and mastery.

It is very important to schedule activities that the client will be likely to carry out. These must be activities that the client has control over and activities that will not be prohibited by parents.

ASSERTIVENESS TRAINING

Assertiveness Training has been found to be effective with problems of depression, anger, resentment, and interpersonal anxiety, particularly in relation to circumstances that are perceived as unfair. The goal is to teach the client to express rights and feelings, and to decrease the frequency of passive collapse or hostile blow-ups (Davis, McKay & Eshelman, 1982). Unassertive adolescents tend to be those who believe that they do not have a right to their own beliefs, feelings, and opinions. As a result, they repeatedly expose themselves to exploitation, mistreatment, or coercion from peers, parents, and others, followed by resentment, anger, or guilt. In contrast, assertive teenagers are able to comfortably stand up for their rights and wishes when appropriate, to ask for clarification, and to openly disagree with someone without behaving in a hostile manner.

Assertiveness training involves several steps. First, the client is taught to distinguish between three basic styles of interpersonal behavior: aggressive behavior (e.g. fighting, accusing, threatening), passive behavior (e.g. doing as told regardless of contrary wishes), and assertive behavior (e.g. expressing true feelings and standing up for oneself). Clients are next asked to specify those situations in which they would like to be more assertive. They are asked to specify *when* they behave unassertively, with *whom* they tend to be unassertive, and *what* they want to achieve that they were formerly unable to achieve with their unassertive style.

Identification and restructuring of dysfunctional cognitions underlying unassertive behavior is an important component of this intervention. For example, unassertive adolescents may believe that it is impolite to question others' actions, that they should never put their own needs before others' needs, or that they will never have any friends if they refuse to submit to peer pressure to engage in certain activities that they consider to be wrong.

Following this, clients are asked to write scripts for change in which they concisely state the problem, their feelings, their goals for change, their requests, and the expected positive consequences if the other person cooperates. This step will require input from the therapist in order to avoid pitfalls such as overly-emotional tone, lack of specifics, and name calling.

Clients will then be asked to rehearse their scripts, using appropriate assertive body language, such as direct eye contact, clear speaking voice, and avoidance of whining or apologetic tone. Finally, clients will be helped to identify manipulative styles of significant others, and they will be taught techniques for responding assertively to these. For example, clients may be taught to calmly repeat a point without becoming sidetracked, to respond to criticism with one-word answers, to agree with the person on some points without giving in on others, and to delay their responses to aggressive remarks until feeling calmer. These techniques are rehearsed during the session, before the client is asked to try them out in daily situations.

BEHAVIOR-ANALYSIS (A-B-C) SKILL TRAINING

The purpose of this intervention is to teach adolescent clients to analyze their own dysfunctional, upsetting behavior patterns, as well as alternative more adaptive behavior patterns manifested by others or suggested by the therapist.

Clients are taught to use a simple A-B-C method of behavior analysis. They are asked to recall specific examples of recent upsetting events and, for each example, they are asked to describe their own (maladaptive) behaviors or response patterns in detail. Next, they are asked to use the following format to record descriptions of their own behavior, and to identify events preceding and following their responses: the Antecedents, or Activating Events, that triggered their responses, and the Consequences following their responses.

A	B	C
ACTIVATING EVENTS	BEHAVIOR	CONSEQUENCES

Antecedents and Consequences reported may be descriptions of responses of significant others, environmental events such as receiving a failing grade, or the client's personal cognitive or emotional behaviors, such as anger, depression, or pleasurable feelings.

CONTINGENCY-AWARENESS TRAINING

This technique is useful for helping adolescent clients to become aware of the probable negative outcomes associated with unwise decisions they may be contemplating or have already made, such as a decision to quit school or to leave home. It is also useful for helping clients to predict the eventual consequences of self-destructive behavior patterns they are currently manifesting, such as drug or alcohol abuse, promiscuity, or other conduct disorders. In addition, Contingency-Awareness Training may also help the client to become aware of probable favorable consequences of alternative decisions or behavior patterns.

Basically, the client is asked to list probable short- and long-term consequences of opposing alternative decisions, behavior patterns, or life styles, using the following format:

BEHAVIOR   SHORT-TERM   LONG-TERM
                           CONSEQUENCES   CONSEQUENCES

Because adolescents often ignore probable negative consequences of self-defeating or self-destructive behavior patterns, it is useful to have the client actually visualize the consequences, both immediate and long-term. For example, a truant student may be asked to visualize being suspended from school, facing the parents' reaction, and being cut off from school friends. The client is encouraged to apply this exercise regularly in order to evaluate current behavior patterns and important decisions.

CONVERSATION-SKILLS TRAINING

Conversation-Skills Training is appropriate for clients who lack sufficient conversational skills to enable them to form satisfying interpersonal relationships. The problem is often compounded by extreme shyness or social anxiety. This intervention has been adapted for individual sessions with adolescent clients from a group training program described by Eckman (1976). Conversation-skill deficits targeted for change may include a low rate of verbal interaction in social situations, lack of verbal spontaneity in groups, failure to elaborate topical content, too frequent change of topic, or speech dysfunctions that interfere with rate or frequency of conversations (such as repetition of content, blocking, and long pauses). The client is taught basic skills necessary to initiate, maintain, and appropriately terminate pleasant, rewarding conversations.

Eckman suggests that the therapist first assess the client's conversational skills in order to identify problems in speech production, nonverbal behavior, and content of conversation. The client is asked to engage in conversations with the therapist on several topics, so that the therapist has a chance to assess the different areas. The checklist based on Eckman's work, shown in Table 3.1, is a useful tool. Following the assessment, one or more of the following training tasks is applied to corresponding skill deficits. For each task, the therapist first models the appropriate behavior and then provides feedback and positive reinforcement as the client imitates the therapist's behavior.

Difficulties in the area of actual speech production may be addressed first. For example, the therapist may introduce tasks designed to increase voice volume and decrease duration of pauses in conversation. Clients are asked to relate recent inci-

TABLE 3.1
Conversation Skills Deficit Checklist*

SPEECH PRODUCTION
  • voice volume and tone
  • duration of pauses
  • verbal fluency

NONVERBAL BEHAVIORS
  • eye contact
  • gesturing
  • posture

CONTENT OF CONVERSATION
  • opening lines
  • initiating new topics of conversation
  • elaborating on answers
  • active listening
  • reflection
  • showing interest in the other person
  • giving compliments
  • encouraging other person to talk about himself
  • asking direct questions
  • asking for advice
  • using open ended questions
  • introducing topics of general interest

Based on Eckman, 1976.

dents they were involved in and, while doing this, to pay particular attention to increasing their voice volume and decreasing pauses.

Another task is designed to provide an opportunity for the client to practice nonverbal conversation skills such as direct eye contact, good posture, and appropriate gesturing. Once again, the client is asked to relate an incident, this time paying particular attention to eye contact and gesturing.

Further tasks are designed to teach techniques for initiating, maintaining, and terminating conversations. In order to increase conversation initiation skills, the client is taught to generate and practice opening lines. Clients may be asked to describe recent situations in which they were unable to successfully initiate a conversation. Possible opening lines are then generated and demonstrated by the therapist, and practiced by the client.

In order to improve skills in maintaining a conversation, the client is taught to use open-ended questions, and to steer the conversation toward certain areas of general interest, such as current events, movies, books, T.V. and sports. In addition, the client is taught techniques for elaborating on answers to questions, active listening, and reflection. The client practices maintaining a conversation with the therapist for increasingly extended periods of time.

Finally, the client may be taught techniques for appropriately terminating a conversation. The therapist models examples of closing lines, exit lines, and exit behaviors, such as excusing oneself in order to keep an appointment.

Clients are also taught skills that will make them more attractive and interesting to peers. Using a role-playing approach, the client practices the following behaviors: showing interest in the other person, giving compliments, asking for advice, and getting the other person to talk about himself by asking direct questions that are neither too personal nor too intense. Training in appropriate techniques for self-disclosure and use of "I" statements are other important components. It is explained that appropriate self-disclosure elicits feelings of affiliation from others. Clients then practice self-disclosure statements, giving information about their feelings, background, goals, and beliefs.

After practicing the above techniques during the session, the client is given the homework assignment of practicing the conversation initiation, maintenance, and termination techniques in daily situations. The therapist suggests possible situations in which the client will be able to try out new skills. The client is asked to arrange these situations in a hierarchy from easiest to most difficult and to practice the newly-learned conversation skills in the easiest situations at first. Clients are asked to observe the reactions of others to their experiments with newly-learned skills, and to note their own private self-statements as they practice these skills.

GOAL PLANNING

This intervention is used to help the adolescent to formulate concrete, attainable short- and long-term goals. It is appropriate for adolescent clients who lack motivation, clients who are drifting, and clients who are anxious or confused about what to do in the future.

The therapist progresses from general open-ended questions (e.g. "What are your goals?"), to more specific questions about one-month, one-year, and long-term goals. Next, the therapist becomes even more specific by asking about short- and long-term goals in the three major areas of family, school, and peer functioning. Clients are asked to describe their immediate goals in terms of relationships with family members, relationships with peers, and school performance. They may also be asked to imagine what they will be doing or what they would like to be doing in terms of family, peers, and school/career in five years time.

Once clients have listed short- and long-term goals, they are asked to prioritize these goals by indicating the most important goals that they would like to begin work on first. The client is then helped to break down both short- and long-term goals into manageable component steps that have to be completed in order to realize these goals. The following format is helpful:

WHAT MUST BE DONE   PLANS FOR IMPLEMENTATION

I. FAMILY-HOME

    short-term goals

    long-term goals

II. FRIENDS

    short-term goals

    long-term goals

III. SCHOOL-CAREER

    short-term goals

    long-term goals

GRADED TASK ASSIGNMENT

This intervention is useful for clients who are overwhelmed by tasks that they must perform, resulting in procrastination or failure to perform the task, followed by negative self-evaluation. The client is helped to break the task down into manageable component parts and to take action on the various components in a step-by-step manner, progressing from easier to more difficult steps. This technique is particularly useful with problems involving social anxiety.

Essential steps in a Graded Task Assignment intervention are outlined below, based on Beck, Rush, Shaw, and Emery (1979):

1. Problem definition;
2. Project formulation and client-therapist collaboration on assignment of tasks in a hierarchy from simple to complex;
3. Client's commitment to carrying out assigned task, proceeding from easier to more difficult tasks, with subsequent report of success or failure in doing so;
4. Reduction of dysfunctional doubts and self belittlements, through clients' realistic evaluations of their actual performance, following success in attaining a goal;
5. Design of more complex assignments by client and therapist.

The first step is to identify the goals that the client wants to achieve. These goals are then broken down into component tasks that have to be completed in order to achieve the goal. Next, these tasks are graded in terms of perceived difficulty. The client may be asked to assign a rating to each task on a five-point scale from "easy" to "extremely difficult." These tasks are then arranged in a hierarchy, and clients commit themselves to one or two tasks per week, moving gradually from easy to difficult tasks. Cognitive and behavioral blocks associated with each task are identified and treated with Cognitive Restructuring interventions.

INTERPERSONAL COPING-SKILLS TRAINING

This intervention is designed to teach the adolescent client adaptive interpersonal coping skills to replace current dysfunctional social-interaction patterns. First, the client is asked to give several detailed examples of recent upsetting, unpleasant interpersonal situations. The following steps are then applied to each example:

1. Identify antecedents (activating events) and consequences eliciting and maintaining the client's dysfunctional interpersonal coping responses.
2. Ask clients why they respond in that particular way, to identify related dysfunctional cognitions.
3. Help the client to generate ideas about possible alternative responses to the Activiating Event. The client may be asked to think of examples of teenagers or adults who manifest alternative behavior patterns in similar situations. The therapist will also suggest alternative behavior styles.
4. The therapist models alternative, more adaptive response styles, and a role-playing technique is used to help the client to rehearse the new behavior during the session.
5. The client is given the assignment of experimenting with the alternative behavior pattern in real-life situations, paying particular attention to the consequences.

First, the client's current dysfunctional coping style is identified and discussed in terms of how this behavior sabotages opportunities for successful, satisfying relationships. Then, by questioning clients about why they adopt identified dysfunctional response styles, the therapist gains a better understanding of underlying attitudes and beliefs that may need to be altered through cognitive restructuring techniques before the client can be convinced to experiment with a new response style. Following this, the therapist models alternative, more adaptive behaviors, and asks the client to imitate and rehearse these using imaginary situations and a role-playing technique. The therapist and client may switch roles, each taking the part of both the client and the significant other. The therapist may also role play the client's current dysfunctional behavior pattern in order to further emphasize self-defeating aspects of this coping style. Following this, clients are asked to experiment with the new behaviors in their natural environment during the coming week. They are asked to note and report consequences, especially in terms of the way others react to them when they are exhibiting the new response styles.

Pro-Social Skill Training

This is a variation of Interpersonal Coping-Skills Training appropriate for adolescent clients with aggressive response styles. Bornstein, Bellack and Hersen (1980) outline five sequentially ordered steps in a skill-training program designed to teach pro-social interpersonal skills to replace aggressive response patterns. First, the therapist explains the rationale for learning assertive response styles to use in place of existing aggressive response patterns. Negative consequences of aggressive responses are identified, such as reciprocal aggression, and contrasted with the more positive consequences of standing up for one's rights by expressing them in an assertive (rather than an aggressive) manner.

In step two, several assertive response styles are described, including, for example, refusal of inappropriate requests such as requests for a fight, leaving the scene of a confrontation, making a request to discuss the situation rationally, listening attentively to the other person's side, agreeing to some parts of the other person's argument, attempting to assess whether the other person can be reasoned with or not, and acting accordingly, and retreating if a talking approach isn't feasible. In step three, the therapist asks clients to describe several actual situations in which they behaved aggressively toward peers, parents, or others. Then the therapist models more appropriate, non-aggressive responses to these situations.

In step four, role-playing is used to help the client to rehearse the responses modelled by the therapist. Particular attention is paid to shaping a non-aggressive tone of voice and non-aggressive gestures. In the final step, the therapist provides feedback on the client's performance, praising adaptive non-aggressive responses and pointing out aspects of the adolescent's performance that still contain aggressive components.

PROBLEM-SOLVING TRAINING

Problem-Solving Training is designed to help the client to discover and implement whatever adjustment strategies are effective in a given situation. The client is taught to follow a logical progression of steps to reach a solution to a given problem (D'Zurilla & Goldfried, 1971). It is one of the most versatile and effective interventions for adolescent clients since it is applicable to a large variety of adolescent disorders, including anger and motivational problems associated with depression, parent-adolescent conflict, school underachievement, and peer relationship problems.

In its simplest form, there are five basic steps:

1) problem definition to help clients clarify their complaints and identify various components of the problem;

2) generation of alternative courses of action, with joint input from client and therapist;
3) evaluation of each alternative by listing the "pros" and "cons" of each;
4) rating of the various alternatives and selection of the best;
5) implementation of the best alternative by planning and carrying out the necessary steps of solution implementation.

At each step, the therapist will need to question the client about relevant beliefs and attitudes related to the various alternatives in order to address dysfunctional cognitions that may impede the success of the problem-solving process.

RELAXATION TRAINING

Adolescents who suffer from tension to the point where it interferes with their engaging in normal teenage activities such as socializing with peers or attending school may be helped by Relaxation Training. Therapists usually have their own favorite relaxation-training approach, with script or audiotape. Clients are instructed to assume a comfortable position, close their eyes, and follow the instructions as the therapist guides the client through the various steps of the relaxation script during the session, until a state of deep relaxation is attained. Therapists may play one of the commercial relaxation tapes for the client or prefer to make their own audiotapes using the commercial audiotape as a model. Clients often react most favorably to the therapist's familiar voice on the tape. When reading the script, the therapist should speak slowly in a calm, monotonous tone of voice.

It is explained to the client that relaxation skills are learned through practice, similar to learning a new sport. The client is given the homework assignment of practicing relaxation skills by listening to the tape once each day. The client is also instructed to apply newly-learned relaxation skills, by listening to the audiotape just prior to engaging in a potentially tension-producing activity.

SELF-MONITORING AND SELF-CONTROL SKILLS TRAINING

Adolescents may be taught self-monitoring and other self-control skills to alter a variety of dysfunctional behaviors. Self-control skills are designed to help clients to gain control over unwanted behaviors under the control of conflicting positive and aversive consequences, where the positive consequences are immediate and the aversive consequences are delayed (Kanfer, 1975). Examples of typical dysfunctional adolescent behaviors in this category include drug and alcohol abuse, overeating, truancy, and avoidance of study behaviors that lead to school failure. In addition to decreasing the frequency of unwanted behaviors, the client may also learn new self-control skills to *increase* the frequency of desired behaviors. For example, Clarke and his colleagues (1990) describe a self-control approach incorporating Self-Monitoring, designed to assist adolescent clients in developing strategies for increasing the number of pleasant activities in their daily lives, in order to improve mood and combat depression.

Kanfer (1975) identifies several self-control skills which may be developed by the client with the therapist's help: (1) self-monitoring, (2) establishment of specific rules of conduct by contracts with oneself and others (standard setting), (3) self-evaluation, (4) seeking support from the environment for fulfillment of contract, and (5) generating strong reinforcing consequences for engaging in behavior which will facilitate achievement of self-control goals. Other self-management methods that may also be taught to the client include: (1) delaying an undesirable act, (2) engaging in competing cognitive or motor behaviors, (3) setting up challenges for oneself, (4) rehearsing positive consequences of self control, and (5) using contingent self-praise or self-criticism.

The underlying rationale for Self-Monitoring is research suggesting that observation of one's own behavior can lead to increases or decreases in aspects of that behavior (Kanfer, 1970). Self-monitoring techniques may be used both as assessment devices and as therapy interventions. As an assessment technique, clients are instructed to systematically record at specified intervals public behaviors and/or private cognitions specified for change. Self-monitoring may also be used to assess therapy efficacy, since measures of behavior may be self-assessed prior to, during, and after completion of the therapy-intervention phase. Clients become involved in the process of identifying the frequency of their own engagement in specified "desirable" and "undesirable" behaviors and they are then in a position to initiate their own behavior change. Once the client has defined the problem, accepted the necessity for change, and defined some initial goals for change, a functional analysis of antecedents and consequences maintaining targeted unwanted behaviors that are part of the identified "problem" may be carried out, and information obtained for use in designing stimulus-control procedures or interventions.

Clarke and his colleagues (1990) outline a simple, straightforward approach for teaching self-control skills to adolescent clients. Clients are taught to use Self-Monitoring to establish a baseline of specific behaviors targeted for change, to set realistic goals for change, and to develop a plan and a contract for implementing behavior change.

First, the therapist introduces the concept and rationale of Self-Monitoring, or "baselining," explaining that the key to changing self-defeating or unwanted behavior patterns (or to increasing a desired behavior pattern), is careful self-observation. The client is told that this may be accomplished through "baselining," which means counting something specific, whether it be activities, social interactions, study sessions, or classroom attendance. It is explained that these data are analyzed through daily totals of specified behaviors and that a person can set goals to increase or decrease these specified behaviors. The client is then asked to record all occurrences of the specified behavior for one week, using a simple format similar to that of the Daily Activity Sheet (Appendix D). After the baseline information has been collected, the client is taught to analyze these data in order to determine the number of times per day that the targeted behavior occurred.

Next, the client is taught to set realistic goals for changes in the frequency of the occurrence of the target behavior. Goals must be specific enough to enable clients to clearly determine whether they have attained them or not. Goals must also be realistic so as to increase client compliance. It is expected that improvement will be attained gradually through increasingly difficult weekly goals. In order that they may increase the likelihood of realizing their goal, clients make written contracts with themselves, with the therapist, or with others in which weekly goals are clearly specified.

In order that they may increase the likelihood of realizing their goals, clients are asked to select rewards that will be contingent upon fulfillment of the contract. It is most effective if selected rewards are things that clients clearly enjoy, that are under their control, and that are immediately available. Clients are instructed to keep a record showing whether goals are achieved or not on a daily and weekly basis, and to reward themselves with the selected rewards each time they are successful in realizing their goals.

TIME-MANAGEMENT TRAINING

This intervention is appropriate for adolescent clients whose ineffective management of personal time results in excessive rushing, anxiety related to a sense of being overwhelmed by daily demands and deadlines, hours of nonproductivity and avoidance, missed deadlines contributing to school failure, or insufficient time for peer interactions and satisfying peer relationships.

Many time-management techniques have been developed by management consultants. Most use the same basic steps: 1) carrying out a time inventory of current activities, 2) establishing priorities, 3) breaking top priorities down into manageable steps, and 4) realistic scheduling of high-priority activities. The following approach based on Davis, McKay and Eshelman (1982) has been simplified and adapted for adolescent clients.

The client is first asked to keep a daily log of all activities engaged in for one week. It is explained to clients that before they can be taught techniques for effective time management, they will need to use this baselining technique to provide an inventory of how they actually spend their time. The therapist then helps the client to identify different categories of activities, such as schoolwork, recreational activities, and peer interactions, and to compute the amount of time per day engaged in activities from each category. The following simple format is useful:

	ACTIVITIES	TIME
MORNING		
AFTERNOON		
EVENING		

After this initial assessment of time spent in various activities, clients are helped to set priorities. They are asked to examine the amount of time spent in specific activities or categories of activities, and to determine if they want to spend more or less time in each of these activities. Clients are asked to list their immediate goals (for the coming days), one-month, and six-month goals, concentrating primarily on goals related to the identified problem areas (e.g. school failure, infrequent interaction with peers, etc.). Using these lists, clients are then asked to circle their most important goals. This step is similar to the Goal-Planning intervention described in this chapter.

Once the goals are prioritized, plans may be made to increase the amount of time devoted to high-priority activities which are related to achievement of the most important goals and to decrease or eliminate low priority activities. Next the client is helped to break top-priority goals down into manageable steps and to set aside time each day to work on high-priority activities. A Self-Monitoring component may be incorporated into the Time-Management intervention at this point. Clients may be asked to use a daily "To-Do" list, on which they list everything they want to accomplish that day. This is especially useful to combat anxiety stemming from feeling overwhelmed with daily tasks and responsibilities, resulting in non-productivity. Activities are then scheduled with appropriate time allowances, including time for interruptions, breaks, and anticipated problems. Clients then commit themselves to implementing the scheduled activities for that day, as planned, and to check off each activity after it is completed.

One important component of Time-Management Training is the identification and restructuring of beliefs and attitudes contributing to the client's failure to carry out top-priority activities. For example, adolescent clients with time-management problems may report that they are unable to say no to peer interruptions or phone calls when studying, for fear of losing friends, that they feel that tasks should be done perfectly or not at all, that they must carry out other less important tasks before engaging in top-priority activities, or that they cannot possibly begin serious studying before 11:00 p.m. Environmental blocks to effective time management must also be identified and altered, such as a noisy study environment.

4

Cognitive-Restructuring Interventions for Adolescent Clients

The primary function of cognitive-restructuring techniques is to teach clients more adaptive thought patterns by helping them to detect their negative and distorted thought patterns, to recognize their deleterious impact, and to replace dysfunctional cognitions with more accurate and adaptive thought patterns. Cognitions are deemed dysfunctional when they appear to be unrealistic or inaccurate, and when they contribute to unwanted behavioral and emotional responses.

Cognitive-restructuring techniques are used by the therapist to alter the client's inaccurate attitudes, beliefs, and assumptions, based on the premise that if clients can be taught to recognize and correct their own distortions of reality, they will then be in a better position to alter their related dysfunctional behavioral and emotional responses. Cognitive symptoms, which may include self-statements, interpretations, beliefs, and cognitive distortion processes, are designated as targets for cognitive-restructuring interventions, just as maladaptive behavioral excesses and deficits are designated as targets for behavioral coping-skills interventions.

An important note of caution should be mentioned here. Cognitive-restructuring interventions are designed to modify *inaccurate* cognitions. However, clients will also report negative cognitions contributing to behavioral and mood disorders that, upon investigation, appear to the therapist to be *accurate*. If this is the case, cognitive-restructuring techniques would not be appropriate, since the object of cognitive therapy is to promote accurate, realistic thinking. Instead, problem-solving and other coping-skills interventions would be used to change aspects of the problem situation responsible for the client's negative cognitions and to alter the client's habitual, but unsuccessful, behavioral responses to the problem situation until there is a decrease in the frequency of negative cognitions.

There are a number of subtle, but significant, differences between the approaches of various leading cognitive-restructuring theorists and clinicians, including Beck and his colleagues (Beck, 1976; Beck et al., 1979; Beck & Emery, 1985); Ellis (Ellis & Grieger, 1977), and Meichenbaum (1977). Three important areas of variation are the relative emphasis placed on formal logical analysis, the directiveness with which the therapeutic rationale and procedures are presented, and relative reliance on adjunctive behavior therapy procedures (Meichenbaum, 1977).

Ellis' approach is essentially one of teaching clients to view their problem behaviors as influenced by maladaptive beliefs, after which the central task of therapy becomes that of challenging these beliefs. Ellis advocates a straightforward didactic approach as the most effective method of changing maladaptive cognitions. In Beck's approach, the therapeutic interaction is structured so that the client can discover for himself that some of his thoughts and thought processes are inaccurate. This is done by means of a "Socratic dialogue," a tactful progression of questions posed by the therapist to lead the client to identify his own irrational thought patterns. Meichenbaum's approach is similar to Beck's, but does not focus to as great an extent on a formal rational analysis of the client's dysfunctional belief system. Relatively more time is spent on teaching the client to employ new problem-solving and coping-skills techniques.

ADAPTATION OF COGNITIVE-RESTRUCTURING TECHNIQUES FOR ADOLESCENT CLIENTS

Several factors must be considered when adapting cognitive-restructuring interventions for adolescent clients. The adolescent's level of intellectual development is an important consideration, since this will affect the capacity for analytical and abstract thought. In general, analytical thinking and self-analysis will still be relatively new processes for adolescent clients, as compared to adult clients. The capacity for self-analysis and analytical thinking would be expected to increase with age and, therefore, be greater during the middle and late adolescent years, as compared to early adolescence. In any case, cognitive-therapy techniques developed by Beck and other therapists working with adults will often need to be modified for adolescent clients by breaking them down into simple steps that are easy to follow. Clients may also be asked to write down important points during the session to help clarify the purpose and content of various interventions. A blackboard may also be used for this purpose.

It is best not to run the risk of overloading adolescent clients with abstract concepts that they may be unable to grasp, keeping in mind normal levels of adolescent intellectual development. For example, given the relatively limited capacity of adolescent clients for abstract thinking as compared to adult clients, the therapist need not go into detailed explanations of difficult concepts such as the constructs underlying Beck's categories of distorted information-processing styles. Instead, the therapist may use simple labels, such as "black-and-white thinking."

An important consideration is that there will be individual differences in the potential for self-analysis among adolescents of similar age. A great deal of variation among adolescent clients has been observed clinically in terms of ability to grasp and benefit from cognitive-restructuring interventions. (This, of course, is also true of adult clients.) As would be expected, a greater emphasis on cognitive-restructuring interventions would be more appropriate with youngsters who are habitually introspective and reflective in day-to-day life, in contrast to clients whose response styles are more impulsive and nonintrospective. The latter would benefit from approaches placing greater emphasis on coping-skills interventions.

Another important consideration is lack of sufficient motivation for self analysis and introspection, characteristic of many adolescent clients. Some adolescents simply do not *wish* to be introspective and, therefore, tend to repond more favorably to a more straightforward, pragmatic, behavioral approach.

The therapist must take all of the above factors into consideration when determining the appropriate level of complexity of cognitive-restructuring techniques for each client and how much time should be devoted to formal cognitive-restructuring techniques, as opposed to behavioral coping-skills techniques. The therapist must assess each client individually in terms of ability to grasp and benefit from cognitive restructuring techniques and willingness to analyze cognitive phenomena.

The above factors, and clinical experience with adolescent clients suggest the benefits of a cognitive-restructuring therapy approach that places less emphasis on formal logical analysis than would be advocated for adult clients and more emphasis on incorporating cognitive-restructuring techniques into behavioral coping-skills interventions. Beck's method of labelling cognitive-distortion processes may be used as a tool by the therapist to identify cognitive targets for cognitive-restructuring intervention, without the expectation that the youngster be able to thoroughly grasp the meaning of these constructs or to independently discover cognitive-distortion patterns. The therapist's approach to cognitive-restructuring with adolescents would therefore be more directive than with adult clients, in terms of the way in which the therapeutic rationale and procedures are presented.

THE COGNITIVE-RESTRUCTURING THERAPY PROCESS

Cognitive-restructuring techniques may be introduced simultaneously with behavioral techniques, or the therapist may decide to delay the introduction of these techniques until later sessions, depending upon the client's readiness for introspection. The proportion of time spent on behavioral as opposed to cognitive techniques will also depend on the unique set of target behaviors presented by a particular client.

A very simple explanation of the rationale for cognitive-restructuring interventions is provided. Basically, the therapist wants to get across the notion that unwanted feelings, such as depression, anger, and anxiety, and self-defeating behaviors, such as truancy or aggressive interactions with peers, are related to negative or distorted automatic thoughts and beliefs. Initially, cognitions may be defined simply as automatic thoughts that spontaneously come into a person's head during upsetting times or situations.

With adolescent clients, it is usually not appropriate to go into lengthly discussions of cognitive processes. Rather, one starts identifying dysfunctional cognitions immediately by asking clients to describe specific upsetting situations and to report accompanying thoughts. It is explained that once a person understands how these thoughts may be contributing to unwanted feelings and behavioral reactions, he or she will then be in a better position to understand why he or she behaves the way he or she does; this will enable him or her to do something constructive about the situation. The purpose of this brief explanation is to provide a convincing rationale for the client's joint participation with the therapist in the cognitive analysis.

The Therapist's Assessment of Cognitive Data

During the sessions, clients will express some beliefs and interpretations that the therapist will recognize as clearly dysfunctional. In other cases, the therapist will hypothesize that certain unreasonable beliefs or distorted reasoning processes underlie identified problem behaviors. Therapists will need to test out the existence of hypothesized dysfunctional cognitions by eliciting further information about attributions, assumptions, and beliefs. They must offer enough guidance to enable clients to recognize their own maladaptive assumptions and beliefs, without imposing their own, as yet untested, hypotheses as to what the client's underlying assumptions might be.

Special attention is paid to extremist statements beginning with "should," "must," "have to," and "always" since these often indicate inflexible cognitive sets. In order to detect the client's causal theories, irrational beliefs, and basic assumptions, Meichenbaum (1977) suggests that the therapist ask questions such as: "Why did you react in that way in that situation?" and "What do you think is the cause of the (unwanted) behavior?" Beck and Emery (1985) advocate a deductive method which starts with identification of unwanted emotions and behaviors and moves to automatic thoughts, then to assumptions behind the thoughts, and finally to major concerns related to dysfunctional assumptions.

Safran, Vallis, Segal, and Shaw (1986) discuss the concept of core cognitive processes, defined as cognitive processes that are related to the definition and experience of the self in some fundamental way. Knowledge of core cognitive processes can help the therapist to predict a client's emotional and behavioral responses to a wide variety of situations. Core cognitive processes of the greatest importance tend to be those that involve self-evaluation, so that the therapist is advised to pay attention to self-referrant statements. The therapist attempts to ascertain the meaning that a particular event or situation has for the client and how this might be related to the client's self-perceptions and evaluations. The therapist may ask: "What does this mean about you as a person?" Particular attention is paid to patterns in the client's automatic thoughts and dysfunctional attitudes that persist across situations, to consistencies in types of situations that the client finds distasteful, to emotionally-laden cognitions, and to those cognitions that are most resistant to change because they tend to be most central for the client.

The therapist will also detect examples of Beck's categories of distorted information processing styles in the verbalizations of adolescent clients: "It's luck rather than hard work or good grades that gets you accepted at university" (arbitrary inference); "I'm no good at math so I'll never be able to get through high school" (selective abstraction); "Because I (once) deceived my parents by skipping school, I can never expect them to trust me again" (overgeneralization); "I'm rotten at school. My grade point average is only 81% this term "(magnification); "If I don't get accepted into medical school my life will be a failure" (dichotomous thinking).

In this chapter, four basic phases of cognitive-restructuring therapy will be used, based on Beck's approach with depressed patients (Beck et al., 1979). These are designed to help clients first become aware of maladaptive cognitions related to unwanted emotions and behaviors, and then modify identified dysfunctional cognitions and cognitive processes by

1. eliciting cognitive data necessary to detect patterns of automatic thoughts, unrealistic beliefs, and distorted information processing,
2. helping clients to analyze the content of their cognitions,
3. challenging dysfunctional cognitions and faulty information-processing styles, and exploring alternative assumptions, beliefs, and causal explanations,
4. setting up experiments to be carried out by the client in order to test identified dysfunctional assumptions and beliefs.

COGNITIVE-RESTRUCTURING THERAPY TECHNIQUES

Many of the following cognitive-restructuring techniques are adaptations for adolescent clients based on interventions developed for adult clients by Beck and his colleagues (Beck et al., 1979; Beck & Emery, 1977; 1985). The work of Clarke, Lewinsohn, and Hops (1990) has also been influential. These authors have adapted a number of interventions for depressed adolescents, using elements of techniques originally developed by Beck et al. (1979) and Ellis and Harper (1961). The order of presentation of techniques in the following sections will conform to the four phases of cognitive-restructuring therapy outlined above.

PHASE ONE: TECHNIQUES FOR ELICITING COGNITIVE DATA

The following techniques are used by the therapist for the purpose of eliciting cognitive data containing distorted perceptions, attributions, expectancies, assumptions, and beliefs, while simultaneously developing clients' awareness of their own internal dialogue. This internal dialogue has been labelled "self talk" by Ellis and Harper (1975), and "automatic thoughts" by Beck (1976). Clients are told that they will be taught to develop an awareness of their automatic thoughts. It is explained that automatic thoughts usually have to do with interpreting, judging, and labelling events occurring in a person's daily life, and that some negative automatic thoughts are related to intense, unpleasant emotions and to unwanted behaviors. It is explained that if a person can be taught to identify negative automatic thoughts, he can later be helped to gain some control over these thoughts and the accompanying unpleasant emotions and self-defeating behaviors.

An explanation such as the following is suitable for adolescent clients:

> Part of helping a person to feel and perform better in daily life has to do with teaching the person to control or change negative or inaccurate thoughts. When we talk about changing our thinking, we are not talking about changing all of our thoughts and ways of thinking, but changing only those negative or inaccurate thoughts that occur over and over again, like bad habits, and are responsible for intense unpleasant feelings such as anger, depression or fear. Negative thoughts may also be responsible for self-defeating behaviors such as avoiding other kids, failure at school, or failure in social situations. For example, Person "A" may typically make negative statements to herself such as "all the other kids think I'm inferior and unattractive," even though this is not true. As a result, she may start to avoid other kids and consequently feel lonely and unhappy because she wrongly concludes that she will always be incapable of making friends and being accepted.
>
> In contrast, Person "B" would habitually make very few of these negative self-statements. Instead she would typically make positive self-statements such as "Most kids think I'm nice and enjoy my company." As a result, she would feel happy around others, and start conversations and get involved in activities with other kids.
>
> Therefore, in order for Person A to feel better and to be more successful, she would need to break the habit of making negative and inaccurate self-statements, and to increase her positive self-statements. This would result in positive feelings and productive friendly behaviors. Part of helping a person to feel and perform better in daily life has to do with teaching the person to control or change his or her unwanted inaccurate, or negative thoughts. These often have to do with interpreting or judging events and situations,

including judging ourselves. Inaccurate thoughts, which are also called irrational or distorted thoughts, are often exaggerations, inaccurate conclusions, or unreasonable expectations, and are often preceded with terms such as "must," "should," or "ought."

Sources of cognitive data include the client's verbalizations of thoughts or images experienced during the therapy session, reports of thoughts accompanying symptom exacerbation or relief between sessions, and automatic thoughts that the clients record in their "Thoughts and Behavior Diary." Often, clients will be unaware of their own automatic thoughts, and must be trained to recognize them. Basically, clients are taught to develop the habit of paying attention to their thoughts during upsetting situations or whenever they find themselves experiencing unpleasant feelings or engaging in self-defeating or unproductive behaviors.

Eliciting Data from Client Descriptions of Problems and Upsetting Situations

During the session, the client is asked to describe upsetting situations, current and past. As he or she does this, he or she is periodically asked: "What is going through your head as you describe this?" "What was going through your head at the time the event occurred?" "What was the meaning of that event for you?"

The client will also be asked to use the " Thoughts and Behavior Diary" to keep a record of upsetting stressful situations as they occur during the week and to record automatic thoughts accompanying each stressful situation. The contents of the diary will be analyzed at the following session each week.

Two additional techniques outlined by Beck and Emery (1977) for eliciting automatic thoughts and images from adult clients during the therapy session are suited for adolescent clients as well.

Instant Replay Technique. When the adolescent experiences negative feelings during the session, but is unable to identify the precipitating or accompanying automatic thought, he or she is asked to replay the upsetting stimulus and his or her response to it. It may work best if the client closes his or her eyes while doing this, and is then asked to try to reproduce a visual image of the event. He or she is then asked to report accompanying thoughts and images.

The "As-If" Technique. To help the youngster identify automatic thoughts related to upsetting events in the past, the therapist asks him or her to "Imagine the event as if it were happening right now." He or she is then asked to report related automatic thoughts.

Clarke et al. (1990) suggest simple exercises to help clients to increase their awareness of dysfunctional cognitions. Clients are helped to identify frequent negative thoughts and moods, and to distinguish between personal and nonpersonal automatic thoughts.

IDENTIFYING NEGATIVE THOUGHTS AND MOODS

The therapist begins by pointing out examples of negative thoughts as the client describes his or her problems and upsetting situations, and reports the thoughts going through his or her head. Afterwards, clients are asked to identify their own negative thoughts, such as "I don't deserve to be happy" or "My father doesn't care about me."

In addition, the list of feeling words shown in Table 4-1, adapted from a more extensive list used by Baucom and Epstein (1990), may help the client to learn to identify negative moods and frequent negative thoughts related to these moods. Clients are asked to keep a list of their habitual negative thoughts as they are identified.

TABLE 4.1
List of Negative Feeling Words

Depression	*Anxiety*
helpless	anxious
hopeless	panicky
worthless	worried
discouraged	nervous
unhappy	shy
bored	confused
exhausted	
Anger	*Other Negative Mood States*
angry	jealous
resentful	ashamed
disgusted	guilty
frustrated	incompetent
critical	alone
	stupid

IDENTIFYING PERSONAL THOUGHTS

Clients are helped to distinguish negative personal thoughts using the words "I," "me," and "my" from negative nonpersonal thoughts about people and events. Clients are asked to circle negative personal thoughts on their lists.

PHASE TWO: TECHNIQUES FOR ANALYZING COGNITIONS

The second step involves a collaborative therapist-client analysis of these cognitions for identification of specific patterns of negative and distorted automatic thoughts.

Initially, the two work together to determine what and how the client thinks, the basis of his or her thinking, and the losses and benefits resulting from this thinking pattern. In addition to identification of recurrent themes and types of logical errors in the client's automatic thoughts, the client will also be taught to identify environmental events stimulating negative thoughts.

Identifying Recurrent Themes

The following format is used to help clients to detect recurrent themes characterizing their automatic thoughts and reflecting their deeper beliefs and attitudes. They are first asked to record automatic thoughts in the left-hand column as they are identified during the session, and to add to this list additional automatic thoughts taken from the "Thoughts and Behavior Diary." Next, they are asked to detect and record in the right-hand column themes characterizing their automatic thoughts. Themes identified in the literature as characteristic of depression and anxiety disorders, characteristic of adolescent clients, and characteristic of parent/adolescent conflict (cited in Chapter Two) provide a useful reference for the therapist.

Identification of themes is illustrated in the following case of a 14-year-old girl who experienced a great deal of anxiety in classroom settings, which prompted her to skip classes and fail courses:

AUTOMATIC THOUGHTS	THEMES
• Nobody in class talks to me because they don't like me	• others critical of me
• I have no friends	• inferiority
• I'm not attractive like others	• inferiority
• I'm undesirable, and incapable of ever making good friends	• self-blame
• Other kids find me unattractive	• others critical of me
• I'll never have friends	• negative expectations of future

Identifying Negative Beliefs

After the following explanation is given, clients are asked to identify negative beliefs among their automatic thoughts:

Many of the negative thoughts that pop into people's heads are really negative beliefs that they have about themselves and others. If you look carefully at your list of negative automatic thoughts and themes, you will notice that many of them are negative beliefs about yourself and others. These negative beliefs can affect how you feel and act, so it is important to study them very carefully.

Identifying Activating Events Related to Negative Automatic Thoughts and Beliefs

Clients are taught to identify activating events preceding their negative automatic thoughts and beliefs. The following explanation and format is used:

When you find yourself thinking negative thoughts, it is important to identify the situation causing you to think that way. We call the situation the
"activating event," because it activates the negative thought. Use the following format to identify activating events associated with or causing the negative automatic thoughts or beliefs you recorded earlier. Sometimes the
"activating event" will not be something someone has said or done recently.
Instead, you may suddenly start thinking of something that happened in
the past or you may start worrying about something that might happen in
the future. If this is the case, your own thoughts or ruminations are the
"activating event."

ACTIVATING EVENT	NEGATIVE (THOUGHTS) BELIEFS
Sitting alone in the classroom watching classmates talking and enjoying themselves, but nobody tries to talk to me	• kids should be talking to me • other kids hate me • I'm undesirable • I'm incapable of making friends • I'll never have any friends

The "Thoughts and Behavior Diary" is designed to aid the client in identifying activating events associated with negative automatic thoughts experienced between sessions. Clients are asked to write short descriptions of upsetting situations experienced each week and to record automatic thoughts accompanying these situations. Clients may first become aware that they are thinking negative thoughts and then identify the event causing the thoughts. Alternatively, they may first experience an upsetting event or interaction, and then identify (and record) accompanying auto-matic thoughts.

Identifying Consequences of Negative Beliefs

Clients are next taught to identify consequences of their negative beliefs, which are generally unpleasant or dysfunctional. This exercise usually increases the client's motivation for examining and evaluating negative dysfunctional beliefs more closely. Once clients are made aware of the connection between their negative beliefs and their dysfunctional emotional and behavioral reactions accompanying these beliefs, they are usually motivated to evaluate and to attempt to alter these beliefs.

An A-B-C Belief-Analysis technique is used to help the client identify the unpleasant consequences of negative beliefs. (This is similar to the A-B-C *Behavior*-Analysis technique for uncovering the consequences of dysfunctional behaviors. However, the "B" now stands for "Belief" rather than "Behavior.")

Now that you have learned to identify your negative beliefs and the activating events that cause these negative beliefs, you can next look at the consequences of the activating event and of your negative beliefs, using the following A-B-C format. Consequences are the results of the activating event or the negative belief. Consequences may be either emotional results (your feelings, such as depression or anxiety) or behavioral results (what you actually *did*, such as skipping classes).

In the case of the 14-year-old girl cited above, unpleasant emotional consequences included feelings of depression and anxiety in the classroom setting. Behaviorally, the girl would avoid others and avoid initiating conversation as a consequence of her negative beliefs. She wrongly assumed that her classmates avoided talking to her because they hated her and considered her undesirable. This was extremely upsetting to her because it exacerbated her major concern about being unpopular and friendless all her life.

A ACTIVATING EVENT	B BELIEFS	C CONSEQUENCES (YOUR FEELINGS AND BEHAVIORS)
Sitting alone in the classroom watching classmates talking and enjoying themselves, but nobody tries to talk to me	• kids should be talking to me • other kids hate me • I'm undesirable • I'm incapable of making friends • I'll never have any friends	• depressed, lonely • anxious • avoid other kids, • avoid initiating conversations

Teaching Clients to Distinguish Between Observations and Interpretations

In order to teach clients to analyze upsetting situations more objectively, they are taught to distinguish between objective *Observations* and subjective *Interpretations* of any given event, situation, or interaction.

It is important to study Activating Events as carefully as possible in order to distinguish between Observations and Interpretations of the event. Observations are reports of *what* events actually took place, without any of your own interpretations about *why* those events took place. Accurate observations are easier to make if you pretend that a newspaper reporter is at the scene. Ask yourself how the reporter would describe the scene in his newspaper column. For example, look at your description of the Activating Event. A newspaper reporter would probably write something like this: "A girl was sitting by herself in a classroom. Nobody was talking to her. Other kids were talking to each other and seemed to be enjoying themselves." Write this in the column labelled "Observations."

Now let's compare the way that *you* interpreted the same events. Look at the negative automatic thoughts and themes that came into your head. Write these automatic thoughts in the other column labelled "Interpretations."

OBSERVATIONS

I was sitting in the classroom. Nobody was talking to me. Other kids were talking to each other and seemed to be enjoying themselves.

INTERPRETATIONS

- Kids should be talking to me
- Other kids hate me
- I'm undesirable
- I'm incapable of making friends
- I'll never make any friends

Teaching Clients to Identify Irrational Interpretations and Beliefs

During weekly sessions, the therapist identifies and labels cognitive distortions in the client's statements as part of the cognitive assessment, and plans cognitive-restructuring interventions to be used subsequently to modify these distortions. As discussed above, Beck's categories of distorted information-processing styles provide useful guidelines for the therapist, but the therapist would not expect most adolescent clients to grasp concepts such as "arbitrary inference" or "selective abstraction." Nor would the therapist embark on a process of a formal logical analysis with the expectation that adolescent clients must discover their own distorted thought patterns for themselves. Instead, the therapist uses simple terms to label these cognitive distortion processes and to point them out to the client. For example, Clarke et al. (1990) use simple, colloquial labels of cognitive-distortion processes that adolescent clients would be likely to be familiar with, such as "overreactions," "unreasonable expectations," and "jumping to conclusions."

Concepts related to cognitive distortions will need to be presented at a very simple level. The therapist will want to get across several points:

1. Many of the negative thoughts people have are actually irrational, inaccurate interpretations of situations (defined as inaccurate or unrealistic thoughts).
2. Thoughts and underlying themes related to, or causing, negative emotions or self-defeating behaviors should be carefully examined to determine

whether they are irrational, inaccurate interpretations of a situation (as opposed to accurate observations of the situation).

3. Irrational, inaccurate interpretations are usually part of larger underlying irrational beliefs held by the person. It is very important to uncover these irrational beliefs because they are probably causing the unwanted negative feelings and self-defeating behaviors.

4. If thoughts or beliefs are found to be irrational, it is possible to learn to replace them with more rational, realistic and positive thoughts.

Once these concepts have been presented to the client, the therapist will then go on to help clients to identify irrational thoughts in their lists of negative automatic thoughts and beliefs, as in the following example:

Examples of irrational beliefs or irrational thinking habits that teenagers often have include things such as (1) overreactions, (2) unrealistic expectations, and (3) the habit of jumping to conclusions. In order to determine whether one of your automatic thoughts or beliefs is irrational or unrealistic, you will find it helpful to compare your automatic thought or belief (your *interpretation* of the event) with a description of the event from the standpoint of a newspaper reporter (*observations* about the event).

Look at the way you interpreted the event, as recorded in the column labelled "Beliefs":

1. Circle the negative personal thoughts (I'm undesirable; I'm incapable of making friends; I'll never have any friends).
2. Circle the negative beliefs about how others feel or behave (Other kids hate me; Other kids should be talking to me).
3. Circle any statements that might be overreactions (Other kids hate me; I'm incapable of making friends; I'll never have any friends).
4. Circle any statements that might be unreasonable expections (Other kids should be talking to me).
5. Circle any statements that might be examples of jumping to conclusions (I'm undesirable; I'm incapable of making friends; I'll never have any friends).

This type of exercise helps the client to understand what is meant by irrational beliefs, while providing the client with practical experience in identifying irrational beliefs. It also lays the groundwork for challenging distorted cognitions and for exploring alternative assumptions and beliefs using cognitive-change techniques.

PHASE THREE: COGNITIVE-CHANGE TECHNIQUES

After clients have learned to identify automatic thoughts accompanying dysfunctional emotions and behaviors, and after they have gained some awareness of beliefs underlying automatic thoughts, they are then helped to reconsider these beliefs more objectively and to alter unrealistic beliefs by using cognitive-change techniques. These techniques are designed for the purpose of challenging dysfunctional negative cognitions and faulty information-processing styles, and for exploring alternative assumptions, beliefs, and causal explanations by means of a joint client-therapist effort.

The following cognitive-change techniques have been found by the author to be effective with adolescent clients. The first two interventions, adapted from Beck, Rush, Shaw, and Emery (1979), complement each other and may be used together.

"What's the Evidence" Technique

This technique is used to help clients to detect faulty logic underlying their distorted interpretations and beliefs. Clients are asked to provide evidence for and against their beliefs and interpretations of events, and to record supportive and non-supportive evidence in the appropriate column, as in the following example:

DISTORTED BELIEF	SUPPORTIVE EVIDENCE "FOR"	NON-SUPPORTIVE EVIDENCE "AGAINST"
• Since classmates don't talk to me, they must hate me	• no evidence	• Kids talk to me in other classes • Classmates never said they hate me • Kids outside of school like me

Both current and past experiences and observations may be used as evidence. In addition, experiments may be designed for the client to carry out between sessions in order to test the evidence. Alternative, more realistic interpretations of the situation may then be considered, using the "Alternative Technique."

The Alternative Technique

This technique consists of teaching the client to search for alternative interpretations of the situation, based on reason and examination of evidence rather than on emotional reactions. Clients are helped to identify and evaluate themes and distortions in their thinking that have prevented them from considering alternative, more adaptive solutions. In addition, clients are helped to search for alternative solutions to the problematic event and are discouraged from pursuing old habitual "solutions." This technique is especially useful with problems of hopelessness and problems that are perceived as insoluble by the client.

DYSFUNCTIONAL INTERPRETATION

- Since classmates don't talk to me, they must hate me

ALTERNATIVE INTERPRETATION

- Classmates are busy talking to each other and don't even notice me
- Since I don't talk to them, they are uncomfortable starting a conversation with me
- If I speak to classmates, they will talk to me

DYSFUNCTIONAL BEHAVIORS

- Sit in class, talk to no one
- No eye contact with classmates

ALTERNATIVE BEHAVIORS

- Initiate conversations
- Look and smile at classmates

Experiments may then be designed for the purpose of testing the validity of the new, alternative interpretations, and for the purpose of trying out new, alternative behavioral responses.

Teaching Correlatives to Distorted Thinking Styles

McKay et al. (1981) summarize several correlatives to distorted thinking styles, based on Ellis and on Beck and his colleagues. These are helpful for planning cognitive-change interventions for adolescent clients:

1. *Arbitrary Inference:* Teach clients to accumulate hard evidence to test their conclusions.
2. *Loss of Perspective:* Teach clients to deliberately shift focus from obsessing about the problem to planning coping strategies for ameliorating the problem.
3. *Overgeneralization:* Teach clients to examine how much evidence there is for their conclusions by having them list (a) evidence supporting the conclusion, (b) evidence against the conclusion, and (c) alternative conclusions.
4. *Minimizing or Maximizing ("Catastrophizing"):* Teach clients to realistically look at the odds of the feared event happening, in terms of percentages (e.g. Is there a 10% or 90% chance of it happening?).
5. *Dichotomous thinking:* Teach clients to ask themselves if they are thinking in "all-or-none" terms. Teach them to think in percentages instead.
6. *Control fallacies:* Teach clients to recognize that each person is responsible for what happens to himself.
7. *Fallacy of fairness:* Teach clients that fairness is usually a disguise for personal wants and preferences. Teach them to tell other people specifically what they want instead of hurling "fairness" accusations. Teach clients to make concrete suggestions, and to be willing to compromise.
8. *Fallacy of change:* Teach clients that their happiness will depend on changes

they make themselves and that they must get into the habit of figuring out ways to make things happen for themselves, instead of relying on others to change.
9. *"Shoulds:"* Apply techniques for modifying the "shoulds," which include: (1) examination of when "shoulds" do and do not apply, (2) comparison of the client's "shoulds" with the client's "wants," (3) counting and recording automatic "shoulds," and (4) exploring the consequences of abandoning the "should" rule.

Increasing Positive Thoughts and Self-Statements

In order to decrease the frequency of negative thoughts, clients may be taught the technique of replacing negative thoughts with positive counterthoughts. After clients have learned to identify their repetitive negative thoughts, they are then taught to generate positive counterthoughts for each negative thought. It is explained that replacing negative thoughts with positive counterthoughts will help to control negative feelings. Positive counterthoughts are simply defined as positive or realistic thoughts about any situation or event. The therapist demonstrates this technique by countering each of the client's negative thoughts with a positive couinterthought. Then therapist and client switch roles. The therapist says: "I'll give you one of your negative thoughts, and you give me a positive counterthought."

INCREASING POSITIVE SELF-STATEMENTS
Decreasing the frequency of negative self-statements and increasing the frequency of positive self-statements is an important cognitive-change technique for problems of poor self-concept, perceived social inadequacy and social anxiety. Clients are asked to identify negative self-statements experienced during upsetting situations, which usually consist of ruminations about their inadequacy. This is followed by a discussion of the way in which these negative self-statements block or inhibit development of satisfying social relationships. The goal is to replace these negative self-statements with positive thoughts about self-value. Clients are helped to make lists of their positive attributes, and to use these lists to help them to generate positive self-statements to combat negative self-deprecatory statements. During the therapy session, clients are asked to practice this technique, while imagining themselves in stressful situations. Following this, they are given the homework assignment of practicing this technique daily in actual social situations.

Changing Inaccurate Social Perceptions

Teaching clients to alter inaccurate social perceptions is an important component of social-skills training for those who repeatedly misinterpret social cues. Clients are taught to distinguish between objective observations of social interactions and their own subjective interpretations of another person's intentions and beliefs, which are often inaccurate. Clients are asked to give examples of upsetting social interactions in daily life and to distinguish between their "observations" and "interpretations" of situations. Clients are taught to describe exactly what the other person did or said, and to label these "Observations." They are then taught to detect their own attributions, assumptions, beliefs, and inferences about the person's thoughts and intentions, and to label these "Interpretations." Clients are then helped to identify and challenge unrealistic interpretations, and to generate alternative, more realistic interpretations of the other person's thoughts, beliefs, and intentions. The therapist may help by suggesting less judgmental interpretations. Clients are then instructed to experiment with the role of accurate observer of other people's behavior in everyday life.

PHASE FOUR: SETTING UP EXPERIMENTS TO TEST INTERPRETATIONS AND BELIEFS

In conjunction with the cognitive-change techniques described above, the therapist designs experiments to be carried out by clients between sessions for the purpose of testing interpretations and beliefs in the natural environment. For example, the client may be given the "homework" assignment of attempting to authenticate automatic thoughts and assumptions by exploring the degree to which others hold the same assumptions. Clients may be asked to interview peers and adults for their interpretations of the same events, and to judge whether their interpretations and beliefs correspond to those held by most other people. Alternatively, they may be asked to systematically observe and record particular events, or to keep a record of how often an event occurs.

Clients are not expected to accept new perspectives automatically. They are more likely to be convinced of the validity of more adaptive perspectives and thinking styles if they have personally carried out experiments designed to put old and new assumptions to the test. It may be presented to the youngster that he or she is to function like a scientist testing hypotheses, by experimenting with new behaviors and noting their consequences.

TEACHING CLIENTS TO COPE WITH ACTIVATING EVENTS CAUSING ACCURATE NEGATIVE THOUGHTS

This approach is appropriate for situations in which a client's negative thoughts causing negative feelings and self-defeating behaviors *are* realistic and accurate. For example, following investigation of the situation, a therapist concluded that the following negative automatic thoughts identified by a girl whose father had a long psychiatric history were probably true: "No matter how hard I try to please my father, he thinks I'm worthless and I will never be good enough for him."

Cognitive-restructuring interventions were not appropriate in this situation, since the purpose of cognitive therapy is to promote realistic, accurate thinking. Instead, when evidence suggests that negative automatic thoughts and beliefs are accurate, clients are taught techniques to help them to cope more effectively with the events or situations activating the negative thoughts and related emotions and self-defeating behaviors. Clarke et al. (1990) present the adolescent with a "package" of five different ways of handing the upsetting activating event:

1. Don't respond to it.
2. Find alternate ways of responding to it.
3. Avoid the activating event as much as possible.
4. Change the activating event.
5. Tolerate the activating event.

COGNITIVE SELF-CONTROL TECHNIQUES

Cognitive self-control techniques are cognitive-restructuring approaches designed to teach clients to give themselves covert instructions for controlling problem behaviors such as angry outbursts, cognitive impulsivity, and anxiety (Goldfried, 1973; Novoco, 1975; Meichenbaum, 1977; Kendall & Finch, 1978). In addition, cognitive self-control interventions (sometimes referred to as cognitive self-instructional training) have also been applied to adolescent conduct disorders, including truancy, aggression, drug abuse, and criminal activities, as well as problems of familial conflict (Snyder & White, 1979).

Most cognitive self-control interventions share the same basic format. First, the conceptual framework is explained to the client in simple terms. The concept of private speech and its effect on behavior is introduced. To illustrate this point, the therapist may point out how athletes talk to themselves and repeat instructions to themselves while learning a new sport. Information about the client's private speech or verbalizations accompanying dysfunctional target behaviors is then elicited using the following format:

SITUATION	MALADAPTIVE VERBALIZATION	BEHAVIOR	CONSEQUENCES
Peer threatening	"I have to hit him or I'm 'chicken'."	Hit peer	Suspension from school

In the next phase, the self-defeating nature of the adolescent's verbalizations accompanying target behaviors is explored with the client and more adaptive self-verbalizations are suggested and modelled by the therapist. These may include a statement of contingencies, statements about the demands of the task, or self-reinforcement for success for completion of a difficult task.

SITUATION	ADAPTIVE VERBALIZATION	BEHAVIOR	CONSEQUENCES
Peer threatening	"If I hit him I'll be suspended. It's not worth it."	Walk away calmly.	Feel good about myself.

Clients are asked to rehearse these adaptive verbalizations, and to re-phrase them in their own language. They are also instructed to rehearse the new verbalizations while role playing difficult situations during the session that include the targeted dysfunctional behavior. Later, they are asked to independently identify their own dysfunctional self-verbalizations and to generate more adaptive statements. In the final phase, the client is asked to apply these cognitive self-instructional skills to daily situations and to keep a record of the consequences, to be used as material for the next therapy session.

Cognitive Self-Control Interventions, applied to anxiety and phobic reactions and to problems of anger, will be illustrated in the following sections.

Cognitive Self-Control Techniques for Anxiety and Phobic Reactions

Cognitive self-control interventions are useful with anxious or phobic adolescents whose fears of particular events occurring are associated with somatic symptoms, anxiety, or avoidance behavior. First, a brief explanation of anxiety and phobic reactions is given. The client is taught to view the problem as having two components: (1) heightened physiological arousal (e.g. rapid breathing, bodily tension, sweaty palms), and (2) anxiety-engendering avoidant thoughts on themes of helplessness, a desire to flee, social embarrassment, and panic thoughts of being overwhelmed by anxiety, or "going crazy." The therapist explains that the client's self-statements during heightened physiological arousal are prime determinants of emotional and avoidant behavior and, therefore, the treatment will focus on teaching the client to control physiological arousal by changing maladaptive self-statements habitually paired with the phobic or anxiety reactions.

In order to make the client aware of anxiety-producing thoughts, he is asked to relive the experience by "running a movie" of it. In order to modify the client's internal dialogue, the therapist helps the client to become aware of his negative self-statements and also models appropriate anxiety-reducing self-statements to be used at each stage, in place of the client's former anxiety-producing self-statements. The new anxiety-reducing self-statements will be used (1) when preparing for the stressor (e.g. "Remember, the situation makes me feel anxious. short of breath and uncomfortable, but it is not life-threatening"), (2) when confronting the stressor (e.g. "Start using the distraction technique"; "Control the anxiety, don't run from it"), and (3) when coping with feelings of being overwhelmed (e.g. "Stay put and distract yourself by counting all the people, 1, 2, 3 . . .").

The client will also be taught behavioral-coping skills in addition to the new anxiety-reducing self-verbalizations. The client is taught direct-action techniques for reducing physiological arousal, such as relaxation exercises, collecting information about the phobic object or anxiety-provoking situation, and arranging escape routes.

In summary, the client is helped to (1) assess the reality of the situation, (2) control negative thoughts and images, (3) acknowledge and relabel arousal he is experiencing, (4) prepare himself or herself to face phobic or anxiety-provoking situations, (5) cope with the fear he or she is experiencing, and (6) reflect on his performance and reinforce himself for having tried. The client may also be given the following task-orientation thoughts to use when feeling overwhelmed (Beck & Emery, 1985):

TASK ORIENTATION THOUGHTS

- Stay focused on what you are doing.
- The anxiety will go down once you get busy.
- Your purpose is to decrease upsetting thoughts and make them more tolerable, so stick with your activity.
- Anxiety and racing thoughts are uncomfortable, but normal, not dangerous.
- This will pass.

During the final stage, the client will be asked to test newly-learned skills under actual stressful situations in day-to-day living.

Stress Inoculation Training for Anger Control

The following approach, based on Novoco (1975) and Meichenbaum (1977), combines cognitive self-instruction and relaxation training. During the initial educational stage, the client is familiarized with the concept of anger as being fermented and maintained by negative self statements made in situations of provocation. Typical themes include: (1) intolerance of mistakes, (2) beliefs about the necessity for success, (3) beliefs about the necessity for retaliation, and (4) unreasonable expectations of others.

Clients are told that they must learn relaxation skills to reduce arousal, along with cognitive controls to control attentional processes and thoughts. They are told that they will be helped to conduct a situational analysis of factors that trigger their anger and that they will learn and rehearse new relaxation and cognitive skills, such as deep breathing exercises and the use of new, adaptive self-statements.

After this explanation, the youngster's personal anger pattern is carefully assessed. The client is asked to give three examples of recent anger situations, and specific people and situations most likely to arouse anger are identified. Typically, these might include a peer threatening the client, a dare or invitation to prove oneself, a situation in which the client feels he or she must adopt a "tough-guy" role to impress peers, or a peer belittling the client with a particular remark or gesture.

Next, the client and therapist identify important internal factors likely to arouse anger, including cognitive factors and somatic-affective factors. The client is asked to pay attention to the things he or she says to himself or herself when provoked, which may take the form of appraisals (e.g. "That guy is really a scum"), attributions (e.g. "He's trying to make me look like a chicken"), expectations (e.g. "He's going to try to pick a fight with me"), and self-evaluative statements (e.g. "I have to prove myself or I'll lose face"). Somatic-affective responses to provocation are next identified, such as anxiety or fear responses. Finally, the client's typical behavior patterns following provocation are identified.

The second phase focuses on skill acquisition and rehearsal. Irrational appraisals and expectations leading to anger arousal are pointed out to the client. Generally, aggressive youngsters are reluctant to take a neutral or positive view of the other person's behavior in anger-arousal situations. The youngster is helped to consider alternative interpretations of the situation. Additional skills taught to the client during this phase include relaxation skills, use of humor, and alternative, non-hostile responses to anger-provoking situations, such as leaving the scene or agreeing with the other person in a neutral way. Clients will also be taught new adaptive self statements to use when their anger is aroused, as illustrated below:

> *Preparing for the Stressor*
> "Remember, I know how to control my anger."
> *Confronting and Handling the Problem*
> "Calm down, take a deep breath, it's not worth getting mad about this."
> *Coping with Feelings at Critical Moment (Being Overwhelmed)*
> "I will stay calm, I won't give in to angry feelings, I'll ignore him."
> *Reinforcing Self Statements*
> "Forget about it now, I can be proud for not getting angry."

The client is asked to practice and role-play new behavioral skills during the session, such as listening to what the person says, keeping an impassive face, maintaining eye contact, and showing interest in the other's point of view.

Finally, clients are helped to construct a hierarchy of regularly occurring anger-provoking situations. They are then asked to try out newly learned skills in real life situations, starting with the less difficult situations in the hierarchy and working gradually toward more difficult situations.

5

Family Interventions

This chapter presents descriptions of family interventions that are consistent with a cognitive-behavioral orientation. Clinicians and researchers have found these interventions to be successful with families of adolescent clients. Two major types of interventions will be discussed: (1) Parent Skill Training, designed for individual sessions with either one or both parents, and (2) Family Therapy Interventions designed for family sessions attended by the adolescent, parents, and other family members.

Although some therapists believe that all work with families should be carried out during family sessions, this is often not feasible, effective, or even appropriate. Parents are often unwilling or reluctant to become involved in family sessions, but will agree to meet with the therapist. Parents may initially deny any responsibility for the adolescent's "problem," and will not see the need for family sessions. However, if the parents are pursuaded to meet with the therapist, they may be helped to see how behavior patterns of various family members are helping to maintain the adolescent's problem. This then paves the way for family therapy.

Even when parents and adolescent are willing to attend family sessions, therapists still have the task of convincing both the adolescents and the parents that they understand and sympathize with each of them. This is often best achieved during individual sessions with the parents and adolescent, concurrently with, or prior to, family therapy sessions.

There may be times when it will be most effective for two different therapists to work with the family, one providing individual therapy for the adolescent and the other providing family therapy. Other times, disagreement between spouses with respect to childrearing practices may be a symptom of severe underlying marital problems. If this is seriously affecting the progress of family therapy sessions, concurrent marital therapy may be recommended.

PARENT SKILL-TRAINING SESSIONS

It is often difficult and inappropriate to address the parents' dysfunctional cognitions and inadequate childrearing techniques during the initial family sessions. Parents become defensive if their mistakes and weaknesses are pointed out in front of their children. Furthermore, effectiveness of family techniques is increased if the parents have had previous exposure, during separate parent-skill training sessions, to behavior analysis skills and alternative childrearing approaches.

Individual sessions with parents also give the therapist the opportunity to assess and challenge attitudes and beliefs underlying current dysfunctional childrearing practices. Parental motivation for change may also be assessed, as well as parental willingness to negotiate solutions with the adolescent. Parents are usually more candid about their own uncertainties and insecurities when critical adolescent children are not present. The parent is not under pressure to make immediate decisions about rules and regulations and is, therefore, in a position to carefully weigh alternative approaches.

Parent Sessions are used for didactic teaching of the rationale and components of specific child-management skills, to be subsequently practiced during family therapy sessions and at home between sessions. During sessions attended by parents and therapist, the parent will be guided in learning and practicing more new, adaptive child-management skills. Examples of new parenting skills that may be taught during parent sessions include: (1) effective verbal response styles, (2) active listening skills, (3) relationship enhancement skills, (4) behavior analysis skills, and (5) effective discipline skills.

Cognitive restructuring of dysfunctional parental beliefs and attitudes related to the parent's failure to successfully implement newly-learned or effective child-management techniques is also important. Identification of parental cognitions accompanying the parent's unsuccessful attempts to implement the new technique is essential. When a new disciplinary intervention fails to gain the desired results, the therapist probes for dysfunctional cognitions that may have affected the outcome: "What do you think went wrong?" "What was going through your head while you were attempting to execute the new approach?" "What were your feelings at the time?" Finally, self-control training for parental anger-management may be another appropriate focus of parent sessions.

It is important at the outset to convey to the parent the underlying rationale for Parent Skill Training, based on theory, research, and the therapist's clinical experience. This explanation should be brief and consistent with the parents' capacity for comprehension. Parent Skill Training should be presented as a collaborative undertaking between parents and therapist, for the purpose of resolving sources of family stress contributing to the adolescent's problems.

Several important points should be conveyed to the parent:

1. The notion of the parent's primary responsibility being that of helping the adolescent to become a competent, happy, independent, and responsible teenager, and that this may require changes in the parent's approach to handling the youngster;

2. The notion that the parent can be taught the steps involved in more efficient methods of parenting that will help to ameliorate some of the adolescent's current problems;
3. The notion that dysfunctional beliefs and attitudes held by parents are often at the root of ineffective parenting patterns and, therefore, need to be examined;
4. The notion that the parents, because of their greater maturity, will need to exercise more patience than would be expected from the adolescent, but that this is not synonymous with allowing the adolescent to manipulate them;
5. The notion that parents may have to compromise on some issues, just as the adolescent will be expected to compromise;
6. The notion that one's own behavior has an effect on the other's behavior, and that certain parenting styles foster particular maladaptive adolescent behavior patterns;
7. The notion that the adolescent's "problem" is a joint family problem, and that interactions between the adolescent, parents, and other family members function to maintain the adolescent's problematic behavior.

Target behaviors for modification are identified and corresponding interventions selected. Interventions must be compatible with strengths and weaknesses of the parents. The therapist must decide if the parents are capable of working together, and whether or not parents are capable of implementing changes on a consistent basis.

FAMILY INTERVENTIONS

Several family interventions consistent with a cognitive-behavioral approach are described in the next section. They are arranged in alphabetical order for easy reference.

Behavior-Analysis Skill Training
Cognitive Restructuring in Parent and Family Sessions
Communication-Skills Training
Conflict-Negotiation Skills Training
Contingency Contracting
Discipline-Effectiveness Training
Expectations-Establishment Training
Independence Training
Problem-Solving Training
Relationship-Enhancement Training

BEHAVIOR-ANALYSIS SKILL TRAINING

Family members may be taught to use the ABC method of analyzing family interactions in parent-adolescent conflict situations, during family therapy sessions or during parent sessions. Parents may be helped through this method to become aware of specific consequences of different components of parenting or discipline approaches. They may be taught to habitually anticipate the consequences that particular childrearing actions and decisions will have on the adolescent. They may also be trained to identify aspects of the adolescent's behavior that elicit unfavorable responses in themselves, such as aggression, or abdicating responsibility.

Parents with vague complaints about adolescent children are helped to pinpoint specific problems. The therapist repeatedly asks the parent to describe what the adolescent actually does, and his or her own response. In this way, the therapist elicits detailed descriptions of the adolescent's behavior, and specific responses of parents and other family members to these behaviors. Through the following format, the parent is asked to observe and record disturbing adolescent behaviors targeted for change, and the antecedents and consequences of each:

ANTECEDENTS   ADOLESCENT'S PROBLEM BEHAVIORS   CONSEQUENCES

Following this, parents are helped to generate alternative parenting approaches that might be tried. Parents are asked to predict consequences of each of these approaches, to select the most appropriate approach, to rehearse it during the session, and to experiment with the selected approach at home.

COGNITIVE RESTRUCTURING IN PARENT AND FAMILY SESSIONS

During sessions with the parents, the therapist helps each parent to identify and alter unrealistic or irrational beliefs and attitudes underlying dysfunctional childrearing approaches. The approach is similar to cognitive-restructuring approaches during individual sessions. Cognitive-restructuring interventions may also be introduced during family sessions.

Cognitive-restructuring interventions in family sessions may follow the format recommended by Robin and Foster (Robin, 1981; Robin & Foster, 1984). Robin describes a four-step approach for restructuring of cognitive distortions underlying parent-adolescent conflict: (1) make the underlying cognitive distortion explicit, (2) challenge the logical premises of the distortion, using direct feedback, exaggeration, humor, and reframing techniques, (3) suggest an alternative, more flexible belief, and (4) ask the family to experiment by implementing a solution to a dispute consistent with the more flexible belief, and later to determine whether the solution was successful.

Through observation of family members' verbal and nonverbal behaviors, the therapist identifies dysfunctional parent and adolescent cognitions that fall into categories of irrational beliefs or distorted reasoning processes. The therapist looks for rigid cognitions, intense, inappropriate emotional reactions, and unrealistic ideas, in addition to typical themes characteristic of parents and adolescents in conflict. Family members are asked to give evidence for and against a particular dysfunctional belief; then the family member holding that belief is asked to try to make a convincing case for the belief. Other family members may also be encouraged to help evaluate the evidence.

The therapist models alternative cognitive sets that are more realistic and flexible. Robin and Foster suggest that the therapist teach family members to transform extremist phrases beginning with "must," "have to," and "always" into more moderate phrases such as "It would be nice if," "I would like you to," and "as often as possible." The therapist suggests logical conclusions based on evidence to replace overgeneralized, arbitrary, and absolutistic reasoning.

Experiments are devised to be carried out by family members to test the veracity of alternative, more flexible cognitive sets. For example, Robin and Foster suggest that family members be asked to carry out a homework assignment of surveying other parents to determine whether their experiences confirm the (irrational) belief in question. Parents may also be asked to implement a solution irrationally feared to be catastrophic, in order to see whether the predicted consequences really occur. In addition, family members may be asked to observe interactions in another family in which a parent holds a directly opposing, but more rational, belief. Steps of the experiment to be carried out at home will need to be planned and rehearsed during the session, prior to implementation.

Epstein et al. (1988) have outlined several cognitive-restructuring procedures appropriate for family sessions. For example, they recommend that family members' distorted thoughts about each other be tested for validity during the family session by means of logical analysis and the collection of relevant data. Family sessions provide a milieu in which family members can give direct individual feedback to challenge each others' distorted inferences and attributions. In addition, evidence for the validity of a belief may be examined during family sessions by means of some of the same techniques used in individual therapy, such as reviewing past and current experiences consistent or inconsistent with a particular belief, or asking family members to list advantages and disadvantages of holding and acting on a particular belief.

COMMUNICATION-SKILLS TRAINING

Communication-Skills Training may be carried out during individual sessions with parents, and also during family therapy sessions. During parent sessions, two types of skills may be taught, to be practiced subsequently at home or during family sessions: 1) effective verbal-response styles, and 2) active listening skills.

In teaching effective verbal-response styles, Gordon (1970) suggests that parents first be made aware of the types of verbal responses they are currently using when interacting with their adolescent children. Parents may be shown the following list, suggested by Gordon, and asked to identify and classify their own habitual styles:

1. Ordering, Directing, Commanding
2. Warning, Admonishing, Threatening
3. Exhorting, Moralizing, Preaching
4. Advising, Giving Solutions, or Suggestions
5. Lecturing, Teaching, Giving Logical Argument
6. Judging, Criticizing, Disagreeing, Blaming
7. Praising, Agreeing
8. Name-Calling, Ridiculing, Shaming
9. Interpreting, Analyzing, Diagnosing
10. Reassuring, Sympathizing, Consoling, Supporting
11. Probing, Questioning, Interrogating
12. Withdrawing, Distracting, Humoring, Diverting

Next, parents are asked to pay attention to the adolescent's reaction to these verbal-response styles. Certain parental styles that elicit unfavorable adolescent responses are then targeted for change. New, more effective verbal-response styles may then be demonstrated by the therapist and taught to the parent. The parent is then instructed to experiment with them when interacting with the adolescent at home or during family sessions.

In teaching active listening skills, the therapist first explains how activive listening on the part of the parent encourages adolescents to discuss their problems and concerns more openly. Many parents complain of their son's or daughter's unwillingness to discuss problems with the parent, but are unaware that their own failure to use active listening skills is associated with the adolescent's reluctance to talk. Gordon (1970) lists several components of active listening, which may be modelled by the therapist and practiced by parents during the session, using a role-playing technique:

Parent is a listener.
Parent is a counsellor.
Parent wants to help the youngster.

Parent is a "sounding board."
Parent facilitates the adolescent finding his or her own solution.
Parent accepts the adolescent's solution.
Parent is primarily interested in the adolescent's needs.
Parent is more passive.

Communication-Skills training during family sessions is aimed at teaching clear communication in order to make views and rules explicit rather than ambiguous. It also tries to enhance the quality of relationship between family members by facilitating supportive communication styles characterized by empathy and attempts to understand the other person's point of view. Robin and Foster (1984) advocate a four-step procedure to modify maladaptive family communication patterns: (1) verbal instructions, (2) modelling, (3) behavior rehearsal, and (4) feedback.

First, maladaptive communication patterns are identified by the therapist during family sessions through informal observation, aided by observational checklists. Another helpful aid is the list of typical problematic communication targets and corresponding alternative, more adaptive behaviors, shown in Table 5.1.

While observing family interactions, the therapist identifies those maladaptive interactions maintaining unwanted parent-adolescent conflict. Next, the therapist introduces and models alternate, more adaptive communication patterns. Family members are then encouraged to use these new communication patterns as they discuss an issue during the session. Robin and Foster (1984) emphasize that

TABLE 5.1
Dysfunctional Family Communication Patterns*

Problematic Behaviors	*Alternative Behaviors*
• Talking through a third person	• Talking directly to another person
• Accusing, blaming, defensive statements	• Making I-statements
• Interrupting	• Listening, raising hand when wanting to talk
• Overgeneralizing, making extremist, rigid statements	• Making tentative statements using "sometimes," "maybe"; accurate quantitative statements
• Lecturing, preaching	• Making brief problem statements, using "I would like"
• Getting off topic	• Returning to the problem
• Commanding	• Suggesting alternative solutions
• Dwelling on the past	• Sticking to present
• Monopolizing	• Sticking to brief statements
• Pedanticizing	• Using clear, simple language
• Threatening	• Suggesting alternative solutions
• Remaining silent; not responding	• Validating; expressing negative affect

*Based on Robin & Foster, 1984

feedback should be immediate, specific, concise, and nonblaming. At times, feedback is best directed at dyads or triads, rather than at individuals, to minimize defensiveness. Modelling and instructions should be adapted to fit the family's educational level and cultural background. Family members should be encouraged to reproduce the modelled verbalizations in their own words, in order to increase the chances of these new behaviors being integrated into the family member's own repertoire.

> Feedback, instructions, modelling, and behavior rehearsal were used successfully with the family of a delinquent boy. The father persisted in addressing all statements and complaints about the adolescent to the therapist or to his wife: "John is never home on time." It was pointed out to the father that he was not talking directly to John, but talking through a third person about John. The father was then instructed to address his concerns directly to John, using "I statements." The therapist modelled this interaction: "John, I get very upset when you do not arrive home on time because I become very worried that something bad has happened to you." The father was then asked to direct a similar statement to John, using his own words and supplying his own reasons for being upset by the boy's behavior.

CONFLICT-NEGOTIATION SKILLS TRAINING

Kifer, Lewis, Green, and Phillips (1974) describe an approach designed to train family members to use more efficient negotiation skills in conflict situations, as well as to modify communication processes maintaining parent-adolescent conflict. Parents and adolescents are encouraged to practice using three types of verbal-negotiation behaviors: (1) complete communications, defined as statements that indicate one's position regarding the situation under discussion, followed by a request for the other person to state his position, (2) statements identifying issues, defined as statements that explicitly identify the point of conflict of the situation and statements that attempt to clarify the other person's position, and (3) statements of options, defined as statements that suggest a course of action to resolve the conflict.

These negotiation skills are practiced during family sessions while family members are in the process of attempting to bring about compliant or negotiated agreements, whereby a person agrees to the original position of the other or a compromise is reached. During training sessions, family members are repeatedly instructed by the therapist to use complete communications, to remember to identify the issues, and to suggest some options. The therapist demonstrates these skills repeatedly until family members begin to use them consistently.

Often, a parent initially refuses to negotiate a solution to a particular problem, such as dating privileges or curfew. If this is the case, the family can first be asked to negotiate a less threatening issue. The therapist attempts to get a nonparticipating parent involved in the negotiations and to encourage parents to back each other up in their negotiated decisions.

CONTINGENCY CONTRACTING

Contingency contracting is a behavior therapy technique whereby agreements are made between family members to exchange rewards for desired behavior. Basically, this involves agreements by parents to make certain changes following changes made by the adolescent. The parents and teenager are asked to specify what behaviors they would like the other to change, and these form the core of the initial contract. Clear communication of content and feelings, and clear presentation of demands for negotiation are important behaviors to be modelled by the therapist and reinforced when emitted by family members.

Stuart (1971) was one of the first to advocate the use of this technique to strengthen a family's control over adolescents manifesting conduct disorders. The basis of contingency contracting is a behavioral contract, which is a means of scheduling the exchange of positive reinforcements between the adolescent and his or her parents. Reciprocal exchanges are structured by specifying who is to do what for whom, and under what circumstances. Reciprocity implies that both the adolescent and the adults have rights and duties, and that the positive reinforcers are exchanged on a "something-for-something" basis.

There are several components of a good behavioral contract. One is the specification of details of the privileges that both adolescent and adults should expect to gain after fulfilling their responsibilities. For example, a girl may be allowed out with her friends on Saturday afternoon (privilege), if she agrees to attend all classes at school (responsibility). The privileges specified in the contract must be highly valued by the adolescent to be effective.

Rewards selected as reinforcers to accelerate desired adolescent responses may consist of activities the adolescent finds pleasant, material rewards, or social reinforcers. It is important to specify details of responsibilities to be fulfilled in order to secure each privilege. If responsibilities can be kept to a minimum, this will increase the likelihood that they will be met.

The responsibilities specified must be monitored by the parents, school officials, or others, so that parents know when to properly grant a privilege. Some responsibilites are more difficult to monitor than others, such as where the adolescent goes after school and whom he or she spends time with outside of the home. If responsible behaviors cannot be monitored, they are probably beyond the scope of behavioral contracts. However, adaptations may be made. For example, reinforcements mediated at home may be contingent on school attendance and performance, if the parents make arrangements to monitor school behavior by means of systematic feedback from school authorities.

Another element of a good contract is the specification of a system of sanctions for failure to meet responsibilities. Planning the sanctions beforehand and building them into the contract helps to insure that the failure of the adolescent to meet the responsibility is not followed by inappropriately severe or light sanctions that would decrease adolescent compliance. Another element of a good contract suggested by Stuart is a bonus clause, which insures that the adolescent receives positive reinforcement for compliance with the contract. The bonus may take the form of added privileges or material rewards.

The following format may be used for the behavioral contract, adapted from Clarke et al. (1990):

CONTRACT AGREEMENT

Teen agrees to do the following: Parent agrees to do the following:

When will teen do these things?   When will parent do these things?

This contract will be valid for _____,

and re-evaluated _____.

Typical privileges used in parent-adolescent contracts include free time with friends, allowance, and free choice of dress. Typical responsibilities include maintenance of adequate school attendance, maintenance of curfew hours, completion of housework chores, and informing parents about activities.

Contingency contracting may also be carried out in the school. The therapist helps to set up contracts between the adolescent client and school personnel.

DISCIPLINE-EFFECTIVENESS TRAINING

Ineffective parental disciplinary approaches tend to rely on negative reinforcement, punishment, and coercion, rather than on positive control procedures. Ineffectual disciplinary patterns include: failure to punish the adolescent's misbehavior and to reward good behavior, parental threats that cannot be followed through, and parental use of punishments that are too mild and have no effect, or too severe, resulting in fear and anxiety rather than discriminative learning. Some parents abdicate responsibility for disciplinary action altogether. They fail to take disciplinary action following the adolescent's unacceptable behavior or they fail to take responsibility for attempts to negotiate solutions to family problems.

Discipline-Effectiveness Training may be carried out during both parent sessions and family sessions. Components of Discipline-Effectiveness Training may include:

1. Rule-Establishment Training
2. Induction-Control Training
3. Behavior-Analysis Skills Training
4. Expectations-Establishment Training
5. Contingency Contracting
6. Family Problem-Solving Training

Rule-Establishment Training and Induction Control will be discussed in this section. The latter four interventions are discussed in separate sections, but may be incorporated into Discipline-Effectiveness Training interventions.

Rule-Establishment Training

A major component of lax, inconsistent discipline is failure to establish and reinforce explicit rules. Difficulties may stem from family rules that are too narrow or too rigid. Difficulties may also stem from lack of explicit rules or lack of consensus among family members as to what the rules actually are.

Parents often need to be instructed, through therapist explanation and modelling, how to set clear rules and regulations, and how to enforce them. First, the importance of consistent enforcement of these rules must be emphasized, in terms of general principles of operant conditioning and social learning theory. The importance of consistent supervision of adolescent children should also be emphasized. After this introduction, parents are assisted by the therapist in setting and enforcing rules during family sessions. Alexander and Parsons (1973) suggest that parents be helped to make rules explicit by the differentiation of rules (limits designed to regulate and control action and conduct of family members) from requests ("asking behavior").

Training family members in solution-oriented communication patterns is a second intervention which facilitates the negotiation of the specific content of rules and requests. The following categories of communication patterns may be modelled by the therapist and taught to family members while they are in the process of establishing rules: (1) interruption for clarification, (2) interruption to increase information about the topic or about one's self in relation to the topic, and (3) interruption to offer informative feedback to other family members. The therapist explains the meaning and purpose of these types of interruptions to the family, and uses verbal and nonverbal praise to reinforce family members for using these communication patterns.

Induction Control Training

Parental induction control is defined as an attempt by the parent to obtain voluntary compliance to parental desires by avoiding direct conflict of wills with the youngster. Operationally, it is defined as a reasoning approach to discipline whereby the parent gives explanations for desired behaviors. Adolescent compliance has been found to be greatest when the parents use induction control and when the adolescent perceives the parent as having a legitimate right to make control attempts.

Rollins and Thomas (1975) conclude, on the basis of their review of literature on the relationship between socialization outcome in children and parental nurturance and control, that a pattern of high parental nurturance, power, and use of inductive control attempts maximizes parental effectiveness, and that this holds across a wide range of age groups and child behaviors. In contrast, the least effective socialization strategy used by parents combines low levels of nurturance with either low levels of induction-control attempts or high levels of power-assertive control attempts. Power-assertion control is defined as force applied by the parent in a contest of wills with the child. It is operationally defined as the summation of parental behaviors, such as physical punishment, deprivation of material objects or privileges, and the direct application of force, where the adolescent perceives the parent as not having the legitimate right to make control attempts.

During family sessions, the therapist requests that the parent provide explanations or reasons for the behaviors expected from the adolescent. The therapist reinforces the parent for providing explanations rather than simply issuing ultimatums. The parent is also reinforced for listening to the adolescent's side of the argument.

EXPECTATIONS-ESTABLISHMENT TRAINING

In troubled families, parental beliefs, attitudes, and expectations with respect to the behavior of adolescent children are often inappropriate for the youngster's age and developmental stage. Parental expectations may be either too great or too minimal. Often, parents are uninformed about aspects of normal adolescent development and are unable to differentiate between what is "normal" and what is "abnormal" adolescent behavior. For example, an authoritarian parent may be unaware that independence-seeking is part of normal adolescent development, along with an increasing desire to spend more time with peers rather than with parents and formation of heterosexual relationships. The authoritarian parent may perceive these behaviors as indicative of rejection and hatred of parents, or immorality, and may respond by placing excessive restrictions and "guilt trips" on the adolescent. The adolescent, in turn, may feel guilty and worthless for these normal desires for independence and peer relationships. Perfectionistic parents are another category of parents who hold unrealistically high expectations for adolescents.

In contrast, overly submissive or overindulgent parents may hold expectations for the adolescent that are too minimal. They may believe that parents have no right to impose their values on an adolescent by restricting certain behaviors and by expecting conformity to reasonable standards of performance. Their failure to establish appropriate and explicit rules and regulations may result in dysfunctional adolescent attitudes and beliefs regarding his or her special right to flaunt societal rules and indulge in behavior excesses characteristic of conduct disorders.

Sessions with parents aimed at changing inappropriate parental expectations would focus on:

1. identifying dysfunctional parental attitudes underlying the inappropriate expectations for adolescent behavior, and altering these through cognitive-restructuring interventions;
2. familiarizing parents with normal adolescent behaviors and crucial developmental tasks of adolescence;
3. assisting parents in formulating more appropriate expectations and helping parents to plan how these new expections will be implemented;
4. helping parents to implement new expectations during family sessions.

INDEPENDENCE TRAINING (ADOLESCENT-AUTONOMY TRAINING)

Developmentally inappropriate parent-adolescent dependency may significantly interfere with crucial developmental tasks, such as formation of peer relationships, development of a sense of responsibility, or preparation for higher education or employment. In some families characterized by lack of privacy and tight mutual contingency control, adolescent independence-seeking is actively resisted by parents. A parent may fear loss of reinforcement if the youngster spends time away from home, or a mother may feel insecure about having to function independently without the adolescent's companionship. Some parents may also have exaggerated fears about the youngster being exposed to dangerous situations. The parent fosters adolescent dependence as a means of alleviating his or her own loneliness or fear. The adolescent fears his or her own inability to cope or loss of control if left alone.

Cognitive-restructuring techniques are used to alter irrational parent and adolescent beliefs. Parents are familiarized with appropriate adolescent behaviors, and Expectation-Establishment Training may be incorporated into Independence Training. Then, a hierarchy of tasks and activities for the adolescent to perform independently is drawn up and a schedule devised for gradual fading of parental participation in these activities. Finally, Assertiveness Training is sometimes an integral part of Independence Training when the youngster is unable to break free from a controlling or overprotective parent.

PROBLEM-SOLVING TRAINING

Gordon (1970) was one of the first to outline a problem-solving training approach to parent-child conflict. A simple version of family problem-solving, outlined by Robin and Foster (1984), consists of four steps, similar to problem-solving interventions for individual therapy:

1. problem definition
2. generation of alternative solutions
3. decision-making
4. planning solution implementation.

There are several components to the problem-definition phase. First, each family member is asked to express his or her own perspective or definition of the problems. Then each member is asked to reflect back to the speaker his or her own understanding of the speaker's problem definition. An adequate problem definition is described as one that indicates what bothers the speaker and why it bothers him or her, while addressing behaviors, feelings, and situations in a nonaccusatory way. The therapist teaches family members how to make adequate problem definitions by modelling adequate problem-definition statements, and by correcting inadequate problem definitions and reflections.

In the next phase, the family members are encouraged to generate alternative solutions to the problem while temporarily deferring evaluation of these solutions. Additional alternatives may be suggested by the therapist. One family member is asked to record these alternatives, preferably the adolescent so that he or she will maintain interest in the activity.

In the evaluation phase, each family member is asked to hypothesize what the possible positive and negative consequences of each of the alternatives might be. Family members are then asked to evaluate each alternative by giving it a plus or minus rating. If a consensus is reached, the alternative is implemented.

If no consensus is reached, the family is next taught to negotiate a compromise. If there is a solution that is rated positively by at least one parent and the adolescent, the therapist starts with it. A list of possible compromises is generated, which family members evaluate in order to reach a solution.

In the final phase, family members specify details and difficulties of putting the solution into practice, and a system is devised that is considered to be best by all family members for evaluating and monitoring successful implementation (either written or oral). The family then tries out the solution at home and reports the results at the next session. Successful implementations are continued, while unsuccessful implementations are renegotiated.

RELATIONSHIP-ENHANCEMENT TRAINING

Gordon (1970) suggests that some parents may have to be taught to demonstrate through words and gestures their inner feelings of acceptance of the adolescent. Often parents do not realize that acceptance must be demonstrated, and that they are not doing this. Nonverbal messages of acceptance include facial expressions, gestures, and hugs. Parents may be asked to inhibit their tendency to intervene in the youngster's activities in order to demonstrate acceptance of what the adolescent has chosen to do. Passive listening (versus verbal interference on the part of the parent) may also be used to communicate acceptance and to foster adolescent independence and confidence. Communication of verbal acceptance can be increased by encouraging the parent to praise the adolescent more frequently during the session, especially in cases where parents are unaware that they rarely or never compliment their son or daughter.

Guerney, Coufal, and Vogelsong (1981) propose tasks to be carried out during family sessions for the purpose of enhancing parent-adolescent relationships. For example, the parent and adolescent may be asked: "Discuss between you: (1) something you would like to see changed in yourself, and (2) something you would like to see changed in the other person." While carrying out this task, the participants are asked to openly express their own feelings on the issue and to help the others to express their feelings. Particular types of responses known to enhance relationships are demonstrated and reinforced by the therapist, including (1) restatement of content responses, (2) feeling clarification responses, and (3) direct expression of feeling responses. Other categories of supportive communication patterns include genuine seeking and giving of information, spontaneous problem-solving, empathic understanding, and equality statements.

On the other hand, defensive communication patterns would be discouraged by the therapist, including judgmental dogmatism, control strategy, indifference, and superiority (Alexander & Parsons, 1973). To foster positive communication, the therapist first models the supportive communication pattern, and then family members are asked to practice these skills. The therapist may also shape behaviors such as thanking or complimenting another person, and giving and accepting constructive criticism (Serna et al., 1986).

Another component of relationship-enhancing training consists of techniques designed to shape and increase parental nurturance. Parental nurturance may be defined as parental behavior manifested toward the child that confirms in the child's mind that he or she is accepted and approved of by the parent. Operationally, parental nurturance has been defined as (1) praising, (2) approving, (3) encouraging, (4) helping, (5) cooperating, (6) expressing terms of endearment, and (7) physical affection.

Family Therapy goals for enhancement of parent-adolescent relationship would include: (1) aiding family members in becoming more helpful and supportive to each other, (2) helping families to plan shared activities, (3) increasing the frequency of positive interactions and decreasing hostile interactions through communication training, and (4) increasing perceived affection between family members by encouraging family members to express feelings of mutual acceptance and affection. In addition, negative labels and attributions that family members attach to one another may be questioned or challenged by the therapist, and replaced by more positive labels.

PART II

APPLICATION TO SPECIFIC ADOLESCENT PROBLEMS

6

Family-Related Problems

Dysfunctional adolescent behaviors and cognitions stemming from family problems will be addressed in this chapter under three overlapping categories of family-related adolescent disorders: (1) disorders related to dysfunctional parenting styles, (2) disorders related to parent-adolescent conflict, and (3) disorders related to chronic family stress stemming from marital conflict and divorce, parental alcohol abuse, and parental violence and child abuse.

ADOLESCENT DISORDERS RELATED TO DYSFUNCTIONAL PARENTING STYLES

Categories of dysfunctional parenting styles and corresponding maladaptive adolescent response patterns outlined by Missildine (1963), (Appendix C), provide a useful guide for identifying target behaviors for therapy intervention. A parent may rely on one or more of these dysfunctional childrearing styles, while an adolescent may manifest one or several of the corresponding response styles.

Components of these dysfunctional parenting styles may be present in milder form in normal families. Manifestations of maladaptive coping patterns may range from mild and transient in normal families to severe persistent patterns in clinical populations. Adolescents may temporarily manifest responses to inadequate parenting for short periods of time without significant interference with resolution of crucial developmental tasks. For example, a youngster may manifest symptoms of depression related to temporary parental neglect caused by a parent's prolonged hospitalization, but the depression subsides once the situation has returned to normal. Harmful long-term effects on the youngster's personality development occur when the severe, persistent, dysfunctional parenting practices shape adolescent coping patterns which ultimately interfere with successful completion of crucial, age-appropriate developmental tasks.

Seven categories of dysfunctional parenting styles are described below: punitive parent, rejecting parent, overcoercive parent, overindulgent parent, oversubmissive parent, neglectful parent, and perfectionistic parent. Brief case examples will be given to illustrate each category of dysfunctional parenting, as well as typical adolescent and parent behaviors and cognitons characteristic of each category. This will be followed by an illustration of the way in which the therapist might go about identifying parent and adolescent behaviors as targets for therapy, with corresponding recommendations for intervention strategies.

Targets Related to Punitive and Rejecting Parenting

These two categories of dysfunctional parenting will be considered jointly, since they often occur simultaneously and are associated with similar dysfunctional adolescent behaviors.

Punitive Parent

Missildine (1963) distinguishes three subcategories of punitive parenting: (1) punitive aggression, (2) punitive guilt engendering, and (3) punitive distrust. Parental punitive aggression usually refers to physical abuse, but may also refer to excessive verbal abuse only. Punitive guilt engendering often accompanies parental aggression. The adolescent is made to feel worthless and guilty because of his or her "bad" behavior or weaknesses. Guilt engendering may take different forms. The parent may blame the child for causing family problems, such as marital breakdown, or the parent may use punitive strict moralizing to label the youngster as "sinful," or "bad." Characteristic patterns of adolescent response to punitive aggression or punitive, guilt-engendering childrearing styles include interpersonal aggression, preoccupation with revenge, retaliation against parents, self-punishment, extreme guilt, approval seeking, assumption of a "victim" role, and fearful obedience.

Punitive distrust is a childrearing style in which parents lecture adolescents endlessly about avoidance of dangerous circumstances that could lead to catastrophes such as unwanted pregnancy or drug addiction. Due to extreme distrust, a parent may falsely blame the son or daughter for engaging in these "dangerous" activities. Adolescents may react to punitive parental distrust by eventual manifestation of the behaviors they have been wrongly accused of exhibiting, or by self-condemnation for minor inconsequential transgressions, accompanied by guilt and self-hate.

The following case examples illustrate maladaptive responses to punitive parenting:

> A 16-year-old boy was beaten regularly by his father during childhood . . . He was too frightened of his father to retaliate against him, but instead developed a physically aggressive pattern with peers, which resulted in a charge of assault and eventual incarceration in training school during adolescence.

> The son of an abusive father became physically abusive toward his own mother. At one point, he threatened to seriously harm both parents and they subsequently had him admitted to an adolescent treatment centre.

A girl wrongly accused by her father of sexual activities with boys was prohibited from even talking to boys. The girl became preoccupied with sexual fantasies; when boys began to show an interest in her, truancy and promiscuity followed.

A girl accused of being a "slut" by her father became severely depressed by her own "evil behavior." She was unable to make a moral distinction between her habit of indulging in sexual fantasies and actual sexual promiscuity, which was not a part of her behavior pattern.

REJECTING PARENT

This parental attitude denies the adolescent any real degree of acceptance. The youngster is viewed as an unwanted burden. One characteristic reaction to parental rejection is excessive approval-seeking from the rejecting parent, from peers, or from others. This is often accompanied by the adolescent's tendency to "test the limits" of a relationship, either by making impossible demands on a person for unconditional love or by behaving in a provocative, hostile, or unacceptable manner guaranteed to evoke rejection. Other characteristic response styles include a tendency to be easily hurt, to be bitter and hostile, to be overly suspicious of a person's intentions or friendly overtures, or to distort the meaning of another person's behavior. Bitter self-depreciation is another characteristic response.

A delinquent boy from a middle-class family had been hyperactive as a child and extremely difficult to handle, in contrast to a younger brother who was described by the mother as a delightful, easy child. After the boy began getting in trouble at school and with the law, the mother refused to have him live with her. The mother's message to her son was that he was not worth her time and effort, which were reserved for the younger brother who was a good student and, according to the mother, destined to become a doctor or lawyer. The boy's grandparents offered to care for him, but after a few weeks he again began to engage in delinquent acts, testing the limits of his grandparents' devotion to him.

The teenage son of parents who had deserted their three children was begrudgingly looked after by his paternal grandmother. The grandmother was bitter about the fact that she had been forced by her irresponsible son to look after her grandson. She repeatedly let him know that he was a terrible burden and that he was worthless just like his father. The boy's repeated attempts to win his grandmother's approval were unsuccessful. He was more successful in proving himself to delinquent peers through daring acts such as car theft.

INTERVENTION

The following targets and interventions would apply to the above cases:

Parent-Adolescent Targets

1. Punitive disciplinary style and adolescent retaliation

2. Parent-adolescent anger

3. Unrealistic parental fears

4. Unrealistic parental expectations

Interventions

• Discipline-Effectiveness Training
• Behavior-Analysis Skill Training
• Conflict-Negotiation Skills Training
• Contingency Contracting
• Communication-Skills Training

• Relationship-Enhancement Training

• Cognitive Restructuring

• Expectations-Establishment Training
• Cognitive Restructuring

Adolescent Targets

1. Delinquent acts

2. Delinquent peer associations

3. Depressive cognitions

4. Excessive demands on others

Interventions

• Cognitive Self-Control interventions
• Contingency-Awareness Training

• Pro-social Interpersonal-Skill Training
• Assertiveness Training

• Cognitive Restructuring
• Activity Scheduling (for esteem-building activities)

• Interpersonal Coping-Skills Training

Targets Related to Overcoercive Parenting

The overcoercive parent constantly directs the youngster's activities in an anxious, nagging manner, so that the teenager has almost no opportunity to pursue his own interests and activities. Overcoercion may also take the form of excessive authoritarianism, with the parent maintaining absolute control and demanding total submission without discussion with the adolescent.

Clinical examples of parental beliefs underlying excessive authoritarianism include: "Parents should have control over all decisions made," "Teenagers are too young to make any important decisions," and "Parents have rights; children don't."

Typical dysfunctional adolescent coping patterns include (1) compliance accompanied by excessive need for direction from adults, (2) active resistance and outward defiance of parents, and (3) passive resistance, or secret defiance of parents.

Adolescents who have never been encouraged or allowed to do things for themselves often fail to develop and practice skills in initiating acitivities and following through. At times, they become so passive that they require an adult's guidance in order to carry out even the simplest age-appropriate tasks.

Active resistance is a pattern adopted by some adolescents in response to over-coercive parenting. The adolescent is forced to listen and comply, but may subsequently rebel by purposely doing the opposite of what the parent demands. For example, in response to a parent's excessive nagging about school achievement and demands that the son or daughter spend an excessive amount of time on homework assignments, the adolescent may purposely underachieve at school.

Passive resistance is another characteristic category of response. It may take the form of dawdling, daydreaming, or procrastination to avoid compliance with parental demands. These patterns may generalize to the school environment.

A teenage daughter of southern European immigrants was forced to abide by restrictions similar to those placed on young girls growing up in the father's boyhood village. Although living in North America, the girl was driven to and from school by her father. She was never allowed to go out with girlfriends, to use the telephone, or to have girlfriends over to the house. The father allowed no discussion around these restrictions, but demanded 100% obedience. The girl began to skip school secretly in order to spend time with peers.

An 18-year-old girl, prohibited by her parents from attending parties or school events, defiantly refused to attend school in an attempt to force her parents to allow her to go out with friends once every two weeks. When school authorities reported the truancy to the parents, they became alarmed by the truancy and reluctantly agreed to meet with school staff and the daughter to talk things over.

INTERVENTION

The following targets and interventions would apply for the above case:

Parent-Adolescent Targets

1. Overcoercive parenting style; adolescent defiance

Interventions

- Discipline-Effectiveness Training
- Contingency Contracting
- Conflict-Negotiation-Skills Training
- Communication-Skills Training

2. Adolescent-parent dependency

- Independence Training

Adolescent Targets

1. Unassertiveness

Interventions

- Assertiveness Training

Targets Associated with Overindulgent/Overprotective Parenting

Overindulgent parents are those who attempt to provide their teenagers with everything they need and desire without setting age-appropriate expectations in return. Overprotective parenting is a variation of overindulgence. The parent tries to protect the teenager from having to endure normal adolescent hardships. Often, these parents have been overindulged themselves and are repeating their own parents' patterns. The overindulgent parent may also be satisfying his or her own needs. The parent may have an exaggerated need to "mother" the child or may direct excessive energy into parenting to make up for an unsatisfactory marriage or job.

Sometimes, parents have had deprived backgrounds and consequently feel they should give their children everything they lacked. Another parent may feel guilty about, or sorry for the adolescent because of hardships that the young person has had to endure, such as ill health, physical deformity, or parental divorce, and may therefore overindulge the youngster in an attempt to make up for the hardships. Sometimes, the adolescent is excessively valued, such as an only child, a child born after years of waiting, or a son born after a succession of daughters. Other parents believe that overindulgence is the only way to demonstrate true love for a child.

Typical adolescent responses to overindulgence include (1) bored passivity, characterized by lack of sufficient interests, and hours of inactivity, (2) expectations that others must fulfill all wishes and desires, (3) abdication of responsibility, (4) lack of persistence when the going gets rough, and (5) a tendency to drift from one thing to another.

By the time they reach adolescence, overindulged children are usually adept at getting what they want from parents, who have been conditioned by the child's unrelenting demands for fulfilment of needs and desires. Frequently, overindulgent parents are also oversubmissive parents.

A 17-year-old boy was referred to a mental health clinic by his worried parents after he refused to attend school, stopped seeing friends, and began to spend long hours sleeping. He had a long history of insufficient application to schoolwork and school failure, but his mother believed that pushing him to do schoolwork would be harmful. She argued that he had always been a delicate child who required gentle handling. For years she had routinely helped her son with his homework, so that the boy never learned to initiate and take responsibility for his own assignments. He became depressed by his inability to cope on his own and by the hopelessness of his academic future.

A 16-year-old girl was fearful of attending school because she dreaded classmates' and teachers' negative opinions of her. Her mother felt sorry for her and allowed her to stay at home when the girl said she was upset and didn't feel like going to school. This pattern had begun in Grade Nine and grew progressively worse. In recent months, the girl had missed weeks of school at a time, with the mother providing written excuses citing illness as the cause of her daughter's absences.

INTERVENTION

The following targets and interventions would apply to the above cases:

Parent-Adolescent Targets	*Interventions*
1. Low parental expectations for adolescent	• Expectations-Establishment Training • Discipline-Effectiveness Training
2. Parental fostering of adolescent dependency	• Independence Training
3. Dysfunctional parent cognitions	• Cognitive Restructuring

Adolescent Targets	*Interventions*
1. Failure to initiate and persist (schoolwork)	• Self-Monitoring Training
2. Expectations for special treatment	• Cognitive Restructuring

ADOLESCENT SOMATOFORM DISORDER

Parental compliance with adolescent somatoform disorders may be viewed as another form of overindulgent parenting. Parents who are unnecessarily preoccupied with their own minor aches, pains, and disease often exaggerate their children's minor aches and pains. Adolescents learn to associate their own bodily sensations and functions with illness and expect them to be incapacitating. In extreme cases, adolescents may feel that they are not well enough to attend school at all, which again is usually supported on some level by the parent. If physical disease is ruled out by medical examination, the adolesent may develop new symptoms to combat pressures to participate in certain activities that were successfully avoided in the past.

A 19-year-old student repeatedly failed courses after poor attendance. This problem dated back to Grade Seven, shortly after she entered a new school after a family move. She complained of pain in her legs and missed seven months of school. Both the girl and her mother had been very unhappy about the move. Doctors were unable to find a physical cause, but eventually the girl was treated by a chiropractor and was able to return to school within four days. Following this, recurrent pain complaints over the years led to prolonged absences from school, although there were few complaints during summer holidays. At first, the mother was not concerned about the school absences, or the daughter's lack of peer friendships and growing social anxiety, since the mother enjoyed spending time with her daughter when she stayed home and considered the girl to be her best friend. Later, however, she became alarmed at her daughter's chronic academic failure and the daughter's almost total social withdrawal.

INTERVENTION

The following targets and interventions would apply to the above case:

Parent-Adolescent Targets
1. Parent-adolescent dependency
2. Adolescent manipulation of parent

Interventions
• Independence Training
• Discipline-Effectiveness Training
• Problem-Solving (family therapy)

Adolescent Targets
1. Pain complaints
2. Social anxiety

3. Absence from school

Interventions
• Medical examination report
• Interpersonal Coping-Skills Training;
• Conversation-Skills Training
• Graded-Task Assignment
• Goal Planning
• Self-Monitoring Training

First, a thorough medical exam was arranged, followed by a discussion of the doctor's report during a subsequent session. (The doctor stated that there was no evidence supporting a physical cause for the girl's symptoms.) Next, the girl was helped to define short- and long-term goals through a Goal-Planning intervention. This was followed by family Problem-Solving Skill Training, which helped the family to generate alternative courses of action to help the daughter achieve her educational goal of finishing high school. The following alternatives were listed:

1. Attend regular classes: full academic program;
2. Individual study program at the school;
3. Take the year off and work;
4. Partial academic program.

The fourth approach was selected and implemented. A combination of Interpersonal Coping-Skills Training, Conversation-Skills Training, and Graded-Task Assignment helped the girl to cope with her social anxiety. The mother-daughter interdependency was addressed through Independence Training in subsequent family sessions.

Targets Associated with Parental Oversubmissiveness

The oversubmissive parent is unable to say no to the adolescent's demands or to set appropriate limits on the adolescent's behavior. The parent fails to impose sufficient rules and expectations, and to administer appropriate consequences following adolescent transgressions. Oversubmissive parents are often unwilling slaves to their children's demands. Some of the same dysfunctional attitudes characteristic of overindulgent parents are also characteristic of oversubmissive parents, such as anxiety about losing the child's love as a result of the imposition of limits, equating love for the child with giving in to his demands, and a belief that a parent does not have the right to impose limits and expectations.

Maladaptive adolescent patterns characteristic of youngsters raised by oversubmissive parents include impulsive response style and failure to persist at unexciting or uninteresting tasks. The adolescent succumbs to desires for immediate gratification and impulse satisfaction. This sometimes results in self-destructive behavioral excesses, such as temper tantrums, thrill-seeking, or substance abuse. Exploitation of others in the belief that it is justified is another characteristic pattern.

Since these youngsters are not used to having limits placed on their behavior, they fail to learn to place limits on themselves. Consequently, they lack sufficient self-discipline to prevent destructive patterns from developing. These self-destructive behaviors may ultimately interfere with completion of essential developmental tasks, such as securing an adequate education or developing satisfying interpersonal relationships.

Adolescent children of oversubmissive parents often have unrealistic expectations for special treatment. The adolescent comes to believe that he is deserving of special treatment due to his superiority or his special circumstances, not only from parents (who may convey the impression to their children that they are unrealistically gifted, unusual, or privileged), but also from peers and teachers. Behaviorally, the adolescent attempts to manipulate or exploit others; this is followed by excessive blaming, rationalization, and denial when these attempts fail to gain the desired effect. Violation of rules and regulations at home, at school, and in the community, may be coupled with a belief that noncompliance with family or societal rules is one's special right.

A teenage boy became a great concern to his divorced mother when he began staying out until 3:00 a.m. with friends, indulging in drugs and alcohol, and skipping school. He said that nobody had the right to run his life. The mother was unable to enforce definite curfews and rules. She said that she did not want to be mean, emphasizing how much her son had suffered when he learned that his father had deserted the family and didn't love him. The mother believed that forcing restrictions on her son would be perceived by him as proof that she, too, did not love him.

INTERVENTION

The following targets and interventions would be applicable to the above cases:

Parent-Adolescent Targets	*Interventions*
1. Inappropriate parental expectations	• Expectation-Establishment Training
2. Insufficient parental rules, limits, and consequences	• Discipline-Effectiveness Training

Adolescent Targets	*Interventions*
1. Impulsive response style and self-destructive patterns	• Cognitive Self-Control
	• Contingency-Awareness Training

Targets Associated with Parental Neglect

Neglect generally involves a parental attitude which precludes adequate consideration of the child's needs. The parent is too involved or preoccupied to give the adolescent the necessary attention and sympathetic support he requires. Sometimes, factors depriving the adolescent of sufficient parental attention are beyond the parent's control, such as prolonged illness or death of a spouse. Parent-adolescent separation is often a contributing factor in the case of parental divorce or desertion.

When neglect is persistent and severe, maladaptive adolescent patterns may include an inability to form close interpersonal relationships due to a lack of true concern for others, a lack of social skills, unrealistic expectations about the way others should behave, or a tendency to place excessive demands on others to prove their love. Failure to form satisfying interpersonal relationships may lead to anxiety and depression and a sense of emptiness. Anger toward the neglectful parent often leads to obsessive preoccupation with retaliation.

Other dysfunctional cognitive patterns might include excessive preoccupation with the missing parent, excessive wishing for recognition from that parent, or idealization of a dead or missing parent. Neglected adolescents may develop a tendency to exploit others, resulting in antisocial patterns and conduct disorders. Excessive striving for success is another maladaptive pattern associated with parental neglect. Self-blame is another response style stemming from the adolescent's belief that something in him caused the parent to neglect him. Finally, a pattern of drifting may develop, characterized by lack of long-term goals and failure to plan and structure daily life.

The son of an alcoholic father and a mother who deserted the father and son ruminated excessively on the possible reasons for his mother's failure to contact him during the past five years, concluding that he had been a disappointing and unworthy son. In addition to these ruminations, he was also handicapped by lack of exposure to normal affectionate interactions in the home, so that he failed to acquire the necessary social skills for forming and maintaining successful peer relationships. He drifted from one fad to another, experimented with drugs, and was truant for days at a time.

A mature-looking 15-year-old girl, who attempted to dress and act like a sophisticated adult, had been angry with her divorced mother for years for not spending enough time with her. Over the years, the girl had competed with a succession of her mother's boyfriends for the mother's attention. In her early teens, the girl began dressing in a provocative manner and succeeded in seducing one of her mother's boyfriends. The girl's truancy and school failure were the factors that eventually prompted the mother to seek psychiatric help for her. The girl subsequently told the psychiatrist that she enjoyed school and explained her truancy by saying, "It's as if I don't want to do well at school because that's what my mother wants me to do."

INTERVENTION

The following targets and interventions would be applicable to the above cases:

Parent-Adolescent Targets

1. Persistent parental neglect

2. Adolescent anger toward neglectful parent
3. Adolescent truancy to manipulate parents

Interventions

• Behavior-Analysis Skills Training (parent session)
• Relationship-Enhancement Training

• Communication-Skills Training
• Conflict-Negotiation Skills Training

Adolescent Targets

1. Failure to establish close interpersonal relationships
2. Depression (self-blame; self-criticism)
3. Drifting

Interventions

• Interpersonal Coping-Skills Training

• Cognitive Restructuring

• Goal-Establishment Training
• Self-Monitoring Training

Targets Associated with Perfectionistic Parent

Perfectionistic parents are characterized by a tendency to exert excessive pressure on the adolescent to "do better." The parent demands more advanced behavior than the adolescent can comfortably achieve; parental approval is withheld until the adolescent is felt to be performing at optimal levels. This may never be achieved, so that real praise is almost totally absent. Excessive parental demands may be reinforced in a variety of ways, from punitiveness and overcoercion to expression of sad disappointment.

The adolescent coping style may be characterized by excessive striving to gain parental acceptance, often to a state of exhaustion. Since parental approval is not given, the adolescent does not gain confidence in his abilities, but develops a basic dissatisfaction with himself and habitual self-belittlement. He begins to impose his parent's perfectionistic demands on himself. The adolescent finds little satisfaction in his own true achievements, because he never believes that he has sufficiently measured up. He sets unattainable standards for himself and experiences guilt because of failure to achieve them.

Parental demands for perfection may be applied to a wide range of adolescent behaviors, such as academic performance, physical appearance, or masculinity or femininity. Parental demands may range from blatant criticism to subtle withholding of approval. Examples of statements reflecting dysfunctional attitudes and beliefs made by perfectionistic parents include: "Children must be pushed to achieve their full potential"; "If a son doesn't excel at school he's a guaranteed failure in life"; and "Children should not be praised."

The 16-year-old son of a depressed father was made to feel that he was never mature, competent, or responsible enough. The father placed excessive demands on the son to contribute financially to the family while simultaneously coping with schoolwork. The boy continually berated himself for his inability to please his father.

The youngest of three teenage sisters berated herself for her inability to achieve high grades like her two older sisters, even though she was a "B" student. Her father was outwardly critical of her grades and the mother subtly conveyed the message that she could have done better with just a little added effort, so that the girl always felt guilty. She was angry at her parents' failure to acknowledge her nonacademic achievements in gymnastics, a sport in which she had received several awards.

INTERVENTION

The following targets and interventions would apply to the above cases:

Parent-Adolescent Targets	*Interventions*
1. Excessively high parental expectations for adolescent	• Expectations-Establishment Training
2. Parental withholding of approval and praise	• Cognitive Restructuring • Discipline-Effectiveness Training
3. Adolescent anger at parents	• Relationship-Enhancement Training

Adolescent Targets	Interventions
1. Excessive striving for parental approval	• Assertiveness Training
2. Depression (self belittlement)	• Cognitive Restructuring

SEVERE PARENT-ADOLESCENT CONFLICT

Severe parent-adolescent conflict is a major component of many of the adolescent disorders stemming from dysfunctional parenting styles described above. Intense, unresolved parent or adolescent anger is frequently present and will be addressed first. This will be followed by a discussion of skill deficits characterizing families with severe parent-adolescent conflict, including aggressive parent-adolescent response style, inadequate family-communication skills, and inadequate problem-solving and conflict-negotiation skills (Guerney et al., 1981; Robin, 1981). Dysfunctional cognitions underlying parent-adolescent conflict will be addressed in the final section.

Parent-adolescent conflict usually takes the form of ongoing verbal arguments about specific issues, characterized by hostile exchanges and failure to come to a mutually satisfactory resolution. These exchanges are distinguished from less problematic parent-adolescent arguments by their greater intensity, higher frequency, longer duration, and greater subjective levels of distress reported by family members (Robin & Foster, 1984).

A comparison of referred female adolescent clients with low self-concepts in relation to family relationships, with non-referred controls with good self-concepts, revealed significant differences in categories of perceived parental evaluations reported by the girls (Zarb, 1990). The following categories of response to the question "How would your father (mother) describe you?" occurred more frequently in the referred group: "promiscuous," "psychologically abnormal," "worthless," and "cruel." In the same study, the following categories of typical adolescent response styles in stressful interactions with parents significantly distinguished referred from non-referred adolescent girls: "abusive name-calling," "disobey (parental) prohibitions," "physically abusive to parent," "manipulative threats," "self-destructive behavior," "prolonged silent treatment," and "passive helplessness."

From a social-learning perspective, parent-adolescent conflict is viewed as resulting from skill deficits and dysfunctional attitudinal responses leading to reciprocally punishing transactions. Kifer et al. (1974) discuss two general types of family interventions found to be effective with severe parent-adolescent conflict: (1) arbitration or mediation of specific conflicts, and (2) modification of the parent-adolescent communication process. In the first approach, which usually involves a form of contingency contracting, the therapist takes the role of mediator in order to facilitate mutual agreement between parent and adolescent with respect to reciprocal exchanges of specific behaviors, reinforcers, and punishers. In the second approach, therapy techniques such as verbal instruction, practice, and feedback are used by the therapist to alter dysfunctional interpersonal behaviors or skill deficits interfering with successful negotiation of conflict. These two approaches may be applied concurrently.

Target: Intense Unresolved Anger

Intense anger is frequently an underlying component of parent-adolescent conflict. The adolescent is angry at the parent for being unfair or rejecting, whereas the parent is angry at the son or daughter for misdemeanors or lack of respect. Both the adolescent and the parent may lack sufficient motivation or skill and understanding to take the necessary steps to mitigate the anger. It is often apparent that the "wronged" party derives some degree of positive reinforcement from wallowing in self-pity. This is particularly true of adolescents, whose penchant for commiserating with peers about unfair treatment from parents is to some degree a part of normal adolescent development. However, when anger at parents is intense and unremitting, stemming primarily from long-standing bitterness associated with aspects of inadequate parenting such as parental rejection, neglect, or parental alcohol or child abuse, it then becomes a crucial target for therapy as a prerequisite to the successful outcome of subsequent interventions.

Similarly, when a parent's anger toward the adolescent is severe and unremitting, it must be addressed as a first step to resolving other components of parent-adolescent conflict.

The following case examples illustrate dysfunctional behaviors and cognitions that typify intense adolescent anger directed at a parent, including deliberate provocation of the parent calculated to punish that parent or to test the extent of the parent's love and devotion, and excessive ruminations on methods of revenge.

A girl who was recently reunited with her alcoholic father was angry at him for having deserted the family several years before and for causing her mother's eventual breakdown. The girl tested her father continually, by placing excessive demands on him, believing that her father was obligated to make up for all the years of pain he had caused her. Regardless of what her father did to improve the situation, it was never perceived as being good enough.

A boy who was physically abused by his father as a child, and who was rejected and labelled "worthless" by his mother, eventually became a ward of the Children's Aid Society. He vowed that he would get even with his father when he was strong enough to do so. He also believed that he could never be happy until his mother was dead. He spent long hours fantasizing about ways in which he would eventually get even.

In many cases, the parent harbors intense anger and resentment toward the adolescent:

> The mother of a rebellious delinquent girl was intensely angry at her daughter because of the girl's ongoing attempts to break up the mother's relationship with her common-law husband, thereby destroying her chances for happiness. The daughter viewed the common-law husband as impinging on her territory, while he, in turn, was angry at the girl, claiming that her behavior caused him to return to his former pattern of alcohol abuse. Delinquent acts were motivated by a desire for attention and revenge.

INTERVENTION

1. Relationship-Enhancement Training (family therapy)
2. Cognitive Restructuring (for parent and adolescent dysfunctional beliefs and attitudes underlying the anger)

Target: Aggressive Parent-Adolescent Response Style

Aggressive response styles are a frequent component of parent-adolescent conflict. Verbal or physical aggression may be habitually resorted to by the adolescent, the parent, or both. At times, family members may not be fully aware that they are using abusive language and that this elicits an aggressive response from the other person. They may be at a loss as to how to avoid aggressive confrontations.

> A tenth-grade student was in constant conflict with her mother over issues of control. One ongoing source of conflict stemmed from the mother's insistence that the daughter assist her three evenings each week in her job as a cleaner in an office building. The girl responded to the mother's angry demands with shouting, threats, physical aggression, and refusal to cooperate. This escalated into a shouting match each time, after which the daughter would feel guilty, give in, and accompany her mother to work, with residual feelings of anger for allowing herself to lose control and be manipulated by her mother.

INTERVENTION

1. Behavior-Analysis Skill Training (Family Therapy)
2. Stress-Inoculation Training (Adolescent)
3. Assertiveness Training (Adolescent)
4. Conflict-Negotiation Skills Training (Family Therapy)

In the above case, Behavior-Analysis Skill Training was used to teach the girl and her mother to identify the antecedents and consequences of aggressive verbal outbursts. The girl learned that her mother's shouting and demands for compliance would elicit aggressive outbursts from her, which would, in turn, be followed by feelings of guilt, leading to compliance. Then, after unwillingly complying with the mother's "unfair" demands, she would feel angry. In order to alter this behavior sequence, Assertiveness Training during individual therapy sessions was helpful in teaching the girl more effective responses to her mother's demands. She was also taught cognitive self-control over her aggressive response pattern through Stress-Inoculation Training.

Target: Inadequate Family Communication Skills

Normal and deviant families have been found to differ in their communication patterns. Deviant families have been found to be more silent, to talk less equally, to have fewer positive interruptions, and to be less active (Alexander & Parsons, 1973). They are also more likely to employ negative communication patterns such as interrupting, mind reading, and talking for another family member. Findings from laboratory studies identify the following characteristics of communication styles in families referred for therapy: defensiveness, commands, ignoring, "put-downs," and overall negative style. In comparison, non-referred families are characterized by higher rates of agreements, evaluations, humor, problem specification, and solution proposals (Robin &Weiss, 1980; Robin & Foster, 1984).

INTERVENTION
Communication-Skills Training is suggested to teach family members solution-oriented communication patterns to increase reciprocity and approximate more closely the communication patterns in better-adjusted families.

Target: Inadequate Conflict-Negotiation Skills

A frequent component of parent-adolescent conflict is inadequate negotiation skills among family members, so that attempts to negotiate solutions to conflicts invariably end in shouting matches. Disagreements generally concern rules, responsibilities, values, and perceived misbehaviors. A combination of Conflict-Negotiation Skills Training, Problem-Solving Skills Training, and parent-adolescent Contingency Contracting during family sessions is appropriate in order to teach family members the art of arbitration or mediation of specific conflicts.

INTERVENTION

1. Conflict-Negotiation Skills Training
2. Contingency Contracting
3. Problem-Solving Skills Training

Target: Dysfunctional Cognitions Underlying Parent-Adolescent Conflict

Once dysfunctional information-processing styles and dysfunctional cognitive themes associated with parent-adolescent conflict have been identified and recorded during the initial data collection phase and subsequent therapy sessions, these are then designated as targets for Cognitive Restructuring interventions. These interventions may be carried out during individual sessions with the adolescent client, or with the parents, or during family sessions. Research reviewed earlier suggests that particular attention should be paid to adolescent and parent beliefs and attitudes with the following underlying themes (Robin & Foster, 1984; Roehling & Robin, 1986):

Parent Themes

1. adolescent ruination
2. obedience
3. perfectionistic expectations
4. malicious intent
5. parental self-blame
6. fear of adolescent disapproval

Adolescent Themes

1. ruination
2. unfair parental treatment
3. autonomy rights

INTERVENTION

Cognitive Restructuring is recommended during both individual and family sessions to aid both parents and adolescents in examining and altering distorted or unrealistic cognitions underlying their conflicts.

MAJOR AREAS OF CHRONIC FAMILY STRESS

Major areas of ongoing family stress often encountered in families of problem adolescents include (1) severe marital conflict, (2) divorce and single parenting, (3) parental alcohol abuse, and (4) child abuse and parental violence. Each of these areas of family stress is characterized by many of the same dysfunctional parenting styles and cognitive and behavioral manifestations of parent-adolescent conflict discussed in the previous sections.

SEVERE MARITAL CONFLICT

Targets for intervention associated with severe marital conflict and resultant adolescent psychological disorders include (1) spouse sabotage maintaining adolescent problems, (2) adolescent manipulations exacerbating marital conflict, and (3) adolescent depression associated with marital conflict.

Target: Spouse Sabotage Maintaining Adolescent Problems

Often, adolescents are drawn into marital conflicts by parents who use the young person as a pawn to punish or manipulate the spouse. For example, a father may purposely sabotage a mother's attempts to impose appropriate limits on the adolescent.

> The mother of a rebellious, only daughter repeatedly blamed the father for failure to set limits and for allowing the girl to flaunt rules by skipping school, getting drunk, and staying out all night. The mother's attempts to impose consequences for truancy were sabotaged by the father who would side with the daughter when she refused to comply with the mother's disciplinary measures. The father, in turn, accused the wife of not understanding the daughter. Both parents competed for the daughter's approval, and fear of losing the daughter was the major factor holding the unhappy marriage together.

INTERVENTION

1. Behavior-Analysis Skill Training (parent and family sessions)
2. Discipline-Effectiveness Training (parent and family sessions)
3. Contingency Contracting (family sessions)

In the above example, the family was taught to identify patterns of marital conflict maintaining the daughter's rebellious behaviors. Both parents were angry and worried by their daughter's self-destructive behavior and her rebellious disregard for parental rules and regulations. However, the parents' determination to hurt each other was so strong that they were unwilling to work together to devise strategies to ameliorate the daughter's self-destructive behaviors. The daughter was benefiting from her parents' power struggle because this left her with almost total freedom. After a few sessions with the parents devoted to Behavior-Analysis Skill Training, the parents were able to gain some insight into the negative consequences stemming from their ongoing marital conflict:

Antecedents	Behaviors	Consequences
School informs parents of truancy.	• Mother attributes truancy to father's weak controls; she adopts disciplinarian role and "grounds" daughter.	• Mother asserts her superiority. • Father is angry at "put down."
	• Father challenges mother saying "grounding" is too harsh (father-daughter alliance).	• Father asserts his superiority. • Daughter escapes consequences for truancy.

Once parents have been taught to analyze the antecedents and consequences of dysfunctional marital interactions, along with their role in maintaining the adolescent's self-defeating behaviors, they are more likely to be open to suggestions for more effective, cooperative childrearing strategies designed to decrease unwanted adolescent behaviors.

Discipline-Effectiveness Training may be initiated during sessions with the parents. This is followed by implementation of newly-learned effective disciplinary techniques during family sessions, aided by Contingency Contracting to help insure the daughter's participation in the joint parental disciplinary effort. In some cases where marital problems are so intense that they prevent parental cooperation on strategies to ameliorate the adolescent's problems, marital therapy may become a necessary prerequisite for successful family therapy interventions.

Target: Adolescent Manipulations Exacerbating Marital Conflict

Adolescents exhausted by exposure to ongoing marital conflict may try to alleviate the nightmare by inappropriate attempts to either break up the marriage or get parents back together. This may take the form of adolescent conduct disorders or adolescent attempts at inappropriate cross-generational alliances.

A daughter periodically extracted promises from her father to leave the mother so that they could get an apartment together. With this agenda in mind, the daughter would "act out" whenever there seemed to be a temporary reconciliation between the parents, in order to insure ongoing marital conflict and eventual separation. The girl held the following irrational beliefs: "If Dad and I leave the family, he'll be able to devote himself to me completely" and "If Dad stays in the marriage, that will mean that he prefers Mom to me."

INTERVENTION

1. Behavior-Analysis Skill Training
2. Cognitive Restructuring
3. Marital Therapy

In this case, marital therapy was recommended to help the parents to make responsible joint decisions about their relationship, including whether to remain together or to separate. Behavior-Analysis Skill Training was initiated to help family members recognize dysfunctional interaction patterns, such as the father-daughter alliance. Cognitive-Restructuring interventions were also carried out during family sessions to clear up inaccurate perceptions.

Target: Adolescent Depression Related to Marital Conflict

Adolescents often feel trapped in a situation of ongoing exposure to parental conflict. Having little or no control over the situation, they begin to manifest symptoms of depression such as self-blame, hopelessness, and anger, as well as symptoms of anxiety (e.g. "It's up to me to find a way to save my parents' marriage"; "If it weren't for me my parents wouldn't fight" "It's not fair that they have to fight all the time" "If my parents split up, it will be too awful to endure").

INTERVENTION

1. Behavior-Analysis Skills Training
2. Cognitive Restructuring
3. Problem-Solving Skills Training
4. Goal Planning

Individual therapy sessions with adolescent clients may be geared toward teaching behavior-analysis and interpersonal coping skills that will help them to better endure the uncomfortable marital situation. They may be taught to analyze their participation in dysfunctional family patterns and to practice new techniques for avoidance of participation in marital conflict situations. In addition, cognitive-restructuring interventions may be applied to depressive themes of guilt and helplessness. Clients may also be helped to explore and structure activities that will get them away from the home situation as much as possible, such as a part-time jobs, sports, and other extracurricular school activities. Goal Planning is another useful intervention, so that clients are helped to make concrete educational and vocational plans that will eventually allow them to become independent and successfully move out of the stressful family home. Clients are taught that although they may be helpless to change the parents' marriage, the current unpleasant living situation is temporary and they can have some control over future living situations. Educational, vocational, and financial counselling may be important components of therapy sessions.

Family sessions may also be undertaken in order to provide a setting in which the adolescent and the parents can express anxious and depressive thoughts. Family Problem-Solving Skill Training will help the family to find partial solutions to components of the problems, even though the marital situation may not be likely to improve.

DIVORCE AND SINGLE PARENTING

Some common problems of single-parent families following divorce include: (1) adolescent adjustment disorder, (2) inadequate parenting following divorce and, (3) manipulative adolescent behaviors.

Target: Adolescent Adjustment Disorder Following Divorce

Adolescents often experience great difficulty adjusting to their parents' divorce. Depression, anxiety, and conduct dissorders are typical, along with school failure, truancy, and difficulty with peer relationships. Adolescents may also get in the habit of using guilt to manipulate divorced parents.

An eighth-grade boy was angry and embarrassed when his mother left his father to live with another man who had two previous divorces. The son chose to live with his mother because she was more dependable and, therefore, better able to look after him. However, he felt guilty for abandoning his father who was severely depressed following the separation. He also began to worry that the mother's boyfriend would eventually leave her for another woman and that the mother would suffer a breakdown. He was unable to concentrate on school work and began failing courses. He also avoided friends due to embarrassment about the separation. He began to dread school and started skipping classes.

INTERVENTION

1. Cognitive Restructuring (family sessions)
2. Problem-Solving Training
3. Cognitive Restructuring (for depressive cognitions; individual sessions)

Family therapy at different stages of the separation process may be appropriate. The therapist can help the family to work through different stages of the separation process. Parents and adolescents may be helped in family sessions to foster honest expression of feelings about the situation. Family members can be helped to resolve irrational beliefs and to accept the inevitability of divorce through Cognitive-Restructuring techniques. Examples of typical parent cognitions include: "This is the worst thing that could happen," "I'm responsible for my children's grief," and "My children will be ruined by this." Adolescents may be plagued by unrealistic fears and beliefs such as "I'll lose my father forever," "If I hadn't behaved badly, my parents wouldn't have split up," or "I'll be disloyal to Mom if I'm nice to Dad." In addition, Problem-Solving Training will help the family to plan and implement supportive arrangements to maintain consistency and former routines as much as possible, and to insure continuation of the adolescent's contact with the absent parent.

Target: Inadequate Parenting Following Divorce

Common forms of inadequate parenting following divorce are parental neglect, overindulgence, and oversubmissiveness. Parental neglect may stem from the parents' own depression and anxiety, or from the parents' determination to have a good time at all costs. Parental oversubmissiveness or overindulgence often stems from guilt about the family break-up. Parents often feel that they have been unsuccessful because of their inability to hold a marriage together and their failure to provide a proper environment for children. The following dysfunctional beliefs were expressed by one divorced mother of a delinquent son: "My son has suffered because our marriage failed, so I have to make it up to him by giving him what he wants," and "I must do everything to insure that he does not suffer any more disappointments."

INTERVENTION

1. Cognitive Restructuring
2. Discipline-Effectiveness Training
3. Expectations-Establishment Training

Target: Inappropriate Parental Expectations Following Divorce

A divorced parent may begin to regard an adolescent child as a sort of replacement for the missing spouse, inappropriately assigning adult role tasks to the young person. A mother may expect a son to listen patiently as she confides in him about personal problems. The adolescent may also be expected to discipline younger siblings or to take on too many financial or mature responsibilities which in turn curtail the adolescent's own social development. A divorced mother may expect her son to be her constant escort at social or recreational functions. Or, the adolescent may be expected to accompany the parent on daily errands such as trips to the store or to doctors' appointments, leaving little time for the adolescent's involvement in age-appropriate activities.

INTERVENTION

1. Cognitive Restructuring (parent)
2. Problem-Solving Training
3. Discipline-Effectiveness Training
4. Expectations-Establishment Trianing
5. Independence Training (parent-adolescent)
6. Assertiveness Training (adolescent)

Target: Custody and Visitation Problems

Disagreement between divorced parents with respect to custody and visitation arrangements for adolescent and younger children is a frequent source of family conflict. This is especially true when parental competence is called into question or when revenge between spouses in involved and adolescents are brought into the parental custody dispute.

Musetto (1978) suggests a number of areas and goals for family problem-solving when conflict stems from custody and visitation problems: (1) to increase parental motivation to cooperate for the good of the children, parents are helped to understand that loyalty ties to both parents are important to maintain and, therefore, that it becomes the parents' responsibility to minimize marital conflict interfering with these loyalty ties, (2) to help the family to reassure the adolescent of continued consistent parenting from both parents, (3) to help the noncustodial parent to predict the negative consequences should he or she decide to abandon the adolescent, (4) to decrease counterproductive patterns such as scapegoating or idealizing a parent, (5) to discourage a parent from using the parent-adolescent relationship to take revenge on the former spouse, by having parents predict the negative long-term consequences of this approach. After these issues have been addressed, family Problem-Solving Training and Conflict-Negotiation Skills Training are useful in teaching the family to generate and implement concrete solutions to custody visitation problems.

INTERVENTION

1. Conflict-Negotiation Skills Training
2. Problem-Solving Skill Training
3. Communication-Skill Training
4. Behavior-Analysis Skill Training

PARENTAL ALCOLHOL ABUSE

Families of alcoholics are prone to low cohesion and conflict. Some of the hardships to which families of alcoholics are exposed include job loss and economic insecurity, marital infidelity, physical violence, family embarrassment and stigma, and ongoing quarrels (Orford, 1980). Hardships described by children of alcoholics include the witnessing of marital rows, the need to intervene during episodes of family violence, chronic fear and apprehension about the effects of drinking on family members, bitterness about the absence of pleasant times in the family, and the necessity of curtailing normal peer friendships due to embarrassment about the alcoholic parent.

Nonalcoholic spouses of alcohol abusers react to the situation in different ways. Coping patterns characterized by avoidance, withdrawal, or action designed to protect the rest of the family have been found to be predictive of poor prognosis in terms of improving the family situation. On the other hand, coping patterns characterized by assertiveness and anti-drink action on the part of the nonalcoholic spouse have been found to be predictive of a more favorable prognosis. The incidence of psychological problems, marital stress, and other abnormalities in the nonalcoholic spouse's family of origin has also been found to be higher than in normal control families.

There is a tendency for children in alcoholic families to develop abnormal behavior patterns in order to cope with the alcoholic parent's irrational and unpredictable behavior. In addition, family routines tend to be organized around the parent's drinking pattern (Steinglass et al., 1987). For this reason, it is unrealistic to expect that family life would automatically become normal if the alcoholic parent were to stop drinking.

Parenting is often inadequate or ineffective in alcoholic families. Inconsistencies exist in parental rules, discipline, and affection during periods of sobriety and drunkenness. Other common parenting patterns include physical abuse, neglect of children, extreme permissiveness, insufficient socialization and inadequate supervision of children. Poor communication between family members, marital tension, and a high incidence of broken homes are additional features.

Target: The Alcoholic Parent

Although no therapist would argue against the benefits of involving the alcoholic parent in individual and family treatment programs, few alcoholic parents actually receive treatment, or the parent's recovery comes too late in the adolescent's formative developmental years to prevent maladjustment (Russell et al., 1985). Although involvement of the alcoholic parent in a treatment program should be an ongoing goal, more often than not the therapist is forced to work with the adolescent alone or with family members excluding the alcoholic parent.

Target: Adolescent Disorders Associated with the Parental Alcoholism

Russell, Henderson, and Blume (1985) review studies comparing children from alcoholic and nonalcoholic families. Therapist awareness of the following symptom patterns, cognitions, and coping mechanisms characterizing children of alcoholics will aid in the identification of problem behaviors for therapy interventions. Depressive cognitions include: sadness stemming from perceptions of being unloved and rejected by parents, anger toward the alcoholic parent, resentment toward the nonalcoholic parent for contributing to the spouse's drinking patterns, and resentment about being part of a family that has no fun together. Symptoms of anxiety often stem from fear of an aggressive drunken parent. Failure to form satisfying relationships may stem from a reluctance to bring friends home in order to avoid shame and social stigma. School failure and truancy often reflect a disorganized, unpredictable, or violent home life interfering with development of adequate study patterns. Other characteristic patterns include excessive dependency on the family, along with conduct disorders such as aggression, delinquency, running away from home, substance abuse, and poor emotional control.

INTERVENTION

1. Cognitive Restructuring (anxious and depressive cognitions)
2. Interpersonal Coping-Skills Training
3. Independence Training (parent-adolescent)
4. Discipline-Effectiveness Training
5. Relationship-Enhancement Training

Target: Maladaptive Family Interaction Patterns Maintaining Parental Alcohol Abuse

Different patterns characterize family members' attempts to cope with various stages and severities of the drinking problem, so that the focus of therapy changes depending on the stage. Stages identified in the literature include the initial stage characterized by denial or minimization of the alcohol problem, a later organization of the family around the drinking behavior, which may function to maintain the alcoholism, deterioration of marital relations as alcoholism-related tensions grow, complete family disorganization coinciding with significant disturbances in the children, and possibly eventual sobriety and problems with reintegration of the now-abstinent parent into the family system (Steinglass et al., 1987).

Problems often arise when an alcoholic parent has made the decision to stop drinking, but the family members still refuse to obey and respect the new authority of the abstinent parent. They need assistance in reintegrating him or her back into the family system, as in the following example of a son who was reluctant to relinquish the adult role he had been playing for some time. Other typical dysfunctional family patterns that work to maintain a parent's drinking problem include family members' passivity and failure to take action to stop the drinking, scapegoating the alcoholic, and payoffs for the martyr role. After the patterns have been identified, more adaptive responses may be shaped during family sessions.

> The older son of an alcoholic father had quit school in order to work and support the family during one of the father's alcoholic binges. The boy was very close to his mother, and both considered the father to be worthless and incompetent, even though the father had recently been attending A.A. sessions and had returned to work. The boy complained bitterly about having to sacrifice his education because of his father's drinking, but could not be persuaded to give up his job and return to school now that the father had returned to work. In contrast, the boy's 13-year-old brother took advantage of the family disorganization, and began staying out late and skipping school.

INTERVENTION

1. Behavior-Analysis Skill Training
2. Relationship-Enhancement Training
3. Cognitive Restructuring
4. Discipline-Effectiveness Training
5. Contingency Contracting
6. Communication-Skills Training

Behavior-Analysis Skill Training during family sessions helped family members to understand how rigid patterns of interaction kept the family in a state that enabled and maintained the drinking behavior. It was necessary through cognitive-restructuring interventions to uncover and alter unspoken family attitudes and rules maintaining the father's drinking. As long as the father was drinking, mother and son were able to "rescue" the family, and the younger son was able to ignore curfews with little interference. A major focus of family therapy was aimed at altering some of the dysfunctional patterns and roles that family members had adopted in order to cope with stress caused by the father's drunkeness. Aspects of the mother's behavior contributing to the maintenance of the drinking pattern were first addressed, such as her pattern of treating the husband like a naughty child. The overly-responsible, parent-like martyr role adoped by the eldest son was also addressed.

Once the family was made aware of these patterns, they were encouraged to experiment with more adaptive interactions through Relationship-Enhancement Training, and Communication-Skill Training. The parents were also taught, through Discipline-Effectiveness Training and Contingency Contracting, to establish consistent rules and disciplinary measures and to provide adequate supervision for the younger son.

CHILD ABUSE AND PARENTAL VIOLENCE

Child abuse involves non-accidental physical injury to the child or adolescent. Parental physical violence and child abuse often accompany parental alcohol abuse. A wide range of parent behaviors have been labelled "child abuse" in the literature, varying in severity and chronicity. These include striking with an open hand or closed fist, hitting with an object, pushing, kicking, or burning the youngster.

Target: Family Patterns Associated with Child Abuse

Friedman et al. (1982) review literature suggesting that abusive parents tend to have unrealistic expectations for their children. They also tend to be socially isolated and unable to call on others for assistance in times of distress. They provide, in general, lower rates of positive reinforcement than nonabusive parents. Research also suggests that nonabusive spouses of abusive parents tend to be passive, actually approving of the abuse in some cases, and that child abuse is often preceded by marital arguments. Cases have been reported in which the abusive parent punishes the spouse by hurting the spouse's preferred child. Assessment of the entire family environment is therefore important.

Like the problem of parental alcohol abuse, parental violence toward children or spouse carries a high risk of relapse. In addition, intergenerational transmission of aggressive patterns within an extended family is a frequent occurrence. Children learn to use violence as a coping technique through observation of a violent parent. At times, family members unwittingly reinforce a child's violent attitudes and behaviors. In addition, emotional deprivation in childhood may lead to an inability to empathize with others, which in turn increases the likelihood of a youngster's reliance on violence to solve problems (Orford, 1980).

It is frequently noted that abusive parents lack effective child-handling skills, so that a violent cycle of behavioral interactions is set in motion. A parent's use of physical punishment increases the likelihood of aggressive behavior and noncompliance in the child, which in turn elicits more aggression in the parent. Abusive parents often inappropriately attribute negative intent to the frustrating behavior of their children. They tend to expect responses from their children that the children are developmentally too immature to perform (Morton et al., 1988).

Friedman et al. (1982) emphasize the importance of a careful assessment of the abusive parent's child-management skills and of his familiarity with appropriate parental expectations consistent with the adolescent's developmental stage. It is also important to assess the parent's anger-management skills and the types of situations that elicit anxiety and anger in the abusive parent. Parental psychiatric disorders must also be identified. Finally, the degree of social isolation of the family should be assessed, as well as available support systems and contacts outside the nuclear family.

Very often, the nonabusive parent is a part of the family's silence conspiracy. An abused wife who adopts a martyr role sets an example for her children of the "correct" way to deal with the problem, which is essentially to accept and endure the physical abuse. The nonabusive parent may fail to take the necessary steps to put an end to the child abuse. In fact, the spouse often indirectly complies with the child abuse, as in the case of the mother who believes that a difficult adolescent deserves, or at least must learn to endure, hardships in life, including child abuse. The nonabusive spouse may be frustrated by his or her own lack of control over the adolescent and may, therefore, encourage the spouse to punish the youngster. Generally, the nonabusive parent denies any involvement in the chain of events culminating in the child abuse. Inappropriate mutual dependency between the nonabusive spouse and the abused adolescent may further impede normal adolescent development.

Herzberger et al. (1981) compared perceptions of physically abused and nonabused children. They found that, relative to nonabused children, abused children described their parents in more negative terms and as emotionally rejecting. However, in some cases, children felt loved, wanted, and cared for by an abusive parent. These authors also cite findings indicating that abused adolescents were more likely than nonabused subjects to feel that their punishments were deserved.

A 12-grade girl was referred for therapy by her teacher who was concerned about symptoms of anxiety in the classroom, and failure to interact with peers. After several individual therapy sessions, the girl disclosed the fact that her father regularly beat her mother. During these violent episodes, the girl would retreat to her room, fearful of calling the police because of the father's threats to severely harm the mother and the girl herself if she were to tell anyone. The girl was also a victim of her father's physical abuse, and her younger brother was already manifesting aggressive behaviors similar to the father's. The mother, who herself had endured a violent alcoholic father, had been taught to pray for strength to accept the situation; this passive victim role was also adopted by the daughter.

The girl felt helpless and guilty for her inability to protect her mother from the father's beatings and for her inability to control her younger brother and prevent him from provoking violent outbursts from the father. Because of the girl's preoccupation with preventing family violence and the mother's plea to the daughter not to leave home and abandon her, the girl had neither the time nor the courage to pursue interests of her own, or to plan and work toward educational goals that would allow her to eventually leave the violent family environment and establish a life of her own. She had also failed to develop social skills or satisfying peer relationships, due to generalized anxiety, family stigma, and family expectations for secrecy. Consequently, she spent most of her free time engaged in solitary pursuits in her room.

Parent training sessions to teach aggressive parents more appropriate childrearing techniques and self-control for anger, combined with family sessions for implementation of newly-learned techniques, would be the preferred intervention approach. Behavior-Analysis Skill Training may also be used to help family members to identify precipitating factors occurring just prior to the aggressive outburst. However, abusive parents are notoriously reluctant to seek or comply with referrals for therapy intervention. In order to increase the chances of engaging the abusive parent in therapy endeavors, the therapist avoids outright criticism of the parent in the initial sessions, while encouraging the family to identify dysfunctional styles of family interaction.

Mental health professionals, teachers, and other school personnel are under obligation to report cases of suspected child abuse to police or Children's Aid Societies, who then have the authority to bring charges against the violent parent or to remove the youngster from the home when appropriate. However, family violence is usually a well-kept secret; although adolescent clients may confide in friends or therapists, they are often unwilling to officially testify against the abusive parent. Many choose instead to endure daily abuse rather than risk rejection from family members for tarnishing the family name. Fear of retaliation is another reason for remaining silent, when the abusive parent threatens to seriously harm family members if the vow of silence is broken.

INTERVENTION

The following interventions are recommended to alter family interaction patterns maintaining child abuse:

1. Report child abuse to Children's Aid Society or Police;
2. Refer abusive parent or spouse for individual psychotherapy;
3. Behavior-Analysis Skill Training (parent and family sessions) to alter patterns maintaining child abuse, such as spouses' compliance in child abuse;
4. Discipline-Effectiveness Training;
5. Parent education about normal adolescent behavior and development;
6. Cognitive Restructuring of characteristic parental cognitive distortions precipitating episodes of child abuse;
7. Self-Control Skill Training to help parent control anger and frustration;
8. Conflict-Negotiation Skill Training;
9. Relationship-Enhancement Training;
10. Independence Training (parent-adolescent);

11. Problem-Solving Training to reduce stresses outside the parent-adolescent relationship contributing to the child abuse.

Additional targets are recommended for individual therapy sessions with the abused adolescent. Symptoms characteristic of adolescent victims of child abuse include chronic anxiety, somatic symptoms, fear of future violence and injury, social isolation, and depression. Typical depressive cognitions include themes of guilt and helplesness, anger at the abusive parent, poor self-image ("I don't deserve to be happy, I deserve the abuse"), passive acceptence of the abuse ("The abuse shows that Dad really loves me"), and fear of rejection ("A good daughter doesn't report abuse and bring shame on the family").

INTERVENTION

1. Cognitive Restructuring to alter dysfunctional anxiety-provoking and depressive cognitions typical of abused adolescents;
2. Goal Planning to increase the adolescent's capacity for self-direction and independence from the abusive family environment;
3. Activity Scheduling for self-esteem building activities outside of the home.

Incest and Sexual Abuse

Incest is another form of child abuse, in which family members are involved in sexual activities with the child or adolescent. Adolescent victims of incest referred for psychological assessment and therapy are, most commonly, adolescent girls who have been abused by a father or stepfather. However, the perpetrator may also have been a brother, stepbrother, cousin, grandfather, or uncle. Generally, adolescent incest victims present with a history of sexual abuse that has taken place in the past. The client may present with symptoms that are initial reactions to the trauma or with long-term effects that are significantly interfering with normal adolescent development in areas of family, peer, or school functioning.

The term child sexual abuse is used in the literature when the following conditions are present: forced or coerced sexual behavior imposed on a youngster, and sexual behavior between an adolescent (or child) and a much older person or caretaker. Browne and Finkelhor (1986) review literature on initial and long-term effects of child and adolescent sexual abuse. Studies reviewed are restricted to female victims, since very few clinincal studies of sexually-abused boys have been reported in the literature. In these studies, the offender may or may not be a member of the family. These authors state that although empirical findings are sketchy due to a lack of standardized outcome measures and adequate comparison groups, certain behaviors are repeatedly associated with sexual abuse.

Initial and long-term effects characterizing victims of sexual abuse include: (1)

anxiety reactions and phobias, (2) depression, negative self-perceptions, guilt, shame, anger, and low self-esteem, (3) somatic disturbances, such as sleep disorders and nightmares, (4) school failure and truancy, (5) conduct disorders, such as running away, promiscuity, inappropriate use of sexual behavior to gain affection and attention, prostitution, and substance abuse, and (6) impaired social functioning, such as social withdrawal, and difficulty forming close relationships, as well as difficulty forming normal heterosexual relationships.

Clinical and empirical studies of the effects of various types of child sexual abuse suggest that the greatest trauma occurs if there are multiple incidents of abuse, if the abuse continues for a long period of time, if the perpetrator is related to the victim (especially fathers or stepfathers), if the abuse is accompanied by aggression, if the youngster participates to some degree, if the family is unsupportive following disclosure of the abuse, and if the victim is removed from the home following disclosure.

Finkelhor and Browne (1986) propose that the experience of sexual abuse may be analyzed in terms of four trauma-causing factors: (1) traumatic sexualization, (2) stigmatization, (3) betrayal, and (4) powerlessness. These provide a useful framework for identifying cognitive and behavioral targets for therapy interventions.

Traumatic sexualization is a process through which a youngster's sexual feelings and attitudes are shaped in a developmentally inappropriate and interpersonally dysfunctional way as a result of sexual abuse. For example, if affection, gifts, attention, or privileges are exchanged for sexual behavior, a girl may learn to use sexual behavior as a strategy for manipulating others in order to gratify her wishes. Or, misconceptions about sexual behavior and morality may be transmitted by the offender to the youngster. In addition, frightening events and memories may become associated with sexual activity, resulting in inappropriate repertoires of sexual behavior.

In the case of incest, a feeling of betrayal often accompanies the youngster's realization that someone she depended on has caused her harm. The awareness may grow into a tendency to mistrust people in general. The victim may also feel betrayed by family members who failed to believe or protect her.

A sense of powerlessness may originally stem from the process through which the victim's will, desires, and sense of efficacy were repeatedly violated by the perpetrator. The sense of powerlessness may continue long after the abuse has stopped because of the victim's inability to make adults believe that the incest took place or because of intense fear of retaliation or further abuse from the perpetrator.

Stigmatization is the fourth effect of sexual abuse identified by Finkelhor and Browne. It is defined as the negative connotation of badness, shame, and guilt communicated to the abused child and incorporated into the youngster's self-image. Stigmatization may come directly from the perpetrator, but may also be reinforced by family members who react with shock or blame the youngster for the situation, labelling her as "spoiled goods."

Dysfunctional cognitions related to underlying depressive reactions to sexual abuse usually take the form of themes of guilt, shame, and intense anger toward the perpetrator or toward family members perceived as critical, unsupportive, or collaborating with the perpetrator.

Loss of ability to function adequately in day-to-day activities is another common effect of sexual abuse, manifested in school failure, truancy, and social withdrawal. Other abnormal behaviors include delinquency, substance abuse, and inappropriate sexual behavior, ranging from "pseudo maturity" to promiscuity, prostitution, or homosexuality. Depressive cognitions usually underlie these behavioral manifestations.

The following case examples illustrate different reactions of adolescent victims to sexual abuse by perpetrators within the family. Many of the dysfunctional behaviors and cognitions described below also characterize victims of sexual abuse by perpetrators outside of the family.

> A teenage girl who had been sexually abused by her step father was enraged because her mother pretended to be ignorant of what was going on, and failed to confront her husband and end the abuse. The marriage eventually broke up, after which the girl sought to repay her mother by lying to school authorities about cruel abuse inflicted on her by the mother, and by repeated suicide threats. Family therapy sessions focused on the daughter's manipulation of her mother through suicide attempts and through elaborate lies to school authorities, and on the daughter's unresolved anger at her mother. Individual therapy was also provided for both the adolescent and her mother to address the girl's depression and the mother's helplessness, guilt, and low self-esteem.

> A 14-year-old girl had been sexually abused over a period of two years by the mother's younger brother, who threatened to kill the girl if she told anyone. The girl was terrified, but finally managed to tell her mother. The mother refused to believe the daughter and warned the girl to never mention this again or she would be responsible for staining the family honor. The girl ran away from home and was eventually sent to a training school. Following her release and return home, she kept the family secret, but continued to suffer intense fear of further abuse. She also experienced ongoing rage at her mother for continuing to refuse to believe her. Family therapy was initiated in order to create a setting in which the girl could discuss the aversive experience and her anger at family members openly, supported by the therapist, and thereby relieve her sense of powerlessness. The family was also helped to develop solutions to ensure that no further abuse occurred.

> A girl who had been abused by her maternal grandfather was labelled a "dirty slut" by her father when this was discovered. The girl perceived herself as a slut and embarked upon a pattern of reckless promiscuity. She was also unable

to concentrate and achieve at school. Cognitive-Restructuring techniques were applied to the girl's view of herself as "damaged goods," and to her excessive need for approval. Self-Monitoring techniques were applied to the girl's impulsivity, and inability to persist at school assignments.

Target behaviors and appropriate therapy interventions may now be summarized, based on empirical findings discussed above and case examples. Depressive cognitions are almost invariably present and may be treated with cognitive-restructuring techniques during individual sessions. In addition to adolescent depression, symptoms of anxiety include intense fear reactions, often related to a sense of powerlessness, and phobias. Sleep and eating disorders are frequent somatic symptoms. Cognitive-behavioral treatment of symptoms of anxiety and depression will be more fully addressed in Chapter Nine.

Incest victims often experience difficulties in forming close, satisfying interpersonal relationships stemming from a generalized lack of trust. They are also frequently terrified of involvement in age-appropriate heterosexual relationships. Some victims suppress their sexuality by dressing and acting in an unfeminine way in order to discourage attention from members of the opposite sex. Interpersonal Coping-Skills Training may be used during individual sessions to help the adolescent to relate in a more normal fashion with same-sex and opposite-sex peers.

Dysfunctional patterns in families of adolescent incest victims include family members' blame or rejection of the incest victim, family members' refusal to acknowledge or discuss the fact that the incest took place, collusion or passivity of nonabusive parent or other family members, inadequate parenting skills, and the incest victim's manipulation of family members through guilt.

Family sessions are usually the preferred setting for addressing issues of stigmatization, blame, and betrayal, as well as the victim's rage against family members' passivity or collusion (misperceived or real). The perpetrator is rarely available or willing to become involved in family therapy, but he or she may continue to wield a great deal of power in the family and this may be an important issue to be addressed in sessions with the remaining family members. An important focus for female victims is the mother-daughter bond, since often the daughter believes that her mother could have stopped the abuse and blames her for not doing so. The mother may be berating herself for not knowing or for not taking action. Often times, a victim's inappropriate manipulation of her mother through guilt hinges on one of these unresolved issues.

7

Peer-Related Problems

This chapter will demonstrate application of a cognitive-behavioral approach to three peer-related problem areas common among adolescent clients: social inadequacy, sex-role behavior disturbances, and dysfunctional peer relationship patterns associated with adolescent Conduct Disorders. Social inadequacy includes both social anxiety and social-skills deficit. Sex role behavior disturbances to be addressed include Gender Identity Disorder and anxiety and depression associated with homosexuality. Finally, two peer-related problems characteristic of adolescents with Conduct Disorders will be discussed: aggressive interpersonal response style and vulnerability to antisocial peer influences.

SOCIAL INADEQUACY

Adolescents who have failed to form successful peer relationships are denied an important source of pleasure, as well as crucial opportunities for acquiring social, physical, and intellectual skills. Adolescents who are rejected by peers may be hampered by an aggressive interpersonal-response style, socially-inappropriate behaviors, or physical unattractiveness. They may also have little in common with peers due to social or intellectual skills that are either far inferior or far superior to those of agemates (Chance, 1989). Adolescents who are true social isolates are those who have been unable to form close relationships with anyone and are upset about it. (They may be distinguished from introverts who prefer their own company, or from adolescents who are accepted by some but rejected by others due to factors such as deviant attitudes or differences in race or social class.)

Social inadequacy has been defined as a deficiency in the ability of the individual to emit behaviors that, in turn, are positively reinforced by others (Lewinsohn, 1975). Social inadequacy leads to rejection and isolation, and subsequently to depression and anxiety. Two major types of social inadequacy have been differentiated: social anxiety or phobia, and social-skills deficit. The first is characterized by excessive anxiety in social situations and a marked tendency to avoid these situations. Social-skills deficit is characterized by awkward behavior, poor self-expression, subjective feelings of unease, and incompetence. It usually involves a long history of poor relationships (Trower et al., 1978). Often, the same client will manifest both types of social inadequacy.

Two major hypotheses have emerged in the literature to explain social inadequacy. The first, influenced by the anxiety-inhibition hypothesis of Wolpe and Lazarus (1966), suggests that interpersonal interactions evoke anxiety that inhibits the expression of normal feelings and the performance of adaptive behavior. A second, the skill-deficit hypothesis, suggests that failure of an individual to exhibit socially-skilled behavior results from never having learned the requisite behavior. Contrasting treatment approaches have evolved from these two hypotheses. Supporters of the anxiety-inhibition hypothesis advocate methods of anxiety reduction. Supporters of the skill-deficit hypothesis advocate social-skills training programs which help the individual to learn appropriate skills and to use them in situations where they will be positively reinforced and thus maintained.

Although there is empirical support for both hypotheses (Eisler, 1976), neither the anxiety-inhibition nor the social-skills treatment approach fully realized its initial promise in establishing long-term, generalized improvement in clinical groups. It has been suggested that failure to address cognitive components of social inadequacy may be partially responsible. Lucock and Salkovskis (1988) review evidence supporting the significant role of cognitive factors contributing to social anxiety and suggest that this may explain why individuals with appropriate social skills fail to use them in some social situations and do not always experience reductions in anxiety when they *do* use them.

Socially anxious individuals have been found to evaluate interpersonal feedback more negatively, as compared to individuals with low levels of social anxiety. They have also been found to remember negative interpersonal reactions, to underestimate their own level of interpersonal skills, and to generate a high frequency of negative cognitions in stressful situations. They have been found to hold unrealistic expectations about their ability to cope with social situations and about the likelihood of threatening social events occurring. This would suggest the importance of identifying both cognitive and behavioral antecedents and consequences of a client's dysfunctional social behaviors, as well as the need to combine cognitive-restructuring strategies with behaviorally-oriented treatments.

Ongoing problems occur when social inadequacy results in chronic social withdrawal during childhood and adolescence. Characteristic behaviors of socially withdrawn youngsters include failure to initiate successful interactions that evoke a positive response from peers, failure to respond to peer initiatives, a tendency to be less verbal than average in social interactions, and a tendency to spend more time than average in solitary pursuits (Hops & Greenwood, 1982).

SOCIAL ANXIETY

Social anxiety is a tendency to be made anxious by social situations. It generally involves fear of social rejection, and a full-blown social phobia may be part of the picture. Major components of the problem are excessive anxiety plus a measurable tendency to avoid certain characteristic social situations, such as situations in which the individual will be exposed to scrutiny by others. The result is an increasing constriction of normal activities as fears or avoidance behaviors dominate the individual's life. Unlike other phobias in which there is very little likelihood of the irrational fear being realized, in social anxieties there is often a reasonable possibility of the fear actually being realized.

Any number of dysfunctional behaviors may be exhibited by the client. For example, the person may begin to stutter or become tongue-tied when attempting to converse in a social situation. Social anxiety may take the form of fear of performing in public or of being the center of attention, fear of conflict, rejection, or disapproval, fear of intimacy, fear of meeting strangers, or anxiety about assertiveness (Argyle, 1980).

The anticipation of the feared outcome makes the adolescent even more inhibited in the social situation, so that the resulting performance is as inept as feared. However, the perceived severity and probability of the dire consequences resulting from the person's inept social behavior *are* exaggerated. Beck and Emery (1985) make a distinction between agoraphobia (in which the fear of losing control, fainting, or going crazy, is primary and fear of social disapproval secondary) and social anxieties (in which the central fear is that of being the center of attention, of having one's weaknesses exposed, or of being judged adversely).

Characteristic cognitive, emotional, and behavioral components of social anxieties include: (1) the individual's belief that others are scrutinizing and judging his performance, accompanied by fears that he will be unable to perform adequately (which is often accurate), (2) physiological responses, such as sweating, or feeling faint, and (3) various types of inhibitions interfering with verbal fluency, thinking, recall, or remote memory.

A 16-year-old girl experienced nausea and stomach pains every day at school. She would carefully time her arrival at school so that there was only enough time to deposit her coat in her locker and go straight to the classroom just before the bell rang in order to avoid anxiety-provoking social situations in which she would be sitting or standing alone, scrutinized by classmates. She left the school at lunchtime, unable to face the lunchroom social scene, and left immediately after school in order to avoid unstructured, socially demanding situations in the halls or outside the school. She found that when peers looked at her and attempted to engage her in conversation she would become particularly anxious. Examples of concurrent self-statements were: "She's seeing how ugly I am," "They hate me," and "I can't stand it here."

Recommended interventions include several behavioral coping skills strategies, such as Cognitive Self-Control interventions, Relaxation Training, distraction techniques, and Graded-Task Assignment, combined with cognitive restructuring. Identification and treatment of components of social anxiety and social phobia will be discussed in detail in Chapter Nine, in conjunction with other adolescent anxiety disorders.

SOCIAL-SKILLS DEFICIT

Some adolescents fail to learn the requisite social skills or behaviors to ensure satisfying peer relationships. Clients who are unable to form satisfying relationships present with a wide variety of dysfunctional interpersonal response styles. This necessitates accurate identification and detailed assessment of the various aspects of deficient social functioning for each client.

The therapist may begin by asking clients to give several examples of upsetting peer interactions they have experienced in recent days or weeks. They are asked to give descriptions of the other person's responses, as well as their own responses in each of these situations. On the basis of this information, client and therapist jointly seek to identify components of the client's interpersonal response style contributing to social failure.

Common targets for intervention with adolescent clients addressed in this chapter include deficits in conversation skills, physical unattractiveness, lack of assertiveness, and distorted social perceptions and beliefs. However, therapists working with adolescent clients will find that patterns underlying social failure are complex, often going beyond these discrete deficit areas. For example, clients may need help in altering jealous reactions, gender-inappropriate behaviors, manipulative behaviors, attempts to "buy" friendship, or a tendency to place unrealistic demands on peers. They may require assistance in changing long-standing patterns that preclude adequate exposure to potentially compatible peers, necessary for the development of satisfying friendships. For example, clients who spend long hours in solitary pursuits may be helped to find peers with similar interests, or they may be helped to make a deliberate effort to expose themselves to more conventional books, music, and T.V. programs currently popular with classmates.

Socially incompetent individuals lack the necessary skills to produce the desired effects on other people in social situations (Argyle, 1980). People with inadequate social skills are often deficient in "person perception." They may not attend to or show much interest in other people, they may be poor at decoding nonverbal signals, they may be inaccurate in the perception of events, or they may fail to recognize approval or annoyance in others. They may inaccurately perceive the other person's perceptions or motives and have difficulty seeing another person's point of view.

Socially incompetent people may fail to produce the right nonverbal signals, by failing to send clear facial and vocal signals or by sending negative sarcastic, superior, or hostile signals. During conversation, certain nonverbal accompaniments of speech may be problematic, such as a very low level of gaze, failure to manage interruptions or pauses in speech, or failure to add sufficient facial, gestural, or vocal signals to speech.

Socially unskilled people may not provide sufficient social rewards, so that their interactions are not enjoyable for the other person. For example, they may fail to be kind, helpful, or interesting. They may also be unresponsive to feedback during social interactions because they do not notice the effect their behavior is having on others or they do not know what corrective action to take if they realize that their behavior is having an unwanted effect on others. Self-presentation may go wrong if the person makes counterfeit claims which are unmasked, sends too little information, sends too much information, is overly dramatic, or presents inappropriately in manner or dress.

The following client had a long history of social isolation, maintained by inadequate conversation skills, unattractive appearance, few interests in common with age-mates, and misperception of social cues.

> A shy, awkward 18-year old was depressed by his long-standing failure to form satisfying relationships with male or female peers. He presented during the initial session wearing ill-fitting clothes that would have been considered unfashionable by classmates at his school. He avoided eye contact, and his responses were minimal, punctuated by long, awkward pauses. Schoolmates privately ridiculed and avoided him. On one occasion, he had attempted to start a conversation with a very attractive girl in his English class, by telling her about his achievements as an artist, but she had walked away from him. Later, he discovered that she had publicly referred to him as "weird." He subsequently persisted in his attempts to date her, but found himself stuttering every time he attempted to speak to her and to schoolmates in general. The therapist learned that he knew very little about girls, having rarely even talked to a girl, and that he incorrectly believed this girl to be "available." He also naively believed that this girl would want to date him once she had been shown some of his impressive art work.

Target: Conversation-Skills Deficit

The Conversation-Skills Deficit Checklist, previously shown in Table 3.1, is useful for precise identification of deficit areas. For example, while attempting to converse with the socially isolated boy described above, the therapist noted that his style of conversing was hampered by long pauses, lack of eye contact, an anxious facial expression, and voice volume that was practically inaudible. There was also a failure to initiate topics of conversation and no attempts were made to maintain the conversation. His responses were restricted to monosyllabic answers to questions. His poor conversation skills were compounded by social anxiety. He described several occasions in which he had become tongue-tied, and felt "trapped" in conversation with peers, embarrassed, and unable to escape.

Poor listening skills and misreading of feedback signals from listeners are other examples of deficits in conversation skills. In the following example, the client was insensitive to the fact that successful, rewarding conversation occurs when *both* parties take turns speaking.

A loud, talkative girl asked the school social worker to help her with her "personlity problem." She explained that she lacked friends and was lonely and unhappy, although she presented herself during the session as a self-proclaimed expert on human relationships and several other topics. Her persistent monologue barely allowed for therapist responses, and when the social worker did manage to interrupt, the girl failed to attend, but simply carried on with her monologue at the first opportunity. The social worker subsequently observed the same pattern when the girl was conversing with peers in the school corridor.

In this case, the girl was particularly unresponsive to peer feedback, failing to notice the effect her behavior was having on others. Argyle (1980) points out that when people are speaking, they need regular feedback on how others are responding so that they can modify their utterances appropriately. The speaker needs to accurately perceive whether the listener understands, believes or disbelieves, is surprised or bored, agrees or disagrees, or is pleased or annoyed. This information is obtained mainly through observing the other person's face for nonverbal signals, or from utterances such as "I see" and "How interesting."

INTERVENTION

1. Conversation-Skills Training

In both cases, the clients were helped to understand how particular aspects of their behavior when conversing with peers affected the way in which peers responded to them. Afterwards, they were taught new skills using a Conversation-Skills Training approach, which they rehearsed over and over again in conversations with the therapist during the session, before trying them out with peers.

Target: Unattractive Appearance, Poor Grooming, Inappropriate Dress

Physical unattractiveness is one of the more obvious blocks to the achievement of satisfying peer relationships during adolescence. Some aspects of unattractiveness are amenable to change through cognitive-behavioral interventions or didactic teaching, such as poor grooming, obesity, or inappropriate dress that deviates sharply from what is considered to be acceptable by peers. Inadequate grooming and inappropriate dress may stem from lack of familiarity with normal procedures or lack of awareness of accepted styles. However, these problems may also stem from dysfunctional cognitions underlying failure to take steps to improve physical appearance, reflected in the following statements of adolescent clients: "People must accept me the way I am" and "I would have to lose 50 pounds to look better so why bother to do anything."

> A tenth-grade student reluctantly agreed to see a psychiatrist after school staff became concerned about apparent depression. The girl complained of having no friends and feeling uncomfortable at school. She had been excluded from various cliques at her new school and after a while made no effort to interact socially. The girl was poorly groomed and overweight, and had an inadequate knowledge of proper nutrition. Self-statements underlying social withdrawal included: "I'm ugly; I don't belong," "They don't like me so why talk to them," "They would rather be with their own group of friends, they don't have anything in common with me," "They could never understand me."

INTERVENTION

Obesity and poor grooming were just two of many identified problem areas for this client, all of which were interfering with successful interpersonal functioning. Alterations in grooming and style of dress were shaped through direct instruction by the therapist, with the use of appropriate books, magazines, and other reading material. The client was also given the assignment of observing the clothes, hair, and make-up styles of socially competent fellow classmates. Distorted and negative assumptions and beliefs maintaining inadequate grooming were then addressed and altered through cognitive restructuring. Finally, the weight-control problem was addressed through a combination of Self-Monitoring, referral to a nutritionist, and referral to a weight-control program run by the school nurse.

Target: Lack of Assertiveness

Lack of assertiveness may contribute to peer-relationship problems of adolescence. Unassertive persons allow themselves to be manipulated or controlled by peers, in spite of wishes to the contrary, rather than express their true feelings and desires.

On the other hand, skills mastered by *assertive* individuals include the ability to say No, the ability to ask for favors or to make requests, the ability to express positive and negative feelings, the ability to initiate, continue, and terminate general conversations, and the ability to stand up for one's rights and to act in one's own best interests (Argyle, 1980).

Unassertive adolescents may be unable to free themselves from unwanted influences and relationships. For example, clients who report that they unwillingly submit to peer pressure to break rules and to perform antisocial acts lack skills necessary for assertive responses. Unassertiveness may also underlie problems in heterosexual relationships, as illustrated in the following case.

A young girl was desperate because she believed that she had no alternative but to marry her steady boyfriend who threatened to harm her. He also threatened to attempt suicide if she were to break off the relationship. She told the therapist that she was responsible for preventing her boyfriend from attempting suicide and therefore she was obligated to marry him even though she didn't love him, and feared him. She felt trapped and viewed her future as hopeless.

INTERVENTION

1. Cognitive Restructuring
2. Problem-Solving Training
3. Assertiveness Training

Cognitive-restructuring therapy is used to help unassertive clients to recognize and accept their own feelings, opinions, and wishes as valid and justified. This is combined with Assertiveness Training to combat coercion or mistreatment by others. In the above case, cognitive-restructuring interventions were first used to challenge the client's belief that she would be responsible if her boyfriend should decide to attempt suicide. This belief had fostered the girl's ongoing passive submission. The client hadn't considered the alternative viewpoint that individuals are responsible for their own self-destructive behaviors.

A problem-solving approach was then used to help the client to generate and evaluate alternative solutions to her dilemma. She decided on the alternative of arranging things so that she would be able to announce to her boyfriend, while her parents were present in the room, her intention of ending the relationship. Her parents could then play a supportive role in helping the boyfriend to cope with her decision. Having decided on this course of action, the girl was then helped, through assertiveness training, to write a script containing a concise statement expressing her feelings and her right to break off the relationship. She rehearsed the script during the session, using newly learned verbal and nonverbal assertive behaviors.

Target: Distorted Social Perceptions and Beliefs Underlying Social Failure

The following examples of dysfunctional beliefs, assumptions, and perceptions were taken from statements of adolescent clients with peer-relationship problems: (1) perception of self as unworthy or undeserving of friendship due to factors such as physical unattractiveness, bad habits, family stigma, or mental instability, (2) perception of self as psychologically "damaged," (3) a tendency to be judgmental and hypercritical of peers, (4) a belief in one's own superiority so that peers are unworthy of one's friendship, (5) unrealistically high expectations of peers, (6) hypersensitivity to perceived slight, (7) the assumption that getting close to peers would lead to rejection and humiliation due to disclosure of family or personal problems, and (8) a belief that socializing is bad or a waste of time.

Many adolescent clients who experience difficulty with peer relationships have a tendency to misperceive social cues and misinterpret the actions of peers. This may take the form of misperceived threats in the case of aggressive adolescents, misperceived rejection in the case of socially anxious clients, or misperception of a wish for romantic involvement, as in the following case of an adolescent lacking experience in heterosocial relationships and skills.

> The 19-year old son of an abusive father was overweight and had been the object of peer ridicule over the years. He was surprised when a female classmate began initiating conversations with him. He discovered that she, too, had been subjected to child abuse, and they began to commiserate with each other on a regular basis. The boy misinterpreted her willingness to discuss family problems with him as a sign that she was attracted to him. He began to fantasize about a future life together and publicly bragged about the fact that they were "going together" and would eventually marry. Lacking experience in even the most basic interactions with girls, he was unaware how inaccurate his perceptions were and was angry and embittered when she began avoiding him after learning of his boasts.

INTERVENTION

1. ABC Belief-Analysis Technique
2. Cognitive Restructuring
3. Interpersonal Coping-Skills Training

Clients are first taught how to identify beliefs and perceptions underlying interpersonal response styles that are counterproductive. They are then helped to understand how they developed a particular inaccurate belief and to understand the consequences of adhering to this belief in terms of negative emotional reactions or inept social responses. The ABC Belief-Analysis Technique is a useful intervention for this purpose. Following this, cognitive-restructuring strategies are used to challenge or alter these unrealistic beliefs and inaccurate social perceptions. In the above case, the boy misperceived the girl's friendly manner as a sign of her wish to become involved in a long-term relationship with him. He failed to notice that the girl behaved in a friendly manner with other boys and that her nonverbal behavior and the content of her conversations with him did not indicate a wish for romantic involvement.

SEX-ROLE BEHAVIOR DISTURBANCES

Types of sex-role deviance patterns encountered with adolescent clients include excessive feminine behavior in boys, excessive masculine behavior in girls, and homosexual orientation. When these patterns are accompanied by anxiety or depression, the adolescent may seek help from a mental-health professional.

Gender Identity Disorder of Adolescence (DSM-III-R) is characterized by persistent discomfort and a sense of inappropriateness about one's assigned sex, along with some degree of cross-dressing in the role of the other sex (but without the more extreme features of cross-dressing for the purpose of sexual excitement or the preoccupation with a need for surgical sex-reassignment treatment). Anxiety and depression are common associated features, and the person may have either a homosexual or a heterosexual orientation. Problems often stem from conflicts with family members and other people regarding the cross-dressing.

Gender sex-role deviance problems are characterized by several chronic behaviors which may be designated as targets for therapy intervention if clients request help in changing (Rekers, 1982). In boys, these may include a history of cross-dressing in girls' clothing or use of cosmetics, feminine mannerisms, gestures, or gait, avoidance of peer activities with other boys or preoccupation with feminine sex-typed activities, and use of a high feminine-like voice or speech content. In girls, behaviors may include: insistence on wearing masculine clothing and chronic rejection of dresses, skirts and cosmetics, masculine behavioral gestures, posture, and gait, avoidance of feminine peer activities, overinvolvement in stereotyped masculine activities, an artificially low voice inflection, predominantly masculine topics of conversation, and use of a boy's nickname.

A 19-year-old girl sought therapy for depression. She was ridiculed by classmates because of her masculine appearance and was mistaken for a boy on several occasions. The girl had a masculine hairstyle, was large and awkward, and wore clothes purchased in the men's section of a department store. She insisted that she would like to dress in a more feminine way, but was afraid to do so, not having worn a skirt for years. Later, it was learned that she had been sexually molested at age eight by a teenage boy who lived in the neighborhood. This had precipitated the onset of cross-dressing, since she decided to adopt masculine attire in order to downplay her feminine features and thereby discourage further sexual assaults. This incident was not repeated, but she continued to wear masculine clothes and to feel anxious when she attempted to wear feminine attire. She failed to form friendships with girls, but played team sports with boys, instead. However, with the onset of puberty, boys no longer wanted to play with her and she began to feel very lonely and rejected. She told the therapist that she wanted to dress and behave like a normal girl so that she could have girlfriends and eventually begin to date boys.

INTERVENTION

1. Cognitive Restructuring of distorted cognitions maintaining cross-dressing;
2. Shaping of feminine dress, grooming, gestures, and conversational skills through didactic instruction, modelling, role-playing, and "homework" assignments;
3. Graded-Task Assignment to gradually mitigate anxiety associated with the wearing of feminine attire;
4. Interpersonal Coping-Skills Training to shape more appropriate feminine response styles;
5. Activity Scheduling of events to increase exposure to female peers and increase the likelihood of forming satisfying same-sex relationships.

Gender Identity Disorders are sometimes accompanied by a stated desire to be a member of the opposite sex or a sexual arousal pattern of homosexual orientation. Development of a homosexual orientation during adolescence may be accompanied by anxiety and depression, precipitating a referral for psychotherapy. Clients often fear condemnation and ridicule from family members and others, and have difficulty dealing with the daily stress of keeping their sexual orientation a secret. Some clients request support in confronting and informing parents and peers, and in coping with the negative responses and rejection of significant others. Other clients seek help in decreasing homosexual behaviors and in acquiring new interpersonal response patterns likely to facilitate development of heterosexual relationships.

There is evidence to suggest that by the time most boys and girls reach adolescence, their sexual preference is already determined, even though they are not yet sexually active (Bell et al., 1981). Those who report pre-adult homosexual feelings typically begin to experience them around the age of 13 for males and the age of 16 for females. There is a tendency for homosexual men and women to find heterosexual experiences during their childhood and adolescent years ungratifying, and a history of gender nonconformity during childhood increases the likelihood of development of a homosexual orientation in later years.

A 16-year-old girl was distressed by her sexual attraction to other girls. After engaging in lesbian behaviors, she would feel depressed and frightened. She referred herself for therapy, and broke down during the initial session stating: "If my parents find out I'm gay, they'll disown me and I wouldn't want to live." She said she was so depressed that she tended to sleep all the time in order to forget her problems. She said that she wanted to end all lesbian relationships forever and start dating boys.

She tended to dress in masculine clothes and said that the odd time when she would wear feminine clothes she found that she would be attracted to boys, but when she dressed like a boy, she would find herself attracted to girls. She said that she had played exclusively with boys as a youngster, mainly team sports, and had few girlfriends because she believed that boys had a much more interesting life-style and that girls were boring. When the boys on her soccer team reached the age of puberty and began showing an interest in girls, she also became aware of her own attraction to other girls.

At the present time, she was spending almost all of her time in the company of lesbian girlfriends and would periodically be involved in physical fights with these girls. She had few heterosexual acquaintances and few interests in typical teenage feminine pursuits.

INTERVENTION

1. Self-Control and Self-Monitoring Skill Training to decrease the frequency of homosexual behaviors and increase heterosexual behaviors;
2. Activity Scheduling to increase exposure to heterosexual peers, and to decrease depressive inactivity;
3. Interpersonal Coping-Skills Training to shape new heterosocial response patterns;
4. Shaping feminine behaviors through didactic instruction;
5. Cognitive Restructuring to alter dysfunctional cognitions interfering with adoption of feminine response styles, and dysfunctional cognitions fostering anxiety and depression.

The therapist will need to clarify the client's wishes and goals with respect to sexual orientation. In the above case, because the client's clearly-stated goal was to eliminate homosexual relationships and form heterosexual relationships, interventions focused on altering behaviors and cognitions maintaining homosexual interactions and on shaping new behaviors likely to foster satisfying heterosexual relationships. (Other clients who express no desire to change their sexual preference, may seek assistance with self-acceptance of their homosexual orientation or with public self-disclosure of their sexual preference). Strategies described in Chapter Nine, designed to alter cognitions and behavior patterns associated with depression, were also part of the treatment package.

DYSFUNCTIONAL PEER-RELATIONSHIP PATTERNS ASSOCIATED WITH ADOLESCENT CONDUCT DISORDER

Adolescent Conduct Disorders are characterized by a persistent repetitive pattern of conduct in which the basic rights of others and major age-appropriate societal norms or rules are violated (DSM-III-R). A variety of maladaptive behavior patterns involving interactions with peers are classified as Conduct Disorders, such as physical aggression toward peers, stealing or destruction of others' property as a delinquent peer-group activity, and heavy use of illegal drugs or alcohol. Some behaviors associated with peer-related adolescent Conduct Disorders are classifiable as adult crimes (e.g. theft, assault, drug abuse), while other uniquely juvenile offenses are not classifiable as adult crimes (e.g. possession of alcohol, failure to attend school).

Target: Aggressive Peer-Interaction Response Style

Adolescents with an aggressive response style have a tendency to react to upsetting incidents involving peers with verbal or physical aggression. Physical aggression may be initiated as a group activity or it may be initiated independently by the adolescent. Insufficient concern for the well-being or feelings of others, and insufficient feelings of guilt or remorse following aggressive responses often underlie the adolescent's callous behavior. Additional features commonly include a history of low frustration tolerance, impulsivity, temper outbursts, and initiation of fights.

A thorough assessment of the problem begins with a detailed analysis of factors that precipitate and maintain the client's aggressive responses. This involves an analysis of environmental stimulus conditions, including types of people, setting, and forms of provocation such as verbal threats or nonverbal behaviors, as well as analysis of consequences following the client's aggressive response. The possible contribution of alcohol or drug consumption is also considered.

This is followed by a cognitive assessment of thoughts and feelings associated with aggressive responses. They may be taught to use a "Thoughts Diary" to record daily situations eliciting anger, along with self-statements preceding and accompanying their aggressive responses. They may be helped to recognize, analyze, and alter misperceptions and distorted beliefs maintaining their aggressive response styles, such as irrational blaming, belief in the necessity of projecting a "tough-guy" image, or perception of another person's behavior as threatening.

INTERVENTION

1. Stress Inoculation Training for anger control;
2. Relaxation Training;
3. Contingency-Awareness Training;
4. Pro-social Interpersonal-Skill Training
5. Behavior-Analysis Skill Training
6. Increased exposure to prosocial peer models
7. Problem-Solving Training
8. Cognitive Restructuring

Basically, interventions for aggressive adolescents focus simultaneously on reducing aggressive coercive behaviors and replacing these with positive prosocial behaviors designed to elicit reciprocal positive responses from peers. Interventions to reduce aggressive coercive behaviors include Stress-Inoculation Training to control anger and impulsive aggressive responding, and Relaxation Training to reduce emotional arousal stemming from anger or rage. Contingency-Awareness Training helps clients to routinely reflect on probable negative consequences that would follow if they respond aggressively.

Prosocial behavioral response patterns are shaped through a combination of Behavior Analysis Skill Training, and Prosocial Interpersonal-Skills Training, based on the rationale that aggressive behavior is partly the result of poorly developed social skills and that the person has not learned more appropriate ways of expressing anger in interpersonal situations (Bornstein et al., 1980; Bornstein et al., 1985). The client is taught new, non-angry and non-antagonistic responses to provocation during the therapy session through therapist modeling and instruction. In addition, an attempt is made to increase the client's exposure to prosocial peer models by encouraging involvement in new prosocial peer activities. There is evidence to suggest that prosocial behaviors (like antisocial behaviors) can be learned through observation of models (Feldman, 1980).

Several Social-Skills Training programs have been designed for aggressive youngsters who lack the necessary skills for successful interaction in prosocial peer groups (Goldstein & Pentz, 1984). Generally speaking, these have focused on training prosocial alternatives to aggression, and on aggression management or aggression-inhibition behaviors. Aggressive clients are taught skills for coping with criticism, negotiation, and problem-solving. Prosocial behaviors taught through direct instruction, modeling, role-playing and performance feedback include:

- asking for help
- giving clear instructions
- expressing affection

- expressing a complaint
- responding to the feelings of others (empathy)
- responding to failure
- responding to contradictory messages
- responding to a complaint
- responding to anger
- dealing with an accusation
- dealing with group pressure

Specific areas to be addressed might also include eye contact, posture, gesturing, appropriate facial mannerisms and affect, directness, refusal of inappropriate requests, and generation of alternative behaviors.

Problem-Solving Training is also applicable. Conduct-disorder children are said to lack adequate social problem-solving skills, such as the ability to conceptualize alternative solutions to problems or to adequately assess the consequences of alternatives to social problems other than aggression (DiGiuseppe, 1988).

Cognitive-restructuring techniques are used to teach clients to identify and alter their own inaccurate social perceptions catalyzing aggressive responses, such as a tendency to mistrust and to blame others unfairly. The magnitude of anger arousal and aggression has been found to be related to the perceived intent of the attacker (Grieger, 1982); attributing arbitrary, nonjustifiable, or selfish motives to the aggressor increases the likelihood of counteraggression.

An 18-year-old victim of child abuse had a long history of aggression toward peers. He had recently been suspended from school for initiating a fight. He gave the following reason for striking the other boy: "He looked at me in that way, and I knew he was thinking he could beat me up, so I hit him first." Other reasons given for initiating fights by the same client were: "Two guys threatened another kid and I had to protect him," "Other kids would think I was 'chicken' if I didn't hit him," "If somebody harms me I have to repay it," and "Something upset me but I don't know what."

The boy said that he had to live with a continual fear of "going crazy," losing control, and harming someone. He said he was unable to control himself and that he would sometimes break things in order to prevent himself from harming others. He said that he sympathized with a boy he read about in the newspaper who was arrested for beating a classmate. He said this aggressive act was not the fault of the boy, but was the fault of the environment.

Target: Vulnerability to Antisocial Peer Influences

Adolescent conduct disorders often involve membership in a delinquent peer group. The youngster is unable to resist peer pressure to engage in antisocial acts, in spite of a stated desire to stay out of trouble. This usually stems from a strong desire for peer acceptance and approval, as well as from fear of rejection or abandonment by friends.

Members of a delinquent peer subculture may engage in activities such as cooperative stealing, initiation of fights, defiance of authority, malicious mischief, drug and alcohol abuse, and habitual school truancy. These youngsters have been labelled "socialized delinquents" in the literature and their delinquent conduct has been traditionally linked to factors such as inadequate parental supervision, disorganized home life, and a minority subculture that reinforces delinquent acts through prestige for such behaviors as successful theft (Jenkins & Boyer, 1968). These youngsters tend to make impulsive decisions to engage in antisocial acts, elicited by cues from peers, without sufficient consideration of the probable consequences of their behavior. They are often motivated by a craving for high levels of stimulation associated with antisocial acts (thrill-seeking), coupled with a low tolerance for activities perceived as boring.

> A teenage boy with a long history of hyperactivity and school failure was unpopular with peers until he joined a motor scooter gang. He began wearing the gang "uniform," and attending all-night parties where members indulged in drugs and alcohol. The boy lived with his mother, but hadn't seen his biological father for years and had little contact with his stepfather, who had recently left the mother for another woman. The mother was overwhelmed by her own problems and unable to supervise or impose limits on her son. After several minor misdemeanors, the boy was arrested with other gang members for theft and assault. Later, the boy reported, "I didn't think ahead. I didn't think the guy would get hurt and me get into trouble. It was like watching T.V. I told the others to leave him alone, but they were in the process of doing it. We just did it for that feeling . . . like being on a roller coaster."

INTERVENTION

1. Contingency-Awareness Training (to shape a more reflective cognitive style);
2. Self-Instructional Training;
3. Assertiveness Training;
4. Prosocial Interpersonal-Skill Training
5. Increased exposure to prosocial peers
6. Parenting-Skill Training

The tendency to impulsively comply with peer requests to engage in antisocial acts may be addressed through a combination of Contingency-Awareness Training, Self-Instructional Training, and Assertiveness Training. Contingency-Awareness Training may be used to decrease delinquent peer influence by teaching the client to routinely consider the probable consequences of impulsive decisions to join in delinquent group activities. During the session, the client is asked to list and to actually visualize the probable negative short- and long-term consequences, such as getting caught or arrested, convictions, reciprocal aggression, school suspension, or parental anger and disappointment. Clients are asked to practice visualizing these consequences each time they are tempted by delinquent peers to engage in antisocial acts; this is expected to function as a deterrent.

However, since antisocial responses tend to be under the influence of conflicting reinforcement contingencies, negative consequences such as arrest or school suspension may be balanced by positive consequences such as recognition and admiration from a peer group that values demonstrations of physical power, or defiance and daring. Therefore, it may be difficult to convince the youngster that antisocial acts are maladaptive.

One approach is to introduce the concept of external control by pointing out to clients that each time they go along with peer pressure to commit delinquent acts, they are, in effect, being controlled by peers, contrary to their own wishes to stay out of trouble. Peers are represented as having the power to elicit antisocial responses in the client. Clients are encouraged to experiment with taking control of their own behavior by refusing to submit to peer pressure for a given period of time and then noting the more positive long-term consequences. They are helped through Assertiveness Training and Self-Instructional Training to develop the skills needed to carry out this "homework" assignment.

Through Self-Instructional Training, clients are first helped to pay attention to what they say to themselves during those moments when considering whether to engage in antisocial acts or not, especially self-statements and beliefs blocking consideration of possible negative consequences of the act (e.g. "What does it matter," "Nothing will happen"). Next, clients are asked to replace these dysfunctional statements with new self-statements that will function as deterrents by reminding them of probable negative consequences of the antisocial act (e.g. "I'll get caught and be sent to reform school," "My life will be ruined," "My parents will be so disappointed in me").

The client is encouraged to formulate and rehearse these new self-statements during the session, and then to practice them in vivo. They may also be taught distracting activities to delay compliance with peers, such as going jogging alone for ten minutes before coming to a decision. As a general rule, in order to increase the chances of convincing the youngster to alter dysfunctional patterns, the therapist should avoid moralizing, and instead endeavor to offer the client practical assistance in staying out of trouble.

Prosocial Skill Training is another major focus. Clients are trained to identify peer-related stimuli eliciting their delinquent responses. They are taught to recognize and avoid temptation and are taught competing prosocial behaviors. They are trained to avoid situations in which delinquent activities occur and to avoid peer associates who model and reinforce delinquent activities. New alternative pastimes will need to be shaped that will provide access to valued reinforcers previously consequent on antisocial activities. Additional approaches that have proven to have some success in reducing delinquent peer influence and decreasing future offenses include: (1) training parents to acquire more effective child-management techniques, (e.g Discipline-Effectiveness Training, Expectations-Establishment Training), (2) teaching parents techniques designed to facilitate the development of prosocial behaviors and associated skills, such as empathy and self control, (3) increased exposure to behavior patterns of prosocial peer models, and (4) effective school programs aimed at cutting down truancy, since many youngsters begin offending when truant from school (Feldman, 1980). The latter would include school programs to provide more positively reinforcing activities to compete with the "fun" of truancy. Other school-related interventions might include teaching job-finding skills, and effective work habits.

8

School-Related Problems

Application of a cognitive-behavioral approach to school-related problems of adolescence will be demonstrated in this chapter. School-related problems are not limited to intellectual deficits or learning disabilities, but are often associated with long-established, maladaptive behavioral, emotional, and cognitive patterns such as erratic attendance, insufficient self-discipline, and anxiety-provoking or depressive self-statements. Environmental stresses in the home or peer environment often exacerbate school problems.

Three major categories of learning and achievement problems of secondary-school students have been documented in the literature: emotional/motivational problems, overplacement, and specific learning disabilities (Vance, 1982). This chapter will be primarily concerned with the first category, since problems in this category are most often referred to mental health professionals. School personnel are generally responsible for dealing with problems of overplacement of a student in a school program that is too demanding academically. However, when a student insists on remaining in the inappropriate school placement in spite of repeated failure, and when anxiety, depression, or rebellious reactions are components of the problem, referral to a mental health professional is indicated.

School personnel are also responsible for dealing with learning disabilities such as developmental arithmetic and language disorders, and Attention-deficit Hyperactive Disorder, through Special Education interventions. Although these are not addressed in this book, it is recognized that a reliable estimate of intellectual functioning and current academic achievement levels is a crucial component of a thorough assessment of school-related problems, so that the extent to which intellectual and academic skill deficits may be contributing to identified school problems can be determined.

Academic underachievement, defined as functionally low levels of school performance unrelated to intellectual ability or skill, is common among adolescent clients referred for therapy for various non-academic presenting problems. Milder forms of academic underachievement may be considered a feature of normal adolescent development, but underachievement becomes clinically significant when it persists in spite of school interventions to remedy a chronic pattern of failure and when it seriously jeopardizes the adolescent's chances of eventually attaining a level of education sufficient for financial and emotional independence from parents in adulthood. Academic underachievement usually involves insufficient application to schoolwork, and this is often combined with truancy. The remainder of this chapter will address targets for assessment and therapy associated with these two major areas.

INSUFFICIENT APPLICATION TO SCHOOLWORK

Various dysfunctional patterns typify adolescents who repeatedly fail several courses each year due to insufficient application to schoolwork. A careful assessment is necessary in order to specify various components of the problem. One client may want very much to succeed academically, but is unable to overcome a tendency to procrastinate. Other clients may find themselves unable to persist at what they consider to be boring study sessions, in light of competition from more attractive ways to spend time such as going out with friends each evening.

Some adolescents are unable to work at home because of pathological family conditions that preclude sustained concentration on homework, such as the disorganization and upheavals associated with parental alcoholism, parental mental disorders, marital conflict, or child abuse. Quiet conditions necessary for productive studying are often lacking in these families. Failure of some clients to apply themselves to schoolwork may also be related to dysfunctional parental attitudes toward homework obligations and academic success, or to the degree and consistency of parental supervision.

Dysfunctional parenting styles may be responsible for shaping and maintaining persistent patterns of insufficient application to schoolwork in the child or adolescent. For example, an adolescent may deliberately underachieve as a form of rebellion against parents who insist upon inappropriately long periods of study at home or unrealistic standards of performance. Passive resistance to overcoercive parents may take the form of task-avoidance strategies such as daydreaming or procrastination.

Adolescent children of overindulgent parents may have developed long-standing patterns of bored passivity, failure to develop diverse interests, failure to persist at unexciting tasks, and expectations to be excused from unpleasant activities. They may attempt to manipulate the school system in the same way they have always successfully manipulated their parents over the years. They may refuse to conform to strict school expectations that require regular attendance, prompt completion of homework assignments, or persistance at tedious academic tasks.

Adolescent emotional disorders may also interfere with application to schoolwork and will need to be treated before school performance may be expected to improve. For example, depressive or anxiety-provoking cognitions may seriously interfere with the adolescent's attempts to concentrate on schoolwork or to pay attention in class.

Some of the most frequently encountered patterns associated with insufficient application to schoolwork in clinical populations will be addressed in the following sections. These include (1) inadequate self-discipline, (2) inadequate organizational and study skills, (3) excessive procrastination, (4) poor time management, and (5) low academic motivation and intent to quit school.

Target: Inadequate Self-Discipline

Clients with inadequate self-discipline fail to independently initiate and persist with study behaviors.

> A 16-year-old boy spent the previous two years trying unsuccessfully to pass his freshman year of secondary school. He was unable to force himself to persist at homework assignments for more than 10 or 15 minutes, after which time he would watch T.V. or find another more pleasurable activity. He wanted to go on to college like his friends, but as the years passed, he found that dream becoming more and more unattainable. He was overwhelmed by depression stemming from self-disgust and a sense of hopelessness. Examples of depressive self-statements were: "There's no point in trying—I'll just fail my year again" and "I'll never be able to learn this material so why begin."
>
> Attempts to study were accompanied by intense feelings of anxiety, from which distractions such as T.V. or going out with friends brought temporary relief. Over the years, neither parent had imposed definite expectations on the boy with respect to school performance. The parents were overindulgent, and the son grew up rarely having to do things he didn't feel like doing. Elementary school records indicated a long history of insufficient application to schoolwork, but teachers allowed the boy to pass on the basis of "potential" and his pleasant disposition. Consequently, the boy was further indulged by the school system, which contributed to his failure to develop the study and organizational skills he needed for secondary school.

INTERVENTION

1. Self-Monitoring Skill Training for study behavior;
2. Family interventions to alter parent-adolescent patterns maintaining self-discipline problems;
3. School-based interventions to increase accountability.

Self-Monitoring Skill Training is recommended for individual sessions, in order to teach clients to monitor their own study behavior. Family therapy and parent-training interventions, such as Contingency Contracting and Rule-Establishment Training may also be appropriate in order to alter dysfunctional parent-adolescent interaction patterns maintaining the problem, especially when clients are in their early teens and sufficient parental control and supervision are important considerations. Arrangements may also be made, through a school-based intervention, for the adolescent client to be accountable to a school counsellor or other member of school staff for completion of school assignments, thus providing an outside, objective frame of reference for the client.

Self-Monitoring may be used as both an assessment and an intervention technique. The client is taught to systematically self-observe and reinforce adaptive study behaviors (Bellack & Schwartz, 1976). First, the client is asked to collect baseline data by recording all instances of study behavior for one week, as well as data on time, place, work accomplished, and situation. The "Daily Activity Sheet" (Appendix D) may be adapted for this purpose. Distracting activities and circumstances are then identified, such as peer or T.V. influences, phone calls, chronic arguing between parents or other family members, or parental demands for chores to be completed, causing disruptions during study periods.

Next, stimulus-control procedures are introduced. For example, a client may be encouraged to change his study environment to a quieter place free from distracting influences and circumstances. If the family home is disruptive, the public library may be the most appropriate place. Clients may be helped to generate other stimulus-control techniques, such as getting up and going to another area for a short break when they find themselves daydreaming, so that when they return to their designated study areas, it will be for the purpose of productive study only.

Clients are then helped to establish self-evaluation guidelines. First, they will show how many hours of study per day they consider to be adequate and realistic. Following this, a schedule of daily study periods is constructed that fulfills the set requirement. A contract is then established between client and therapist, with clients committing themselves to the number of hours they will study each day. Self-reinforcement procedures are introduced next. Positive reinforcement for productive study may take the form of permission to watch a T.V. show or to take a snack break. Clients are taught to establish criteria for deciding whether their performance has been adequate and deserving of positive reinforcement, based on their study schedule contracts.

Target: Inadequate Organizational and Study Skills

Inadequate organizational and study skills are frequent components of problems of insufficient application to schoolwork. Students who fail tend to avoid taking responsibility for keeping a clear, up-to-date record of homework assignments and tests, and they do not bother to obtain and clarify important details, such as material to be covered on upcoming tests and teacher expectations for written assignments. They also lack efficient study skills, which are needed in order to use study time productively.

INTERVENTION

1. Organizational-Skills Training;
2. Study Skills Training

The client may be referred to school staff for organizational- and study-skills training. However, if this is not available, mental-health professionals often undertake this task themselves. Although some therapists may consider organizational- and study-skills training outside their domain of expertise, the approaches outlined in the following section are straightforward and easy to implement.

INTERVENTION: ORGANIZATIONAL-SKILLS TRAINING

Organizational-skills training essentially consists of teaching the client to keep a record of pertinent information about school assignments. The client is taught to list details of all chapters and materials that have to be learned. Contacting teachers and classmates for information is often a part of the process of keeping an accurate record of assignments. The client is then taught to break down assignments into component tasks or steps, to prioritize these, and to schedule specific study times for particular tasks. The following format is useful:

RECORD OF ASSIGNMENTS

COURSE	ASSIGNMENTS AND TESTS	DATE DUE	PREPARATION TIMES

In addition to improving organizational abilities, this will also foster accountability and responsibity for schoolwork. Once tasks and activities have been identified, clients are taught long-term planning. They are helped to schedule study sessions for the coming days and weeks, using the "Daily Activity Sheet" (Appendix D). They are cautioned to be practical and realistic, scheduling in only what they will be committed to and capable of carrying out. A Self-Monitoring approach may then be used to insure commitment to scheduled tasks.

INTERVENTION: STUDY SKILLS TRAINING

Richards (1985) outlines a concise study-skills training approach that is easily adapted for use with adolescents. Four areas are covered: where to study, how to read textbooks, what to do during class, and what to do before and during tests. Because of the didactic nature of this intervention, clients should be encouraged to keep written notes on each topic for subsequent reference and review when implementing newly learned techniques.

Assessment of current study locations for the presence of distracting influences should first be undertaken. Sources of distraction in current study locations need to be identified, as discussed earlier. Plans must then be made to insure regular study periods in optimal locations.

Next, efficient methods of reading textbooks are taught, in order to insure a high degree of comprehension and retention of material. The client is asked to note the following steps: (1) Survey, (2) Question, (3) Read, (4) Notes, (5) Review. The therapist demonstrates these study steps by using one of the client's reading assignments. The client is taught to first survey the whole reading assignment, paying attention to headings and study questions at the end of chapters, in order to get an idea of how much time the reading assignment will require and the important points that will be covered. Clients are taught to predict what they think the important points will be and what the teacher will consider to be important.

Clients may then be instructed to read part of a chapter during the therapy session and are taught to take notes on the material read. It is explained that this aids retention of material and provides a study guide for future reference in preparing for tests. Finally, they are instructed to review their notes at the end of the study period and during subsequent study periods; it is explained that material reviewed regularly is more likely to be remembered.

Next, clients are taught skills to be used in the classroom. They are advised to attend all classes and to take detailed notes during class. It is explained that this will serve the purpose of forcing them to concentrate during class and will decrease the tendency to daydream. It will also provide essential material for test preparation, based on what the teacher considers to be important. It is explained that paying close attention in class will cut down the amount of home-study needed. It is also recommended that the client place a sheet of paper in the front of each notebook on which to record daily assignments and the due date of each. The need to obtain notes and assignments promptly for any missed classes is also emphasized.

The final topic concerns tips on test preparation. The client is advised to avoid waiting until the night before the test to begin studying, since this tends to result in increased levels of anxiety. A schedule for test preparation should be devised and written out, and the client may be taught to do this during the session for an upcoming test. The client will then be given the assignment of finding out from the teacher what form the test will take (e.g. multiple choice or essay) and what topics will be covered. This information should be brought to the following session.

Tips for test-taking are then discussed, including careful reading and rereading of test instructions, noting which questions are given the most weight. (If this is not indicated on the test, the client is instructed to predict which items seem to be most important). Next, clients are taught to allot the amount of the total test time to be spent on each question, leaving five or 10 minutes at the end of the test period for completing unfinished questions and for reading over and correcting answers. Finally, the importance of writing something for each test question is stressed, to insure at least partial credit for each item.

Target: Excessive Procrastination

Clients who report that they can never get down to work even though they may make detailed lists and schedules, adolescents who fear that a project won't be up to standard and therefore put off starting it, and clients who find all sorts of other tasks that must be done before starting homework assignments may all be manifesting different forms of excessive procrastination. Procrastination itself is usually accompanied by self-belittlement, depression, or anxiety.

In order to be fully understood, excessive procrastination must be placed in its correct context for each client. Frequent patterns of procrastination observed in adult clients by Beck and Emery (1985) are also observed clinically with adolescent clients who fail to get down to their schoolwork. Procrastination may be associated with rebellion against being told what to do by adults. For example, one adolescent client regularly refused to start homework when told to do so by his mother, who attempted to run every aspect of her son's life. He enjoyed the fact that schoolwork was one area over which the mother had little control.

Procrastination may also stem from anxiety, as in the case of a client who spent so much time compulsively making perfect, comprehensive lists and schedules of assignments that she would become overwhelmed with anxiety and unable to begin. Procrastination may be related to a shift in life circumstances not yet fully accepted. For example, a boy coerced into transferring to an easier school program by his counsellor felt humiliated by this and put off beginning assignments that he considered too easy and beneath him.

Procrastination may also stem from fear of rejection, as in the case of a client who was so sure that his classmates would consider his oral presentation inferior that he was unable to begin work on it.

Dysfunctional beliefs usually underlie procrastination. For example, one girl believed that everything must be in order before she could begin to work. She would tell herself that there was no point in starting her homework assignment before everything in her room was in place. She would then convince herself that she didn't have sufficient time to complete the assignment, given all the other housework tasks she had to do first.

INTERVENTION

1. Identification of blocks to initiation of study behaviors
2. Problem Solving Training to generate more adaptive solutions to problems maintaining procrastination
3. Cognitive Restructuring of dysfunctional beliefs underlying procrastination

The first task is to identify "blocks" preventing initiation of homework tasks. Clients are asked to describe recent situations in which they had intended to get down to work, but ultimately failed to do so. They are helped to identify people, circumstances, or self-statements blocking productive study in each of the situations described. They may also be asked to give detailed accounts of their daily activities. This will help the therapist to determine how often clients are actually in situations conducive to serious study, what types of activities they pursue in lieu of studying, and what obligations precluded study behaviors. The therapist will also listen for statements reflecting dysfunctional beliefs underlying procrastination, such as: "I can never work mornings . . . I'm not a morning person" or "I can't start my essay until I've read all the material there is on the topic."

Problem-Solving Training is used to help clients deal with problems blocking initiation of study behavior. For example, one boy identified the following "block": "Whenever I sit down to study at home, I start worrying that my father will come home drunk again." The boy was helped to find a more appropriate place to study. He made arrangements to work at his aunt's house each evening to insure prolonged periods of uninterrupted time before returning home. He was taught a thought-stopping technique of allowing only five minutes of ruminations about father, after which he would order himself to "stop" and to begin to study. He was also referred to a support group for children of alcoholics.

Target: Poor Time-Management

Poor management of time is a frequent component of chronic school failure. The adolescent tries to do too much, and ends up accomplishing very little.

A 16-year old son of an unemployed father was preoccupied with a need to make money doing odd jobs to help support his mother and younger brothers. The mother continually accused her husband of being an inadequate provider and the boy felt it was his responsibility to remedy the situation by providing enough money to relieve the marital conflict. As a result, the boy worked until midnight on school nights cleaning office buildings. He also worked weekends. He was too exhausted to study or to concentrate in class; consequently, he was failing most of his subjects at school.

INTERVENTION

1. Time-Management Training
2. Cognitive Restructuring

Often adolescent clients are unaware of the discrepancy between the amount of time spent in what they say are "top-priority" activities and time spent in "low-priority" activities. The boy in the above example said that his education was his top priority, but was surprised to discover the discrepancy between what he verbalized and the amount of time he devoted to his studies.

It is also important to address unrealistic beliefs and dysfunctional family inter-action patterns contributing to poor time-management. In the above case, during a family session attended by the boy and his mother, the therapist challenged the boy's belief that he should be personally responsible for the family's financial recovery. The therapist also addressed the mother's failure to dispel this belief and the mother's excessive dependence on her son as a sounding board for venting her own frustrations with her husband.

Target: Poor Academic Motivation and Intent to Quit School

Clients whose insufficient application to schoolwork stems mainly from a strong aversion to academics and a desire to quit school may be helped by the therapist to gain a realistic perspective on probable short- and long-term job opportunities, as well as probable changes in social life and family relationships should they decide to quit school.

A careful assessment should also be undertaken to determine whether the strong aversion to academics stems primarily from dysfunctional behavioral patterns that can be altered, such as inadequate study skills, procrastination, and self-discipline problems, or from an habitual pattern of giving up when faced with difficult situations.

The client's age, work skills, and severity of current and past school failure record are also important factors to consider. Older adolescents with long histories of chronic school failure, little chance of earning a high-school diploma, some job experience and marketable skills, and parental support for the decision to quit school would be more appropriate candidates for early school leaving than younger, rebel-lious teenagers with no concrete plans or social supports. If clients persist in their determination to quit school, a combination of Problem Solving, Contingency-Awareness, Training and Goal-Planning interventions may be used to guide them in making a responsible decision.

INTERVENTION

1. Problem Solving
2. Contingency-Awareness Training
3. Goal Planning

Clients are encouraged to talk about their aversion to school and to give specific examples to illustrate different aspects of the problem. After components of the prob-lem are identified, the therapist uses a Problem-Solving approach to guide the client in listing the pros and cons of dropping out of school and in generating and evaluating a variety of possible alternatives to leaving school. For example, one client listed the major advantages of dropping out of school as relief from school-failure anxiety, a chance to work and assume an adult role, and the opportunity to live independently from parents. Major disadvantages reported were restricted long-term earning capacity and angry parent reactions.

The client was then helped to explore two possible alternatives. One involved dropping two classes and channeling energy into the remaining classes for the rest of the school year. Another alternative was a work-school program. Exploration of these alternatives also involved family sessions to obtain input from parents and a meeting with the principal to discuss the possibility of dropping a course. Contingency-Awareness Training was undertaken in order to provide the client with new perspectives on long-term consequences of the alternative courses of action. Goal Planning was useful in helping the client to articulate and formulate short- and long-term career goals and to determine how to implement the steps necessary for realization of these goals.

TRUANCY

Truancy in early adolescence has been found to be associated with stress related to home, school, and peers (Nielson & Gerber, 1979). Stresses in the home associated with truancy included parental divorce or separation, unemployment, serious illness, parental discord, and alcoholism. Difficulties at school reported by truants included dislike of school, limited academic abilities, and negative experiences with school personnel, such as teachers perceived to be unfriendly, authoritarian, and unresponsive to students' needs. Close association with other truant peers is another factor highly correlated with persistent truancy.

Truancy has been classified as a Conduct Disorder since it violates a major societal rule of mandatory school attendance up until the age of sixteen (DSM III-R). Truancy may be the only conduct problem manifested by a client, but it is often just one of several conduct disorders manifested by a single adolescent. Although school nonattendance after the age of 16 does not technically violate school rules, it may still be viewed as an adolescent behavior problem significantly limiting opportunities for higher education and successful career development.

Factors contributing to a youngster's failure to attend school on a consistent basis vary for each case. However, psychologists working with truant adolescents recognize several recurrent patterns, characterized by different maladaptive behaviors and cognitive themes, which may be designated as targets for therapy intervention.

One common pattern is a history of insufficient application to schoolwork, resulting in chronic failure. This is often compounded by serious deficiencies in academic skills necessary to cope successfully with demands of the current academic program. Academic success is deemed impossible by the adolescent, resulting in avoidance of the school setting that serves as a reminder of repeated failure. Clients in this category typically report that they skip classes because they are unprepared for tests or homework assignments. Therefore, they have no hope of passing the course.

A careful assessment of academic skill levels and reasons for insufficient application to schoolwork is the first step. After this, appropriate interventions for problems such as inadequate self discipline, procrastination, and inadequate study and organizational skills are applied, as discussed in the previous section. If the client is currently misplaced in a school program that is too demanding, a change of schools may be considered. Improvement in academic performance produced by these interventions should also result in improved school attendance.

Other common patterns include vulnerability to influences of truant peers, truancy as a form of rebellion against parents or school personnel, and truancy as a part of a pattern of irresponsible drifting, often associated with lax or inconsistent parental discipline. Truancy may also be associated with somatoform disorders or with anxiety disorders such as school phobia.

Depression may be a component of any of these patterns. Clients may report difficulty getting to class on certain days due to fatigue or insomnia accompanying depressive mood and thoughts. Depressive inactivity may be responsible for the client missing several consecutive days or weeks of school. Therapy interventions must be directed toward the major symptoms of the depressive disorder before school attendance would be expected to improve.

Regardless of the form it takes, a client's persistent unexcused absences from school, either alone or in the company of truant peers, may usually be conceptualized as a self-control problem in which the school-avoidance behavior is under the control of conflicting positive and negative consequences. Positive consequences often involve a sense of relief following avoidance of the oppressive or anxiety-producing school setting where one is forced to endure teacher or classmate disapproval, persistent academic failure, or intolerable boredom or frustration. Positive reinforcement for some clients stems from being approved of and accepted by fellow truant peers, along with the excitement and fun of skipping classes together. Aversive consequences of truancy tend to be delayed, such as parental disapproval when informed of the son's or daughter's attendance pattern, or school failure at the end of the year.

Target: Dysfunctional Parenting Patterns Fostering Adolescent Truancy

Overindulgent or oversubmissive parenting, characterized by inadequate parental expectations for school attendance and lax or inconsistent discipline, is commonly encountered in clinical work with families of truant adolescents. The adolescent adopts a "rudderless" life-style characterized by ill-defined goals and a tendency to drift from one thing to another. Definite parental expectations for standards of school achievement and clear rules about school attendance are lacking or have been stated in such vague terms that the adolescent feels no real need to comply with these standards or rules. This is usually accompanied by parental failure to follow through with negative consequences after learning that the son or daughter has been truant. As a result, the adolescent comes to view the parent as a person who is easily manipulated.

Often, the parents had been willing to tolerate minor acts of noncompliance when the child was young, but suddenly find themselves alarmed at their inability to control more serious adolescent noncompliance problems such as truancy. Often, too, there is a lack of sufficient parental supervision or involvement with the adolescent. One or both parents may be absent, either in a physical sense due to divorce, marital separation, or parental illness, or in being unavailable or unable to devote much time to the adolescent due to preoccupations with other matters.

> The single parent of a 14-year-old boy was so overwhelmed with her own emotional problems when her husband died that she had provided very little supervision or expectations for her son during pre-teen years. In the past, she had regularly given in to her son's demands and allowed him to stay home from school whenever he insisted that he needed to sleep in. Recently, the school informed the mother that her son had been remaining at home after she left for work and that he had missed almost two months of school. This came as a complete surprise to her and she was unable to persuade her son to start attending school again.

Some overprotective parents attempt to cope with their son's or daughter's truancy by ignoring or denying the seriousness of the problem. Often, they believe that their first duty is to be supportive. Consequently, they reluctantly give in to the adolescent over and over again in order to protect the adolescent from disappointments and uncomfortable situations. Some parents sympathize excessively with the truant adolescent, perhaps recalling their own negative school experiences. Other parents blame school personnel and others for the adolescent's truancy, thereby indirectly supporting school nonattendance. Truant adolescents use a variety of ploys to manipulate their parents into allowing them to miss school, including "guilt-trips," physical complaints, and sickness.

INTERVENTION

A variety of family interventions are available to alter dysfunctional parent-adolescent interaction patterns fostering truancy:

1. Contingency Contracting
2. Independence Training
3. Discipline-Effectiveness Training
4. Conflict-Negotiation Skills Training

5. Cognitive Restructuring of dysfunctional parental beliefs
6. Expectations-Establishment Training
7. Relationship-Enhancement Training

Parents who fail to impose definite expectations for school attendance may be helped through Expectations-Establishment Training and Discipline-Effectiveness Training to differentiate between definite rules (i.e. "You must attend school every-day") as opposed to requests ("I'd feel better if you were attending school"). Parents are taught how to define, impose, and enforce explicit expectations for school attend-ance, and these newly learned parenting skills are practiced during family sessions, assisted by the therapist. Cognitive therapy techniques during family sessions may also be used to identify dysfunctional beliefs contributing to parental reluctance to make explicit demands and to set reasonable limits. For example, one mother of a truant son stated: "It's my son's choice, I don't want to interfere with his rights." Parents who have been unable to set and enforce appropriate rules for school attend-ance often make statements reflecting beliefs that parents have no rights, that ado-lescents should be motivated to attend school regularly without any parental supervision, and that it is necessary to shield one's children from exposure to anxiety-provoking or uncomfortable school situations, even if it severely jeopardizes the ado-lescent's education.

Target: Truancy as Rebellion

Truancy may be used as a form of rebellion against parents who are perceived by the adolescent to be unfair. It may be a manifestation of either overt or secret rebellion against parents who are overly coercive, cruel, punitive, or neglecting. For example, one daughter of excessively strict parents who prohibited her from socializing with peers after school or on weekends skipped classes regularly in order to spend time with friends. Another boy was angry because he had been forced by his parents to enroll at a school which was not his choice. He would leave for school each morning, but would spend the day with truant peers at a shopping mall as a form of protest.

Sometimes truancy is used by adolescents for the purpose of manipulating parents into complying with their desires or wishes. For example, one girl told her parents that she would refuse to attend school if they failed to allow her to go out with her friends every Friday night. The parents still refused to allow her to go out, and were angry and embarrassed when contacted by the school about their daughter's truancy.

Sometimes truancy is used to protest against behavior or decisions of school per-sonnel perceived to be unfair. One student at a technical school was angry because he was denied entry into the Printing Program on the basis of his poor grades. He was put into the less popular Foods Program instead, but refused to attend any of these classes. Another student who was failing three classes was denied her request to change to a partial schedule for the remainder of the term in order to concentrate exclusively on passing her other courses. She was told she must attend all courses or face suspension from school, so she refused to attend school altogether.

INTERVENTION

1. Conflict-Negotiation Skills Training
2. Communication Skills Training
3. Contingency Contracting
4. Problem-Solving Training
5. Relationship-Enhancement Training
6. Discipline-Effectiveness Training

The above family interventions may be used to help the adolescent to resolve parent-adolescent conflicts without resorting to truancy. Contingency Contracting may also be used for school-based interventions when adolescents use truancy as a form of rebellion against school personnel. In one case, a successful contract was drawn up between a school vice-principal and the adolescent client in which the vice-principal agreed to allow the student to drop math class in return for the student's promise to attend all other classes with no absences for three straight weeks.

Target: Vulnerability to Truant Peer Influences

Adolescents with truant friends may succumb to peer pressure to skip classes even though at times this may be contrary to their own stated wishes. A history of difficulties in forming satisfying peer relationships and failure to win approval and acceptance from non-truant peers in the past adds to the youngster's vulnerability to truant-peer influences. Truancy as a group activity is thus bound up with conflicting reinforcement contingencies: immediate positive reinforcement following impulsive pleasure-seeking with friends, combined with recognition, status, and praise from truant peers for flaunting school rules, pitted against future negative consequences of possible school suspension, angry disapproving parents, or a failure report card.

A 15-year-old girl was on her own for long periods of unstructured time after school and during the evenings while her mother was working late. To fill her time, she began to hang around a neighborhood snack bar where she made new friends. She subsequently began to skip afternoon classes to spend more time with these friends. The girl had never had many friends in the past, a fact she attributed to having been a fat child. She believed that most of her classmates considered her inferior, whereas fellow truant peers seemed to accept her.

The mother was eventually informed of her daughter's truancy, She confronted the daughter and accused her of letting her down. Although the girl felt guilty for disappointing her mother, the truancy continued because she was able to deceive her mother quite easily and positive feelings stemming from peer acceptance were more powerful than the negative guilt feelings. However, after the school threatened to suspend her, she resolved to change, and tried unsuccessfully to resist peer invitations to skip classes. After skipping, she would berate herself for being weak.

INTERVENTION

1. Self-Monitoring of school attendance
2. Cognitive Self-Control Techniques
3. Contingency-Awareness Training
4. School-Based Interventions to facilitate participation in pro-social school activities
5. Assertiveness Training to resist peer pressure to skip class

The client was taught two self-control techniques: Self-Monitoring and Cognitive Self-Instruction. During the assessment phase of the Self-Monitoring intervention, the girl kept a record for one week of each occurrence of impulsive yielding to truant peer pressure. She identified two recurrent patterns: skipping the first period each day to have coffee with her truant friends and failure to return to school after lunching with truant friends at the snack bar.

Next, two stimulus-control procedures to increase first-period and afternoon attendance were devised—arranging to walk to school each morning with a former non-truant friend from grade school and eating lunch in the school lunchroom rather than at the snack bar. The next step involved the establishment of goals for change and self-evaluation guidelines. The girl committed herself to attending her first-period class every morning and to eating in the school lunchroom every Monday, Wednesday, and Friday. This was written into a joint client-therapist contract. Self-reinforcement contingencies were then established by the girl. She decided that she would use the money saved by not buying morning coffee and lunches at the snack bar to buy herself a gift after she had succeeded in achieving her goals for three weeks.

Cognitive Self-Instruction techniques were also taught to the client. The girl was asked to identify her private speech (self-verbalizations) accompanying submission to peer pressure to skip classes. Reported verbalizations included: "If I refuse to skip classes, they won't consider me a friend," "This will be fun, and class is so boring," and "I'll feel embarrassed walking into class again."

More adaptive self-verbalizations were then suggested. These included statements reflecting probable negative long-term consequences, and the mother's reaction if she were to find out: "I'll be depressed when I get my report card," "I'll be suspended from school," and "Mother will be so hurt." These were rehearsed during the session and then practiced the next day at school. The girl's motivation to persist with self-control techniques was strengthened through Contingency-Awareness Training.

Scheduling of potentially enjoyable school activities was then explored. After determining which extracurricular school activities would be of interest to the client, they contacted school personnel for help in facilitating the girl's participation. It was explained to school personnel that one way of "treating" a truancy problem is to structure pleasurable school activities into the client's day to compete with positive reinforcing contingencies of skipping classes with truant peers. These activities would also be expected to facilitate new friendships with non-truant peers.

Target: School Phobia

"School phobia" is a label used in clinical studies to describe a pattern of behavior characterized by partial or total refusal to attend school in response to intense feelings of anxiety, dread, and panic associated with the school environment (Weiner, 1970). The characteristic features of dread of the school setting, psychophysiological reaction, and rationalization have been likened to symptoms of a classical phobia: persistent unrealistic fear, coupled with a desire to avoid the phobic situation, along with increased anxiety or panic attack when approaching the phobic stimulus. The phobic component is important in distinguishing school phobia from school non-attendance problems due primarily to other psychological causes, such as depressive inactivity.

It is important to obtain information about how the phobia developed, visual fantasies evoked by the situation, connections between past or ongoing traumatic events and current fear of the phobic stimulus, and social-evaluation anxieties related to the phobic stimulus (Guidano & Liotti, 1983). Clients will have a better chance of identifying maladaptive thoughts, images, and feelings while actually exposed to the phobic stimulus since once out of the situation, they usually acknowledge that the fear is unrealistic and they may have difficulty identifying dysfunctional self-statements accompanying phobic reactions.

There is often a precipitating event that initially elicited the phobic reaction. It may be a past traumatic experience in the school setting, or simply the increased demands for independent functioning when an adolescent moves from a structured elementary-school setting to a less structured secondary-school environment.

Somatic complaints are a common feature of school phobia. These are most severe as the adolescent approaches, or anticipates approaching, the school. Conversely, they tend to subside with successful avoidance of the school setting. Different forms of social evaluation anxiety are often components of school phobia, such as fear of public speaking or a more generalized fear of judgmental or unfriendly peers or teachers. Absence of satisfactory peer relationships is sometimes a feature.

Characteristic patterns of family interaction have been identified as contributing to the maintenance of school phobia—most notably, the overprotective mother who fosters the adolescent's dependence on her. Unlike truants who dislike and do poorly in school, and who skip classes in order to engage in pleasurable activities without parental knowledge or consent, school phobics tend to remain at home with parental knowledge and partial consent, unable to get himself to school even though they claim to like school and in spite of the fact that their academic performance has been adequate in the past.

Often, the overprotective mother's own insecurity in her maternal role leads to the mother-adolescent interdependence. The father is frequently passive and fails to counteract the mother's overprotectiveness. He tends to be detached from the family and is likely to blame the wife for the adolescent's school avoidance, without getting involved himslf in handling the adolescent. Concrete parental expectations and rules, along with a consistent framework for discipline, are usually lacking. School phobics become adept at manipulating parents into allowing them to miss school; complaints of illness are often used for this purpose.

Many agoraphobic adults have an earlier history of school phobia (Guidano & Liotti, 1983). Dysfunctional cognitions of school phobics are similar to those of adult agoraphobics and tend to reflect themes of loss of control, serious threat to physical or psychological well-being, and inability to deal with perceived external danger.

Fear of losing control may take the form of loss of control of physiological functions (e.g. vomiting, fainting, or suffocation) or loss of control over one's social behavior (e.g. suddenly crying, shouting, or "going crazy" in front of others). These stem from an underlying fear of social disapproval and the imagined criticism and condemnation of bystanders. Consequently, there is avoidance of the school setting where these events are perceived as likely to occur. If school phobics are forced to enter the school setting, they usually feel they must be accompanied by a trusted family member or friend who can come to the rescue if the feared event occurs.

A girl who had suffered a diabetic reaction at school several months before became preoccupied with a recurrent image of herself lying on the floor close to death, while classmates stared at her in shock, but failed to take any action. She was convinced that classmates still discussed the event and thought she was crazy. She began to avoid school for fear of this recurring, and experienced nausea and difficulty in breathing as soon as she entered the school building. Even though she admitted that there was very little likelihood of a recurrence of the feared event with proper diet and medication, she could not bring herself to enter the school.

She reluctantly agreed to let her mother accompany her to the entrance of the school, but found this very embarrassing. The mother actually quit her job in order to be available to accompany the daughter to school. On a few occasions, the girl managed to remain in class for an hour, but would then become upset and return home by herself after the first class. She began complaining of nausea upon waking in the morning and the mother would reluctantly agree that she was not well enough to go to school that day, after which the nausea would subside. The father blamed the mother for babying the daughter, but made no attempt to change the situation.

INTERVENTION

Interventions for school phobia are aimed at two major areas: the actual avoidance behavior (refusal or reluctance to enter the school or classroom) and the maladaptive family system. After targets for change in these two areas are identified, a combination of individual, family, and school-based interventions is undertaken.

Intervention techniques to alter the avoidance behavior
1. Cognitive Self-Control for phobic reactions
2. Relaxation Training
3. Training in distraction techniques
4. Graded-Task Assignment
5. School-based interventions to facilitate Graded-Task Assignment
6. Cognitive Restructuring

The initial goal is to normalize school attendance as much as possible, even if significant others are initially utilized for the purpose of getting the adolescent back to school and then faded out at a later date. In the above case, an overall coping plan was formulated, aimed at helping the girl tolerate the school setting, which included Cognitive Self-Control techniques, Relaxation Training, training in distraction techniques, and Graded-Task Assignment.

Cognitive components of the avoidance behavior targeted for change through Cognitive Restructuring included the girl's somatic reactions, her frightening visual fantasies, her distorted beliefs about the high probability of having another diabetic reaction while at school, and her distorted beliefs about peer evaluation, namely her perception that classmates were still discussing the event daily, and that they thought she had mental problems. A detailed discussion of interventions for treatment of phobic avoidance behaviors characterizing social phobia and agoraphobia is provided in the section on anxiety disorders in Chapter Nine; therefore, treatment of the avoidance component will not be addressed further here.

School interventions may be initiated by the therapist in order to enlist the cooperation of school personnel in the therapy endeavor. For example, classroom teachers may be asked to refrain from drawing attention to sensitive clients when they first return to class, and to volunteer to provide clients with information on missed assignments. It may also be necessary to negotiate with the school for permission for partial attendance for the initial days or weeks, in keeping with the schedule devised as part of the Graded-Task Assignment. In the above case, the school's expectations for client attendance had to be flexible enough to allow the client to gradually return to a full-day school program over the period of one month.

Intervention Techniques for the Maladaptive Family System
1. Discipline-Effectiveness Training
2. Independence Training
3. Contingency Contracting

The above interventions are recommended to alter dysfunctional family patterns such as inadequate parental expectations for school attendance, inadeqate parental disciplinary skills, and mutual parent-adolescent dependency. Discipline-Effectiveness Training may serve to address the parent-adolescent control issue by helping parents to establish firm rules for school attendance, with appropriate consequences for nonattendance. Parents are helped to stand up to the adolescent's attempts to manipulate them. Formerly non-involved parents are helped to take an active role in implementation of disciplinary measures. Parent-adolescent Contingency Contracting may be undertaken to insure that privileges sought by the adolescent are made contingent on school attendance.

Cognitive Restructuring during family sessions helps parents to reconceptualize the school phobia as a family problem in which parents play a part in maintaining the youngster's ongoing school avoidance. In the above case, several of the mother's unrealistic beliefs were challenged. These included her belief that she would be neglecting her responsibilities as a supportive mother if she were to demand that her daughter attend school, the more general belief that a parent must never force a child to do anything, the exaggerated fear of catastrophic consequences if the daughter were made to tolerate the stressful school situation, the belief that a good mother must sacrifice her own career in order to be available to to help her daughter at all times, and the belief that a mother should be her daughter's "best friend."

After these dysfunctional beliefs were addressed, Independence Training was initiated, which involved stimulus fading of the mother as a protective companion for the daughter and facilitation of independent activities for the daughter. The girl began attending a youth group at the church and arranged to sleep over at a girlfriend's house for the first time.

Dysfunctional family patterns maintaining the school avoidance may also be addressed during family sessions. In the above case, these included the mother's tendency to take the daughter's side against the father in any discussion of the school avoidance problem, the father's tendency to blame the mother for "babying" the daughter while failing to take any action himself, the mother's use of her "need" to devote all her energies to her daughter as an excuse to ignore her husband's requests that she devote more time to him, and the mother's reliance on the daughter as a "best friend" to fill an otherwise empty life.

9

Adolescent Emotional Disorders: Depression and Anxiety

Cognitive-behavioral treatment of adolescent depression and anxiety disorders will be addressed in this chapter. A marked increase in the frequency of depressive conditions, bipolar affective disorders, and attempted suicide has been found to coincide with the onset of adolescence, whereas anxiety disorders show little change in frequency from childhood to adolescence (Rutter, 1986). The coexistence of anxiety and depression is well documented (Maser & Clonniger, 1989), suggesting that in some cases treatment of anxiety will result in improvement in depressive symptomology, and vice versa.

A cognitive-behavioral perspective recognizes the crucial role of perceptions and appraisals in producing emotions. The individual's cognitions and emotional responses are interrelated, so that the specific content of a person's interpretation of an event influences the person's particular emotional response to that event. Clients feel glad, sad, anxious, or angry, depending upon their interpretations of particular events. Cognitive therapy is concerned with the empirical investigation of the client's interpretations (i.e. automatic thoughts, inferences, conclusions, and assumptions), and their relationship to dysfunctional emotional and behavioral patterns. The correction of distorted inferences and assumptions is necessary in order to alter dysfunctional emotional responses.

ADOLESCENT DEPRESSION

Adolescent depression encompasses a heterogeneous group of problems not inherent in "normal" adolescent development. Research reviewed by Clarke et al. (1990) suggests that up to 20% of all teenagers have at least one episode of clinical depression by age 18. Adolescent depression has been linked to (1) poor social skills, (2) social anxiety and high levels of anxiety related to other sources

176

of stress, (3) drug and alcohol abuse, (4) insufficient involvement in "pleasant" activities, (5) suicidal ideation, (6) academic problems, (7) exposure to frequent stressful events and interpersonal problems, (8) conduct disorders, and (9) eating disorders in adolescent girls.

Research reviewed by Clarke et al. (1990) also suggests that core features of adolescent depression are similar to those of adult depressive disorders. DSM III-R criteria for a major depressive episode in adults include one or more distinct periods with dysphoric mood or pervasive loss of interest or pleasure, with at least five of the following symptoms present during the same period representing a change from previous functioning:

1. Depressed mood
2. Markedly diminished interest or pleasure in almost all activities
3. Increase or decrease in appetite or weight
4. Insomnia or hypersomnia
5. Psychomotor agitation or retardation
6. Low energy, fatigability, tiredness
7. Feelings of worthlessness or excessive or inappropriate guilt
8. Diminished ability to think or concentrate
9. Recurrent thoughts of death or suicide

Dysthymia is a similar disorder, characterized by a chronic mild depressive syndrome for at least a year in children and adolescents, with two or more of the following associated symptoms: poor appetite or overeating, insomnia or hypersomnia, low energy or fatigue, low self-esteem, poor concentration or difficulty making decisions, and feelings of hopelessness. The boundaries between Dysthymia and Major Depressive Episode are unclear, particularly in children and adolescents.

A depressive disorder is labelled "minor" when the most prominent disturbance is a prevailing mood of depression with some, but not all, of the other features of the depressive syndrome. Since major adult and adolescent depressive disorders may require pharmacotherapy interventions, this major-minor distinction is important.

The unipolar-bipolar distinction is also important, since treatment of bipolar depressions, involving one or more manic episodes of elevated or expansive mood, may require pharmacotherapy. Pharmacotherapy is also considered appropriate for psychotic depressions accompanied by hallucinations or delusions, depressions characterized by inhibition of the pleasure/reward system to such a degree that the person no longer has the capacity for enjoyment, and nonpsychotic, unipolar depressions characterized by severe somatic symptoms). A combination of pharmacological and cognitive-behavioral therapy may be appropriate for major depressive episodes, whereas minor affective disorders may be treated exclusively by cognitive-behavioral interventions.

Correlates of Adolescent Depression

Clinical studies of adolescent depression reviewed by Chartier and Ranieri (1984) failed to reveal a clear-cut syndrome of depression, suggesting that depression in adolescence accompanies a variety of other disorders. A number of behaviors and symptoms accompanying adolescent depression have sometimes been referred to in the literature as "depressive equivalents." These include: (1) "acting out" or delinquent behavior in the home or the community (e.g. aggression, antisocial acts, disobedience, temper tantrums, running away from home, compulsive drug abuse, or sexual promiscuity), (2) school problems (e.g. school phobias, failure to achieve, truancy, and suspension from school, and (3) peer relationship problems such as social withdrawal.

Other depressive equivalents frequently mentioned include hypochrondriacal reactions, pervasive boredom, restlessness, reluctance to be alone, and frantic seeking of new pleasurable activities. However, Chartier and Ranieri (1984) concluded on the basis of studies examining the relationship between these so-called depressive equivalents and diagnoses of adolescent depression, that the frequently presumed function of underlying depression as a cause of depressive equivalent symptoms cannot be sustained empirically. Adolescent depression may be observed prior to, coincident with, or subsequent to other problems, and may or may not be prominent in presenting complaints.

Crook et al. (1981) review findings supporting the frequent clinical observation that a depressed person's negative view of self develops partly in response to an unsatisfactory early parent-child relationship, characterized by parental rejection and by parental control through techniques of derision, debasement, negative evaluation, withdrawal of affection, and parental manipulation through anxiety and guilt.

In early adolescence, clients are less likely to display the classical introspective preoccupations characteristic of depressed adults. Younger adolescents are more likely to behave in ways that indirectly reflect the psychological toll of depression. They may manifest hypochondriasis, fatigue, and concentration difficulties. Their behavior patterns may reflect efforts to ward off depression or represent appeals for help (Weiner, 1970).

Efforts to ward off depression typically take the form of restlessness, or a flight to or from people. The restlessness is seen in a high activity level that seems driven rather than productive, and in a constant need for new and different kinds of stimulation, with limited tolerance for anything familiar or routine. Depressed adolescents may exhibit a constant need for companionship and a continuous search for new, more interesting friends.

Appeals for help may take the form of problem behaviors such as temper tantrums, running away, stealing, truancy, and rebellious, antisocial, or delinquent acts. These acts gain attention from others and force some recognition of the need for help, but differ in several ways from aggressive, impulsive behaviors of adolescents diagnosed as having conduct disorders: the acts are uncharacteristic of the youngster, the onset can be traced to some depressing experience, and the misbehavior is intended to be carried out in ways that guarantee being observed or caught.

Older adolescents have developed a greater capacity to think about themselves critically and to express these self-critical thoughts to others. Consequently, they are more likely to manifest traditional adult symptoms of depression. They may also manifest self-destructive behaviors such as drug abuse, sexual promiscuity, alienation, and suicide attempts. When depressed adolescents are unable to achieve a satisfying degree of excitement, companionship, or attention through more adaptive pursuits, they may turn to sex and drugs as a way of combatting their depression. Alternatively, they may withdraw from efforts to be competent and successful, and become apathetic and cynical because of depressive concerns about their adequacy.

Beck's Model of Depression

Beck (1963) compared depressed with nondepressed adults and found the cognitions of depressed patients to be characterized by particular themes, processes of reality distortion, and cognitive patterns. Characteristic themes included low self-esteem, self-blame, overwhelming responsibilities, and desire to escape. Characteristic processes involved in the distortion of reality included arbitrary inference, selective abstraction, overgeneralization, exaggeration, and inexact labelling. Beck concluded that depression results from the client's negative or inaccurate interpretation of his or her experiences. Three major themes are prominent: viewing the world as cruel and punishing, seeing oneself as worthless, and viewing one's future as hopeless. Beck's cognitive therapy approach seeks to relieve emotional distress and other symptoms of depression by focusing on the client's misinterpretations, self-defeating behaviors, and dysfunctional attitudes, and by helping clients to observe the relationship between their negative thoughts and negative feelings.

Development and maintenance of the affective depressive response is determined by characteristic ways in which depressed patients structure their experiences. Beck coined the term "cognitive triangle" to describe three major cognitive patterns of depressed adults. The depressed patient tends to view himself or herself, his or her experiences, and his or her future in a negativistic way. He or she views his or her environment as a burden, sees himself or herself as inadequate, undesirable, and responsible for his or her negative experiences, and expects no improvement in the future. He or she tends to systematically misinterpret, exaggerate, and distort his or her life experiences in keeping with his or her belief system. Behaviorally, since he or she expects the outcome of his or her activities to be negative, he or she avoids setting goals and engaging in constructive pursuits.

Chartier and Ranieri (1984) review research suggesting that Beck's perspective also applies to adolescent depression. Depressed adolescents have been found to have poor self-images, and to report feelings of worthlessness, low self-esteem, and hopelessness.

Beck's cognitive therapy approach concentrates on identifying and correcting particular cognitive distortions hypothesized to be contributing to a client's symptoms. The therapist progresses from focusing on the client's symptoms and behaviors to a focus on situation-specific thoughts, and finally to a focus on central beliefs and philosophy espoused by the client. Many of the cognitive schema recurrently found in depression reflect themes of excessive self-blame, "shoulds" and "musts," passivity, and helplessness (Shaw & Beck, 1977; Beck et al., 1979).

For moderately to severely depressed clients, Beck's advice is to focus initially on the core symptoms of depression. For clients whose depression is less severe, the initial focus may be on external problems related to the depression, such as difficulty with a personal relationship, failure to achieve a goal, or deprivation of a pleasurable activity.

The therapist seeks to identify themes reflecting the three major cognitive patterns of depression described by Beck. The therapist also notes the client's characteristic patterns of distorting current and past experiences, which may take the form of arbitrary inference, selective abstraction, overgeneralization, magnification, minimization, or personalization. The therapist also notes self-statements accompanying emotional responses such as sadness, anger, and fear, and helps clients to understand the relationship between their own emotional responses and the maladaptive cognitive patterns.

Cognitive-behavioral interventions for many of the typical family, peer, and school-related problems coexisting with, and contributing to adolescent depression have been outlined in earlier chapters. These include problems associated with dysfunctional parenting practices, poor school performance, social withdrawal, and conduct disorders.

Beck organized target symptoms of depressed adults into the following categories: cognitive symptoms, affective symptoms, motivational symptoms, behavioral symptoms, and physiological symptoms. These symptom categories are also appropriate for adolescent clients. Clinical samples of depressed adolescents are characterized by (1) cognitive features including a tendency to view oneself and one's future negatively, (2) emotional features, such as sadness and lack of gratification or pleasurable experiences, (3) motivational features, including social withdrawal and suicidal ideation and acts, and (4) behavioral and psychophysiological features, including inactivity, changes in appetite, sleep disturbances, and complaints of tiredness (Chartier & Ranieri, 1984). Prompt relief of symptoms of the depressive syndrome and prevention of recurrence are achieved by teaching clients to identify and modify their faulty thinking and dysfunctional behaviors using cognitive restructuring and behavioral interventions.

COGNITIVE TARGETS

Cognitive targets include distorted or negative statements, attitudes, and beliefs reflecting a negative view of the world, of oneself, or of the future. (Concentration, attention, or memory problems may also be reported by the client.) Basically, the therapist determines what kinds of logical errors a client is making, his or her view of himself or herself, his or her particular world, and his or her future. In this way, recurrent depressive themes are identified, and targeted for cognitive-restructuring interventions.

Target: Negative View of the World

Examples of themes reflecting a negative view of the world include a view of one's problems as overwhelming, exaggerations of one's difficulties and minimization of corrective action, perceived inability to control one's environment or one's own self-destructive behaviors, and a belief that more is expected of one than is actually the case.

> The eldest daughter of an abusive father was anxious at school due to fears that her father would harm her mother and she would not be there to protect her from the father's beatings. The girl believed that she was responsible for protecting her mother and felt guilty for being away from home during school hours. The girl said she would hold herself responsible if anything happened to her mother since it would be her fault. She was unable to concentrate at school because of intrusive images of violence and the recurrent thought that she should be at home at all times. She often failed to attend school, and avoided spending time with friends after school. She was unable to fill out application forms for college for the coming year, since acceptance might necessitate living away from home, and the mother had begged the daughter not to abandon her. At the same time, the girl was depressed by the prospect of being stuck at home indefinitely in the years to come.
>
> Examples of distorted cognitions reflecting guilt, self-criticism, helplessness, and exaggerated sense of responsibility were: "I'm responsible for what Dad does," "There's nothing I can do about the situation," "Nothing can change Dad so I have to give up college to stay at home."
>
> Interventions included: (1) cognitive restructuring of the above distorted beliefs, (2) Problem-Solving Training to generate possible courses of action for improving the home situation, such as helping her mother to get in contact with a battered women's support group, and (3) task-oriented thoughts and cognitive restructuring to combat intrusive thoughts and frightening recurrent

images of possible disaster occurring at home in her absence interfering with her ability to concentrate, at school.

INTERVENTION

1. Coping-Skills therapies for taking *action* on problems perceived by the client to be insoluable (e.g. Problem-Solving Training; Graded-Task Assignment; Self-Monitoring)
2. Cognitive Restructuring of distorted and negative cognitions (e.g. exaggeration of difficulties; perfectionistic self-expectations)
3. Assertiveness Training to challenge unrealistic expections and behaviors of significant others

The client is helped to identify the specific problems or components of the over-whelming situation and to generate possible solutions for each of these problems by using a Problem-Solving technique. Once the best solution has been determined, this solution may be broken down into tasks, from very simple to complex, and these tasks may then become homework assignments, beginning with a task that the therapist is quite sure that the client can accomplish. This is combined with cognitive restructuring of distorted exaggerations of difficulties or of perfectionistic self-expectations. Finally, Assertiveness Training may be appropriate to teach some clients to challenge unrealistic expectations placed on them by others, indirectly contributing to the overwhelming situation.

Target: Negative View of Self

The adolescent's negative self-concept may be related to themes of excessive self-blame, guilt, or shame underlying feelings of anger, or to unrealistic self-expectations reflected in statements beginning with "I must" or "I should." These themes are reflected in statements made by clients during therapy sessions. Excessive self-blame usually involves a tendency to assume total responsibility for failures and to selectively discount responsibility for success: "I don't deserve to be happy because I've been so bad," "I'm lazy and worthless like my dad who could never keep a job," "I deserve to fail. I waste so much time socializing instead of studying." Anger toward significant others frequently underlies a negative self-concept: "Dad used to beat me as a kid and damaged me so much that I always vowed I'd get even with him some day," "My mother ruined me and my life. Now she has to make it up to me," "Nothing I do is ever good enough for my family."

Guilty feelings underlying negative self-concept may stem from wishing ill on someone ("Dad is so mean to us when he's drunk, I wish he were dead"), from an unrealistic assumption of responsibility for the behavior of others ("I can't get Dad to stop drinking"), or from engaging in self-defeating behaviors such as drug abuse, overeating, or promiscuity (e.g. "I watched T.V. all evening and didn't study. I deserve to fail") and "When I'm with kids, I can't stop myself from taking drugs, and afterwards I hate myself," and "Dad's right, I *am* a slut for going out with boys").

Unrealistic "musts" and "shoulds" contributing to negative self-evaluations are frequently detected in statements of adolescent clients: "Children should love their parents but I can't help hating my father." Shame underlying negative self-concept occurs when clients believe they are being judged weak, or inferior ("I failed math again. I'm mental and stupid like Dad says. I've ruined the family name").

A 19-year-old boy whose mother had commited suicide two years before held himself responsible for her death. He believed that he should have gotten a job in order to provide his mother with some financial security so that she would not have become so desperate and killed herself. At the same time, he felt angry at his mother for abandoning him and angry at his father for being a helpless alcoholic. He had been forced to live with the mother's sister who disliked him. The boy hated this living arrangement and was infuriated by the aunt's daily complaints about having to look after him, but saw no way out. In addition, even though he was a "B" student, he considered his school performance inadequate and belittled himself after each exam for not doing better. He considered himself worthless and was unable to form successful peer relationships because he believed that schoolmates would find him undesirable.

INTERVENTION

1. Cognitive Restructuring of distorted beliefs reflecting self-blame, shame, and guilt, and techniques for increasing positive self-statements.
2. Problem-Solving Training to teach the client to take appropriate action to alter problems and situations activating chronic anger.

Cognitive restructuring interventions for adult clients manifesting excessive self-criticism, guilt, and shame outlined by Beck and his colleagues (Beck et al., 1979; Shaw & Beck, 1977) have been found to be clinically effective with adolescent clients. Three "Reattribution" techniques for problems of self-blame have been recommended by Beck and his colleagues. Basically, the facts are reviewed, the patient's double standard or other beliefs and assumptions representing manifestations of faulty thinking are identified, and the dysfunctional beliefs are then challenged.

The first technique is concerned with increasing client awareness of success experiences by having clients keep logs of activities in which they have demonstrated some degree of mastery. Reverse Role-Playing is a second technique. The therapist role-plays another person emitting the same behavior for which the client previously degraded himself or herself. If the client is more sympathetic toward another person with the same problem, the discrepancy is then pointed out between the excessively high standards the client has set for himself or herself and the lesser standards he or she sets for others. A third reattribution technique is the identification of excessive responsibility. Clients are taught to distinguish between situations which they can and cannot control. Then, the validity of the client's assumption that he or she is totally responsible for an upsetting situation is challenged.

When depression stems from guilt feelings for wishing ill on someone else, clients are helped to understand that thoughts are not actions. Clients experiencing guilt feelings for engaging in self-defeating behaviors are helped to see that guilt feelings are counterproductive since they do not prevent one from engaging in these behaviors. Instead, the client is taught coping techniques, such as Self-Monitoring, for altering the frequency of unwanted behaviors. Clients whose depression stems from shame are helped to understand that shame is self-created. They are asked to identify self-behaviors that they are ashamed of, but which others would not consider shameful. They are also asked to recall things they were ashamed of in the past for which they no longer feel ashamed. Again, they are taught techniques for decreasing the frequency of "shameful" behaviors.

Finally, clients may be taught cognitive restructuring techniques for modifying unrealistic "shoulds" and "musts" related to guilt and shame, as discussed earlier in Chapter Four.

Target: Negative View of Future

A negative view of the future is reflected in the following statements of adolescent clients:

- "I can never be successful because of my abnormal childhood."
- "Mom has given up on me. It's too late to do anything worthwhile."
- "Even if I graduate from high school, the failure would just start all over again."
- "I hate living with my father and putting up with his beatings, but I can't leave because I have nowhere to go and I can't survive without him helping me when I get down."
- "I can never leave home and make a life for myself. I must always be there to take care of mom."
- "I can never graduate now and get into college. It's too late for me."
- "Friends are progressing toward goals, I'm not."
- "I'll end up like Dad, because I have the same bad qualities: no friends, and a bad temper."
- "I'm crazy like Mom. I'll end up in an asylum."

The following is a case in which the client perceived her future to be too painful to endure:

A high-school English teacher was alarmed when she read a student's journal entry containing the following depressive and suicidal statements: "Life holds nothing for me," "I can't do anything good," "There are too many chances and decisions," "I'll always be rejected," "If I don't improve, I can't think of any other solution but dying, nobody will care." The student was referred to the school psychologist who learned that the girl perceived several of her problems to be insolvable. These included her unattractiveness and obesity, her parents' hatred for her, and her inability to make friends. Songwriting was her one source of achievement and pleasure, but she was angry at her parents for ridiculing her songs, and for refusing to support her wish to attend music school after graduation, as well as for favoring her older brother.

Therapy interventions focused on helping the girl to devise and implement solutions to her overwhelming problems. First, she was taught Self-Monitoring to control her food intake, combined with a referral to a weight-control clinic. Next, she was helped through a combination of Interpersonal-Skills Training and Conversation-Skills Training to establish a positive relationship with two classmates. She was also helped through cognitive restructuring to gain a more realistic perspective on her distorted beliefs concerning negative parent and peer evaluations of her.

INTERVENTION

1. Cognitive Restructuring
2. Problem-Solving Training
3. Family Sessions: Communication-Skills Training, Relationship-Enhancement Training, Conflict-Negotiation Skills Training

In addition to Cognitive-Restructuring and Problem-Solving interventions during individual sessions with the client, dysfunctional beliefs of family members contributing to the adolescent's negative view of the future may be addressed in family sessions.

EMOTIONAL, MOTIVATIONAL, BEHAVIORAL, AND PHYSIOLOGICAL TARGETS

Target: Overwhelming Sadness

Overwhelming feelings of sadness are usually accompanied by frequent crying spells. The following interventions have been found to be useful with adolescents:

INTERVENTION

1. Self-Monitoring of Mood (i.e. daily periods of sad feelings and crying spells)
2. Cognitive Restructuring of distorted beliefs and assumptions correlated with sadness
3. Activity Scheduling to establish distracting pleasant acitivities

The client may also be asked to keep a "mood diary" for a precise record of periods of sadness and crying spells during the day, along with accompanying self-statements and cognitions. If sadness occurs regularly at a particular time each day, the clients may be asked to use an Activity-Scheduling technique to plan pleasant diversions, such as meeting with friends or having phone conversations, for those times when they tend to feel sad. Activity Scheduling also helps the client to carry on with normal routines in spite of sad feelings. Clients are asked to behave like "robots" in order to go through the motions of normal activities, even though they may not feel like doing so. They are told that improvement in mood will follow. They may also be asked to limit crying spells and ruminations about sad feelings to particular times of the day, thereby decreasing their frequency. Cognitive restructuring of client exaggerations of the catastrophic significance of periods of sadness, combined with humor, may be used to help clients gain a more positive perspective, and to increase their tolerance for periodic feelings of sadness. At the same time, cognitive techniques are used to restructure underlying beliefs associated with self-criticism, anger, guilt, or shame contributing to the feelings of sadness.

Target: Low Rate of Positively Reinforcing Activities (Loss of Gratification)

Depressed adolescents often report that they never enjoy anything they do. Frequently, this is tied to themes of guilt or shame, which must first be addressed through Cognitive restructuring. Perfectionistic self-expectations are also common. The therapist may help the client to discover how perfectionistic expectations originated. For example, they are often associated with excessively high parental expectations for their children, which clients then adopt for themselves.

In addition to Cognitive restructuring, depressed clients often need help in identifying potentially satisfying activities which they may then schedule into their daily lives by using an Activity-Scheduling intervention. Lists of activities generally found to be satisfying to adolescents are sometimes helpful.

INTERVENTION

1. Cognitive Restucturing
2. Selecting Pleasant Activities
3. Activity Scheduling of Pleasant Activities

Target: Suicidal Ideation and Acts

Adolescents attempt suicide for a variety of reasons, including isolation, loneliness, shame, rage, guilt, loss of a loved one, and loss of self-esteem (Hatten et al., 1977). In some cases, adolescent suicide attempts represent the person's way of solving a problem, the intention being not to die but to draw attention to something the adolescent wants (e.g. a problem solved, a relationship changed, relief from isolation and discomfort, or relief from feelings of helplessness and hopelessness). However, Weiner (1970) cautions that it is a common myth that adolescent suicide attempts are only shallow, histrionic, and impulsive reactions to immediate distress, such as the breakup of a relationship or exam failure. The current disappointment may be the last straw, but it has been demonstrated that suicidal behavior is more complex in its origins, stemming from ongoing conflicts and concerns that the adolescent cannot resolve, from increasing family instability and discord, and from collapse of formerly supportive relationships outside of the family. A substantial number of adolescent suicidal attempts reflect a wish to die rather than solely manipulative attempts to bring about changes in how they are being treated by others. Sometimes adolescents call attention to their needs by means of rebelliousness or withdrawn behavior before finally resorting to suicidal acts as a drastic measure of problem-solving.

ASSESSING SUICIDAL RISK

The following risk factors for adolescent suicide have been identified in the literature (Anderson, 1982) and are helpful as assessment guidelines:

- a long-standing history of problems escalating in adolescence
- failure in coping techniques, related to loss of hope
- progressive isolation from meaningful social relationships
- a history of prior suicide attempts
- symptoms of depression
- poor impulse control
- a history of suicide attempts in the family
- a specific suicide plan

The following categories of adolescents are most vulnerable:

- loners with poor social skills and communication abilities
- "acting out" adolescents, especially drug and alcohol abusers
- adolescents unable to cope with crises or traumas
- psychotic adolescents who experience delusions and hallucinations
- boys programmed early for a particular role and pushed beyond their endurance
- intense, gifted, rigid, compulsive, overachieving adolescents
- victims of sexual abuse

A boy who had repeatedly failed Grade 10 due to poor study skills, excessive procrastination, and low academic aptitude became preoccupied with thoughts of suicide. When it became more and more clear that he would be unable to attend college, he believed that he had irreversibly ruined his chances for a successful life and became alarmed at his preoccupation with suicide. He said his concern for his mother and the suffering that his suicide would cause her had prevented him from carrying out his suicidal wishes in the past. However, the breakup of a short-term relationship with a girlfriend provided him with an immediate excuse for a suicide attempt, and he phoned his counselor late at night saying he was afraid he would harm himself.

The 18-year-old daughter of an authoritarian father was deeply depressed about the father's lack of trust in her. The father refused to allow her to date boys, resulting in intense daily family conflict, with the mother secretly taking the daughter's side. When the father discovered that his daughter had been skipping school to spend time with a boyfriend, he called her a "slut" and insisted on driving her to and from school every day. The girl eventually began to believe that she was no better than a prostitute, but still longed to see her boyfriend. Prevented by the father from doing this, she viewed her situation as hopeless. She swallowed several aspirins before showing up for her scheduled appointment with her psychiatrist.

The therapist's immediate task of determining the suicidal motive is facilitated by his or her paying close attention to client statements reflecting themes of hopelessness, helplessness, self-criticism, self-blame, shame, loss, and revenge. Interventions focus on helping the client to control the impulse for self-destruction and on teaching alternate problem-solving strategies.

INTERVENTION

1. consider hospitalization, medication, and/or informing significant others
2. Problem-Solving Training applied to problems perceived as insolvable
3. Cognitive Restructuring of irrational beliefs associated with suicidal ideation

4. Formulation of a coping plan for the client to use when experiencing self-destructive thoughts

If the client's life appears to be in immediate danger, the therapist considers interventions such as hospitalization, medication, or informing significant others of the adolescent's suicidal wishes, even though these may be perceived by the client as a breach of confidentiality and may temporarily weaken the therapeutic relationship. Hospitalization and medication should definitely be considered when the adolescent manifests a rapid deterioration of functioning or a high degree of suicidal impulsivity.

Clients who are frightened by their own potential for self-destructive behaviors may be helped to formulate an emergency coping plan. They may compile a list of phone numbers of supportive friends, therapists, or crisis intervention "hot lines." One client, who was afraid of his self-destructive wishes even though he had never carried through with suicidal acts, was accompanied by his therapist to a hospital emergency department so that he would learn the correct bus route.

Family sessions are often necessary in order to alter destructive family patterns and beliefs fostering the adolescent's suicidal preoccupations. Additional issues for families of suicidal adolescents include parental inability to assess suicidal risk, parental denial of suicidal risk, and parental dismissal of the son's or daughter's suicidal acts as being merely manipulative.

Cognitive-restructuring interventions during individual sessions may be used to challenge beliefs reflecting a negative self-concept, as well as perceptions of life as overwhelming and the future as hopeless. Following this, the client may be taught problem-solving skills for resolving seemingly overwhelming problems leading to feelings of despair. Another useful technique is to ask the adolescent to list pros and cons of going through with suicidal plans. This forces the client to consider consequences that may serve as deterrents, such as the devastating effects that the suicidal act might have on friends and loved ones.

Target: Inactivity

Inactivity is usually accompanied by loss of gratification when attempting to engage in formerly pleasurable activities and by long hours of depressive ruminations. The client experiences difficulty performing simple activities of daily living, increased dependency on significant others, and withdrawal from peer interactions.

Teachers were concerned about an apathetic 17-year-old boy who sat passively in the classroom, not bothering to follow the lesson or to interact with other students. He was absent from school several days each month, always with a written excuse from his mother citing minor illnesses. When the boy was interviewed by the school social worker, he was lethargic and gave "yes-no" answers to questions in a flat, expressionless voice. He said that he no longer enjoyed activities with friends that he had previously considered fun, and in recent months he had been avoiding friends and school, spending long hours watching T.V. and sleeping, unable to get out of bed until noon. He said that school bored him, and that he had no hope of passing. He said he had always had problems disciplining himself to do schoolwork, and that after entering secondary school he was no longer able to scrape by and had failed almost everything for the past two years. He said that his father called him lazy and "no-good," and that this was true. He said his mother always defended him against the father, and did everything for him. For the last few weeks he had been unable to dress himself and to get to school without his mother's assistance. He had lost 10 pounds due to poor appetite. He said that friends wouldn't want to bother with someone so helpless and disgusting, and that he didn't deserve to have fun.

INTERVENTION

1. Activity Scheduling to combat inertia by establising a routine of normal school and peer activities, and to increase performance of simple activities of daily living
2. Pleasant-Activity Scheduling, to increase frequency of pursuits likely to lead to feelings of pleasure and mastery
3. Cognitive Restructuing of depressive and distorted beliefs reflecting themes of hopelessness, helplessness, and self-condemnation
4. Family therapy to alter family members' dysfunctional cognitions and interaction patterns contributing to the client's inactivitiy
5. Self-Monitoring Skill Training to decrease excessive sleeping and to increase school attendance
6. Goal-Establishment Training to increase motivation for regular school attendance, peer activities, and recreational activities
7. Possible pharmacotherapy

Target: Physiological Symptoms of Depression

Increased or decreased sleep or appetite are manifested by some depressed adolescents, as illustrated in the following example. When poor appetite stems from depression, adolescents complain that they have no appetite and don't feel like eating (in contrast to perfectionistic preoccupations with body image characteristic of anorexic clients).

A girl was angry with her parents because they disapproved of her boyfriend and tried to prevent her from seeing him. Angry ruminations had prevented her from getting adequate sleep at night for the past two months. She complained of being unable to fall asleep until four a.m., and on two occasions she had been unable to fall asleep at all. She developed a pattern of sleeping in the morning to make up for nighttime insomnia and began missing school. This led to academic difficulties, which compounded the depression. She also complained of nausea when she attempted to eat, and she had developed a pattern of skipping breakfast and lunch and eating only a light supper each evening.

INTERVENTION

1. Self-Monitoring of eating or sleeping patterns
2. Activity Scheduling
3. Relaxation Training

Clients may be taught to use Self-Monitoring techniques to increase daily food intake. The rationale presented to the client is that "feeling" like eating is not an essential condition for healthy, daily food intake, and that normalization of body functions through Self-Monitoring is an initial step toward overcoming depression. Depressed clients who *overeat* may also be helped by a combination of Self-Monitoring and Activity Scheduling of distracting activities for times when there is a tendency to binge. Referral to a weight-control program or clinic may also be appropriate.

Clients who sleep too much or clients who have attempted to cope with insomnia by sleeping during daytime school hours may be helped through Self-Monitoring to reestablish normal nocturnal sleep patterns. Clients are instructed to get up and go to bed at the same time each day, seven days a week, until normalization of sleep patterns is achieved. They are helped through an Activity-Scheduling intervention to plan morning activities for weekends and holidays, in addition to weekday class attendance.

For clients who have been sleeping much of the day for some time, it may be necessary to devise a schedule that requires them to wake at earlier and earlier hours each day until a more normal pattern is established. Clients are instructed to get up and carry on with scheduled activities regardless of the number of hours they have slept. They are also instructed to avoid taking long naps and to rely instead on 15-minute "catnaps" until more normal sleep patterns return. In addition, Relaxation Training provides the client with exercises that may be used when he or she is experiencing difficulty falling asleep.

These interventions were used successfully with the girl in the above case. In addition, family therapy sessions were initiated to help resolve the parent-adolescent conflict stemming from the issue of the girl's relationship with the boyfriend.

ADOLESCENT ANXIETY DISORDERS

A pervasive sense of vulnerability is the core symptom in anxiety disorders. The person believes that something bad is going to happen that he or she will be unable to handle. This vulnerability often manifests itself in a tendency to devalue one's own problem-solving ability and to exaggerate the degree of threat in certain problematic situations. These situations usually have to do with perceived threats to a person's social bonding, sense of individuality, freedom, and identity. Dysfunctional avoidance behaviors, such as staying at home for days, may be viewed as strategies used for self-protection. A combination of behavioral, cognitive, and physiological symptoms is typical. (Beck & Emery, 1985). A thorough medical examination is recommended as part of the diagnostic process, since there is always the possibility that a purely physical condition is producing symptoms similar or identical to those involved in adolescent anxiety disorders.

Overanxious disorder of adolescence is characterized by excessive unrealistic worry about future events such as examinations, the possibility of injury, inclusion in peer-group activities, worries about meeting expectations or performing chores, or concerns about past behavior (DSM III-R). Preoccupations usually focus on more general forms of judgment, such as peer, social, or athletic acceptance, as well as on school grades. The disorder may persist into adulthood as an anxiety disorder, such as Generalized Anxiety Disorder or Social Phobia. The DSM III-R classification of adult anxiety disorders is applicable to adolescent clients since the essential features are the same (American Psychiatric Association, 1987).

Anxiety disorders most commonly encountered with adolescent clients to be addressed in this chapter include: phobias, such as social phobia and agoraphobia, and generalized anxiety disorder. (Obsessive-compulsive disorders, characterized by recurrent persistent ideas, thoughts, or images, or by ritualistic behaviors significantly interfering with normal daily functioning, are less common and will not be addressed here.) Panic attacks are often a feature of anxiety disorders. These are characterized by sudden intense apprehension, fear, or terror, accompanied by physiological symptoms.

Fears and phobias change in nature from childhood to adolescence, with a marked increase in agoraphobia and social phobias (Marks & Gelder, 1966). These often affect school attendance and compromise school performance. Social anxiety, and high levels of anxiety related to other sources of stress have been linked in the literature to adolescent depression (Clarke et al., 1990). Treatment of adolescent anxiety disorders described in the remainder of this chapter relies heavily on the work of Beck and Emery (1985). The interventions outlined have been simplified for use with adolescent clients.

PHOBIAS

A phobia is a persistent, excessive, unrealistic fear of an object or situation. This fear is also perceived by the client as unrealistic. Components of the problem usually include a desire to avoid the situation, increased anxiety, and desire to escape when approaching the phobic situation. Acute anxiety attacks may be manifested in rapid breathing, palpitations, abdominal pains, and difficulty concentrating (Beck, 1976).

Cognitive phenomena commonly reported by phobic clients include (1) a visual fantasy (e.g. of a disaster) evoked by the stimulus situation, (2) a visual image of onself as the victim of the event, (3) a tendency to hold simultaneous contradictory beliefs about the situation being both harmless and harmful (i.e. harmless when away from the phobic situation, with increasing expectations of harm as the client gets nearer to the situation), and (4) somatic imaging (having an experience simulating the feared situation). A phobic reaction may be conceptualized as stemming from fears, not of the situation itself, but of the expectation of the consequences of being in that situation. In terms of past history, careful questioning often reveals an understandable connection between a previous traumatic experience and current fear of being in the phobic situation (Beck & Emery, 1985). Social phobia and agoraphobia are examples of phobic disorders of adolescence.

SOCIAL PHOBIA

Social Phobia is characterized by the client's persistent fear of situations in which he or she is exposed to possible scrutinization by others, along with fear of doing something that will be humiliating or embarrassing. Examples include fears of being unable to perform public-speaking tasks, of trembling in public, of saying foolish things, or of being unable to answer questions in social situations. Exposure to the phobic stimulus provokes an anxiety reaction such as panic feelings, tachycardia, or shortness of breath. This is followed by avoidant behavior, which may interfere with school attendance or with usual social activities or relationships.

A 15-year-old girl was referred for psychological counseling after missing several weeks of school in all classes except history, which she continued to attend once or twice a week because she had a friend in that class. The onset of this student's school avoidance problem occurred a few weeks after the accidental death of the girl's aunt the previous year, which was reported in the newspaper. Classmates and teachers became aware that the niece of the accident victim was in their school and whispered about it for several days. The girl, who had always been shy, was very upset about suddenly becoming the center of attention. She began to feel extremely uncomfortable in the school setting and began avoiding school.

Even though one year had passed, and the event was no longer a topic of conversation, the girl continued to mistakenly imagine that others were talking about her. When she entered the classroom, she would experience physical symptoms of anxiety including racing heart and shortness of breath. When classmates attempted to initiate conversations with her, she would tremble and become speechless because she imagined that they were judging and criticizing her. One day she walked out of the classroom when her anxiety became intolerable. Afterwards, she was bothered by a recurrent image of herself becoming so uncomfortable in the classroom full of "hostile" peers that she would suddenly get up and flee from the room, leaving classmates with the impression that she was crazy. When classmates failed to talk to her, she interpreted this as evidence that they despised her for being such a "baby," afraid to come to school. She began to use illness as an excuse in order to justify staying at home.

AGORAPHOBIA

Agoraphobia is a multiple phobia. Clients may report fears of leaving their homes, of being on public transportation, or crowded places, or even of being alone in the house. Acute panic attacks and somatic complaints may occur in several situations. These clients are characterized by dysfunctional beliefs about the need to be in control, and a fear-motivated dependence on others for protection (Guidano & Liotti, 1983).

Agoraphobic clients fear being in places or situations from which escape might be difficult or embarrassing, and situations in which a panic attack might occur when help may not be available. The client either restricts travel or needs a companion when exposed to the phobic stimulus. During adolescence, this often results in prolonged absence from school. The person may be afraid of developing symptoms such as dizziness, depersonalization, loss of bladder or bowel control, vomiting, or cardiac distress. These symptoms may have occurred in the past so that the client becomes preoccupied with fears of recurrence or may fear symptoms that have never occurred in the past.

An 11th-grade boy who had been an excellent student with good attendance began missing school regularly after transferring to a new secondary school.

The new school was far from his home, requiring him to take the subway. The boy was frightened of being trapped in the confined space of the subway, suffocating, and "going crazy." He experienced palpitations, difficulty breathing, and a choking sensation when he appoached the subway station. At times, the boy would reluctantly agree to attend school if his older sister accompanied him on the subway, although he found this embarrassing. He began staying home from school for several days at a time, eventually becoming more and more reluctant to take buses, go out on his own, or meet friends outside of the home.

Eventually, he even began to experience shortness of breath every time he left the house alone. At one point, he decided to quit school for the remainder of the year. During sessions with the psychologist, the boy berated himself for his foolishness and acknowledged that his fears of suffocation were unrealistic.

A cognitive-behavioral approach to phobic reactions and other anxiety disorders involves assessment and modification of behavioral, cognitive, and physiological symptoms accompanying anxiety reactions. The major behavioral target is avoidance of the phobic stimulus or situation.

Target: Avoidance Behavior

Information about aspects of the phobic stimuli and the avoidance pattern is first collected. In the above example of the "social-phobic" girl, the phobic stimuli were a combination of scrutinizing glances of classmates, perceived negative evaluation by classmates, the classroom setting itself, and classmates' attempts to initiate conversations with her. For the agoraphobic client, phobic stimuli consisted of the subway station, subway trains, and to a lesser extent buses and most places outside of the home, if unaccompanied.

INTERVENTION

1. Prepare Coping-Techniques Package
2. Cognitive Self-Control for Phobic Reactions
3. Relaxation Training
4. Distraction Techniques
5. Graded-Task Assignment

Anxious adolescents, in general, and phobic adolescent clients, in particular, benefit from having a "package" of newly learned and rehearsed coping techniques at hand to use when faced with the phobic stimulus. Cognitive Self-Control techniques and Distraction Techniques are two types of anxiety-reducing coping skills that are frequently part of a phobic client's coping package. Adolescent clients may be asked to compile an actual folder consisting of notes on coping techniques that they have learned during therapy sessions and outlines of the actual steps involved in these coping techniques.

The social phobic client was taught Cognitive Self-Control, Relaxation, and Distraction Techniques to help her to get herself into the classroom each day and to remain there for the duration of the class. She was taught to use Task-Orientation Thoughts to increase her tolerance for classmates' stares and probing questions. A combination of Interpersonal Coping-Skills Training and Conversation-Skills Training was also used to help the girl learn and rehearse what she would do and say when scrutinized or addressed by classmates. For example, the girl was taught verbal and nonverbal responses to help her to maintain, tolerate, and end social interactions. She was taught to use simple, nonverbal "yes-no" responses when she became tongue-tied and to terminate conversations with such phrases as, "I must go now and read over my notes."

Interpersonal Coping-Skills Training was applied to specific examples of recent stressful interpersonal interactions. The girl described each interaction in detail, after which she was helped during the session to learn and rehearse new techniques for handling each situation, which she later tried out in vivo. Finally, she was taught Distraction Techniques to be used in the classroom to help her tolerate the anxiety; these included counting desks or other objects, or taking copious notes during teachers' lectures.

After a coping package is compiled and techniques rehearsed, the client is ready for the Graded Task-Assignment intervention. The following hierarchy of tasks from the simplest to the most difficult was constructed as part of the Graded Task-Assignment intervention to help the social-phobic client to attend her current class regularly and to begin attending a second class.

TASKS (FROM EASIEST TO HARDEST)

1. Attend History class three days per week; sit next to the friend. Use Cognitive Control, Relaxation, and Distraction Techniques to help tolerate "scrutinization" by classmates.
2. Attend history class five days per week; sit apart from friend; use above techniques.
3. Attend English class three days a week in addition to History class. Use Cognitive Control and Distraction Techniques to facilitate entering and remaining in the new classroom.
4. Initiate a brief conversation with a classmate in History class, using newly learned conversation skills (e.g. ask for information about forthcoming assignments).

A coping package was also devised for the agoraphobic client, which again included Cognitive Self-Control, relaxation, and Distraction Techniques. While in a relaxed state during the therapy session, the boy pictured himself traveling on the subway, while he distracted himself from anxiety-provoking thoughts by counting the number of people in the subway train and reading all the signs and advertisements thoroughly. He then pictured himself calmly getting up and leaving the train after riding the designated number of stops. Then the client constructed the following hierarchy:

Tasks (From Easiest to Hardest)

1. Enter subway station and stay there five minutes before going out again.
2. Enter subway train accompanied by sister and ride one stop together before sister gets off. Continue one stop on subway unaccompanied after sister gets off. Then get off the train and walk home.
3. Same as #2, but go two stops unaccompanied before getting off.
4. Enter subway station alone, get on train, go one stop, then get off and walk home.
5. Same as #4, but go two stops.

Phobic clients pose a real challenge to the therpist in that they tend to come up with numerous excuses to justify their noncompliance with the assigned homework tasks on the hierarchy, even though these were mutually generated and agreed on by client and therapist. Beck and Emery (1985) provide excellent suggestions for motivating clients to carry out the hierarchy tasks: (1) It is demonstrated to the client that avoidance behavior strengthens anxiety and accompanying unrealistic fearful thoughts, and that confronting the situation (i.e. doing the task) decreases the anxiety. This is done by having the client recall and compare past situations in which he avoided threat, as opposed to situations in which he confronted it, and then to review the consequences of each in terms of reduction of anxiety level; (2) The client is encouraged to stay in the phobic situation and put up with the anxiety until it subsides. He is instructed that if he weakens and leaves the situation, he is to immediately carry out a lower, less threatening step on the hierarchy, rather than avoid the situation altogether; (3) The importance of completing the hierarchy tasks is stressed by emphasizing that those who do the "homework" assignments eventually overcome the problem, whereas others fail to get better; and (4) Obstacles to successful completion of hierarchy tasks are assessed by asking the client to identify the reasons for failure to complete tasks (e.g. "I was too tired," "I was too busy," "I didn't feel like it"). These are probably some of the same factors that maintain the avoidance behavior.

Target: Dysfunctional Cognitions and Imagery Maintaining Avoidance

One common theme for phobic clients, as well as for anxious clients in general, is an unrealistic recurrent thought that something awful is going to happen. The thought is often accompanied by a disturbing image. For example, the social-phobic girl feared that she would break down and run from the classroom while being scrutinized, thus making a fool of herself, even though she had left the classroom in a quiet manner on only one occasion in the past year in spite of her extreme discomfort. The agoraphobic boy feared that he would go "crazy," start shouting and yelling, and be unable to catch his breath, although this had never happened in the past.

INTERVENTION

1. Cognitive Restructuring
2. Image-Modification Techniques

Beck and Emery (1985) recommend three cognitive-restructuring strategies to be used in helping clients to restructure typical distorted "phobic" beliefs, such as the unrealistic belief that something awful is going to happen that one will be unable to handle or the belief in the need for the presence of another person for protection in the presence of the phobic stimulus. In addition to the "What's-the-Evidence" technique and the "Alternative" technique discussed earlier, a third technique is specifically designed for anxiety problems: the "So-What-If-It-Does-Happen" technique. During the therapy session, clients are asked to picture the worst scenario and to describe it in detail. They are then helped to devise and practice coping strategies to be applied if the feared event were to actually occur.

Using the "What's-the-Evidence" and the "Alternative" techniques, the anxious client may be helped to examine and restructure his or her unrealistic beliefs that the highly unlikely, greatly feared catastrophic event will actually occur. The therapist may challenge distortions in the probability of the event actually occurring, the degree of catastrophe if it does occur, and the client's reasons for believing that he or she will be unable to prevent it from happening or be unable to handle it if it does occur.

The therapist may also use the "What's the Evidence" technique to demonstrate to the client that the self-protection device of being accompanied by another person when exposed to the phobic stimulus actually leads to more anxiety in the long run because it increases the fear of being alone. Clients are helped to recall situations in the past in which they successfully acted independently. Clients are also helped to discover for themselves that the antidote to anxiety and avoidance is taking action by going into the phobic situation alone, and experimenting with newly learned skills from the "Coping-Techniques Package."

INTERVENTIONS FOR MODIFYING UPSETTING IMAGERY

Beck and Emery (1985) also recommend techniques for modifying anxiety-provoking images. The client is asked to picture the situation in detail and to describe it, including descriptions of sounds, colors, and emotional activity. From this description, the therapist is able to identify related cognitive distortions, such as expectations for failure or possible death, which may later be corrected through cognitive-restructuring techniques. Next, the client is asked to modify the induced image by repeatedly picturing the threatening image and altering it to make it less catastrophic—for example, by picturing a more pleasant ending to the situation. Through repetition and alterations, the client is help to lessen the impact by "decatastrophizing" the image and changing negative images into more positive ones.

In the case of the phobic client, the girl was asked to picture the image of herself being scrutinized or questioned about her absences by peers in the classroom setting and to picture herself getting more and more upset, speechless, and panicky, ready to run from the classroom. She was then asked to picture herself resolving the problem by successfully using the coping techniques from her Coping-Techniques Package in order to remain in the classroom until the end of the class. She was asked to picture herself tolerating the anxious feelings, thereby gaining some control over them.

By imagining this over and over again, the girl was able to lessen the negative impact of the image. An escape route was planned, but only as a last resort. This consisted of the girl getting up and walking quietly out of the classroom, and subsequently leaving a note in the teacher's box explaining that she had had to leave the classroom in order to keep a dental appointment. Just the knowledge that "escape" was possible reduced the girl's fears to a significant degree.

Target: Physiological Symptoms

Physiological symptoms accompanying anxiety and phobic reactions include shortness of breath, dizziness, palpitations, sweating, choking, nausea, and chest pain, often accompanied by fears of dying, going crazy, or doing something uncontrolled.

INTERVENTION

1. Relaxation Training
2. Cognitive Self-Control Techniques for toleration of physical discomfort

Physical symptoms accompanying anxiety may be treated with a combination of Relaxation Training and Cognitive Self-Control Techniques. Relaxation exercises my be used in both a longer form (with relaxation tape), and also in a shortened form. The latter may consist of just imagining a relaxing scene while combining this with deep breathing.

GENERALIZED ANXIETY DISORDER

Generalized Anxiety Disorder (GAD) is characterized by unrealistic, excessive, apprehensive expectations related to two or more life circumstances. Anxiety is often accompanied by signs of motor tension, autonomic hyperactivity, vigilance, and scanning, but without specific symptoms of phobic, panic, or obsessive compulsive disorders. Generalized Anxiety Disorders lack the central feature of panic attacks, which is the misreading of internal physiological sensations as indicating a serious threat to life. Clients may report sleep difficulties, concentration difficulties, or that the mind suddenly "goes blank." Adolescent clients suffering from Generalized Anxiety Disorder may report worries about academic performance, social performance, fears about dying, or various other worries.

Generalized Anxiety Disorder may also be accompanied by mild depressive symptoms, but it is distinguished from clinical depression by the person's more optimistic view of the future, and more pleasant recollection of past experiences. Anxious clients tend to criticize themselves for specific deficiencies, as compared to depressed clients' more global self-blame. Maladaptive cognitions of clients with Generalized Anxiety Disorder often reflect issues of acceptance, competence, and control. Vague fears alluded to by clients can often be better understood if viewed from the standpoint of assumptions reflecting these three issues, which are usually framed in all-or-none terms (Beck & Emery, 1985).

A boy was referred to a psychologist by his high-school counselor because of persistent debilitating apprehension related to several aspects of his life. At school he suffered from severe test anxiety and fears that he would fail courses, even though he had a maintained a consistent C+ average. He would experience insomnia before a test. He frequently missed tests because of stomach pains, although he always managed to pass the make-up test.

School-related insecurities dated back to kindergarten, when he would cry and cling to his mother when she attempted to leave him in the classroom and go home. Fearfulness at school persisted throughout elementary-school years and he was absent a great deal. Another residual fear lasting until the present day was a fear of the dark when going to bed at night, so that he still slept with the light on. In addition, the boy felt apprehensive when he was farther than walking distance from his home. This occurred at school, at movies, or at a friend's house. He felt uncomfortable around peers at most times, fearing that they would find out that he was afraid of the dark, that his parents were divorced, or that he had other characteristics they would consider undesirable. He also stated that practically every day he would wake up with the thought that he would be involved in a car accident and die that day.

Intervention strategies for Generalized Anxiety Disorder are similar to those discussed above for phobic reactions. They are applied to anxiety-related cognitions, avoidance behaviors, and physiological symptoms. Interventions for cognitive symptoms include Cognitive-Restructuring and Cognitive-Control techniques. Interventions for behavioral avoidance consist of teaching the client a variety of coping strategies for a Coping-Techniques Package. Interventions for physiological symptoms include Relaxation Training and teaching the client strategies for increasing tolerance for uncomfortable physiological symptoms while continuing with normal routines.

Target: Cognitive Symptoms and Interventions for GAD

Beck and Emery's (1985) approach to identifying and altering core cognitive distortions is helpful. The therapist seeks to identify the person's major preoccupations, his or her "habitualized, fixed, and largely automatic ways of thinking, acting, feeling, and responding to the world." Several methods are suggested for identifying the client's deeper anxiety-provoking assumptions. The therapist might formulate hypotheses about core cognitions on the basis of the client's automatic thoughts, behavior, coping strategy, and personal history, and then ask the client whether or not these hypotheses fit.

Another method of eliciting more information is to ask clients to recall, picture, and describe their earliest memories of distressing experiences that are similar to current anxiety-provoking experiences. Clients are asked to describe feelings and sensations that accompanied the earlier experiences and to compare them with current unpleasant experiences.

Finally, clients are asked to try to remember underlying beliefs they were working from at that time. This helps clients to discover how they may have developed a life-style based on their major preoccupations, which encompass past memories, present fears, and underlying beliefs.

Cognitive therapy interventions help clients to see how they may have learned dysfunctional assumptions at stages in their lives when they lacked the maturity to see things clearly and realistically and when immature thought processes were operating. These immature thought processes and the content of the beliefs or assumptions may now be analyzed from a more mature point of view. For example, it was learned that the boy described above had been fearful of staying at kindergarten because he feared that nobody would come to pick him up and he would be unable to get home. Once this was identified, the client realized how unrealistic this residual fear was at the present time, since he travelled to and from school alone on the bus each day.

Components of school-related anxiety for this client also included test anxiety and fear of school failure. The underlying "catastrophic" feared event was that he would "draw a blank" after being handed an exam and that he would not be able to answer a single question on the test paper. Other underlying fears were that failure on the next test would would preclude his being accepted at university in three years time and that classmates would learn that he had failed the test, which would be unbearably humiliating.

It was learned that when the boy attempted to study for exams, he would become overwhelmed with palpitations and other physiological manifestations of anxiety, which he found intolerable. The "paralysis" that followed was related to an inability to decide what material to study first and to a belief that he must learn everything thoroughly without skipping one sentence. These patterns reflected "control" themes, typical of anxious clients. The "Alternative Technique" was used to challenge the boy's belief that he must be in control by thoroughly learning everything that may possibly be asked on the test. Instead, the boy was helped to tolerate the idea of covering only 80 percent of the material, given time constraints.

At the same time, he was helped through Study-Skills Training to learn to study more efficiently. Test-taking strategies and test-preparation skills were practiced during the session. Fact-finding "homework" assignments were also suggested, such as speaking to the teacher to ask for guidance as to what to study for the exam.

In order to address the boy's indecisiveness, it was proposed that he spend no more than 10 minutes at the beginning of a study session revising his list of topics that he thought may be covered on the test and underlining the three most important topics. After this, the boy was to begin work on the first topic. He was instructed to use a "Just-Do-It" technique. He was told that when he started to ruminate about where to start, he was to go directly to the first topic on his list, and "Just-Do-It." He was also asked to spend no more than 30 minutes on each topic in order to decrease his "perfectionistic" but inefficient tendency to learn everything there was to know about a topic. These strategies were labelled "Action" techniques and were part of his Coping-Techniques Package.

Task-Oriented Thoughts, and other Cognitive Self-Control techniques for anxiety-provoking self-statements during study sessions and during test-taking situations were also part of the package. These were designed to help the client to gain some control over the anxiety and to tolerate it and carry on rather than insist that he wouldn't be able to study until the anxiety went away. Cognitive-Restructuring Techniques were used to alter the boy's anxiety-producing self-statements reflecting the belief that he would certainly fail (unrealistic "catastrophizing") and that one failure would mean that he would have lost his chance to go to university (unrealistic generalization).

Components of the peer-related anxiety for this client included evaluation anxiety, centering around concerns that peers would find out about his childish fear of the dark or that peers would ask him embarrassing questions about his parents' divorce. Cognitive restructuring was used to help the client to approach these fears from a more realistic point of view. He was asked to estimate the probability of either of these events happening and was helped to formulate a stock answer to terminate the conversation if the event did occur. Humor was used to help him gain a more realistic view of the degree of "catastrophe," should these events occur. Finally, he was asked to research and then to estimate the probability, based on current statistics, of his being involved in a car accident and dying. Afterwards, he was able to grasp the unlikelihood of this event happening and to use the statistics as part of a Cognitive Self-Control coping technique.

APPENDICES

APPENDIX A
INITIAL PRESENTING PROBLEMS INTERVIEW

(Use with adolescent client, parents, or other referring sources.)

Part A. Problem Definition

Directions:
Encourage the person to talk freely about the problems and complaints, by asking, "What do you see as the major problem?" while simultaneously guiding the interview as outlined below:

1. Request examples to illustrate each of the problems and concerns.
2. Elicit information regarding frequency, intensity, and duration of each problem.
3. Elicit and record the person's cognitions associated with each problem (e.g. beliefs, attitudes, causal attributions, etc.). Ask: "What causes the problem?" "Why does the problem behavior occur?" "What goes through your head when the problem occurs?"

Description of Presenting Problems	Frequency, Intensity, Duration	Related Cognitions

Part B. Reinforcement Contingencies of Identified Problems

Directions:

1) List identified target behaviors in column 1.
2) Elicit information about the typical responses of Significant Others when the problem behavior occurs. Ask: "When the problem occurs, how do others react?" (e.g. mother, father, classmates, etc.). Inquire about other consequences and events, and about the client's own reaction. Ask: "What else happens?" "How do you feel afterwards?"

3) Elicit information about antecedents. Ask: "What situations or events precede the problem behavior?"

Target Behaviors	*Antecedents*	*Consequences*

APPENDIX B
THE FAMILY-PEER-SCHOOL BEHAVIOR INTERVIEW

ADOLESCENT CLIENT FORM

Part A. *Influence of Significant Others*

Directions:
The following questions should be asked with respect to each Significant Other:

1. "Describe your mother" (father, sister(s), brother(s), best friend, etc.). (Elicit descriptions of personality factors, rather than physical descriptions. Record client's responses in column 1.)
2. "How would this person (e.g. mother, sib, etc.) describe you?" (If the person says that he doesn't know, encourage him to hypothesize about what the person's description of him might be. Record client's responses in column 2.)

	Description of Significant Other	*Significant Other's Description of Client*
MOTHER		
FATHER		
SIBLINGS		
BEST FRIEND		
CLASSMATES		
TEACHERS		

What teenager do you admire most? describe the person.

What adult(s) do you admire most? describe the person.

209

Part B. Adolescent's Characteristic Stress Interaction Patterns with Significant Others

I. ADOLESCENT'S INTERACTIONS WITH SIGNIFICANT OTHERS

Directions:
The following question should be asked with respect to each Significant Other: "How do you typically deal with upsetting situations involving mother (father, teachers, etc.)?"

Think of a typical upsetting situation involving your mother.
- a. "Describe the upsetting situation." (Record answer in column 1.)
- b. "What was your response? Was that typical? If not, what would be your typical response in that situation?" (Record answer in column 2.)
- c. "What were the consequences following your response?" (Record answer under "Consequences" in column 3.)
- d. "What thoughts were going through your head at the time?" (Record answer in column 4.)

	Describe Situation	Adolescent's Response	Consequences	Adolescent's Cognitions
MOTHER				
FATHER				
SIBLINGS				
BEST FRIEND				
CLASSMATES				
TEACHERS				

II. PARENTAL DISCIPLINARY STYLES

Directions:
Collect information about the parent's disciplinary style. Ask: "If you do something that your mother (father) disapproves of, what is her typical response?"
- a. "Describe a recent typical situation when your parent was disapproving of you."
- b. "What was your response to your parent's disapproval?"
- c. "What were the consequences?"
- d. "What thoughts were going through your head at the time?"

	Describe Situation	Adolescent's Response	Consequences	Adolescent's Cognitions
MOTHER				
FATHER				

Part C. Typical Activities of Daily Living

Directions:
Say to the client: "Describe a typical weekday from the time you get up in the morning until the time you go to bed at night. For example, describe everything that happened yesterday in detail (if yesterday was a 'typical' day). Next, describe a typical weekend day. For example, describe last Saturday or Sunday, if they were 'typical' weekend days."

	Typical Weekday	*Typical Weekend Day*
MORNING		
AFTERNOON		
EVENING		

What activities or aspects of your life do you enjoy most? What are you most successful at?

What activities or aspects of your life do you enjoy least? What are you least successful at?

Part D. Pre-Adolescent Behavior

I. STRESSFUL SITUATIONS AND COPING STYLES

Directions:
Ask the client: "What were the events or ongoing situations that were most upsetting and stressful for you during previous years, either at home, with other kids, or at school? What was the cause of each? What was your way of coping with these situations?"

	Description of Situation	*Perceived Cause*	*Coping Strategies*
ELEMENTARY SCHOOL YEARS			
JUNIOR HIGH SCHOOL YEARS			

II. CLIENT'S PERCEPTION OF SIGNIFICANT OTHERS' DESCRIPTION (EVALUATION) OF HIM DURING ELEMENTARY AND JUNIOR HIGH SCHOOL YEARS

Directions:
Ask the client: "During your elementary and junior high school years, how do you think you would have been described by (1) your parents, (2) other children, and (3) teachers?"

	Elementary Years	*Junior High Years*
S.O.'S DESCRIPTION		
PARENTS' DESCRIPTION		
PEERS' DESCRIPTION		
TEACHERS' DESCRIPTION		

Part E. Client's Perception of School Behavior

I. SELF-RATINGS OF ACADEMIC PERFORMANCE, ATTENDANCE, AND INTERPERSONAL RELATIONSHIPS

1. How are things at school? Describe your life at school.
2. Generally, how are you doing academically? How would you rate your current academic performance? (Poor; Fair; Very Good)
   Please Explain:
3. How would you rate your school attendance? (Poor; Fair; Very Good)
   Please Explain:
4. How would you rate your relationship with classmates? (Poor; Fair; Very Good)
   Please Explain:
5. How would you rate your relationship with teachers? (Poor; Fair; Very Good)
   Please Explain:

II. Specific Information About Current Academic Subjects

What subjects are you currently taking? Describe each course, and your academic performance and attendance pattern in each subject.

Subject	Current Mark	No. Days Absent to Date	Major Reason for Failure
1.			
2.			
3.			
4.			
5.			

THE FAMILY-PEER-SCHOOL BEHAVIOR INTERVIEW

PARENT FORM

Parental Disciplinary Styles

1. Who makes the rules in your family? Who is the disciplinarian?

2. What disciplinary methods are used in your family?

3. In your view, what are the best methods of handling adolescent sons and daughters?

4. If your son (daughter) does not comply with your rules or does something you disapprove of, what is your typical response?

Directions:
Use the following method to collect more information about parental disciplinary styles:

    a. "Describe recent typical situations when your son (daughter) did something that you disapproved of, or when you became angry or upset with your son (daughter)."
    b. "What was your response?"
    c. "What were the consequences?"
    d. "What thoughts were going through your head at the time?"

Describe Situation	Parent's Response	Consequences	Parent's Cognitions

Adolescent's Typical Activities of Daily Living

1. How does your son (daughter) spend his (her) days? Describe a typical weekday *and* a typical weekend day, from the time he (she) gets up in the morning until he (she) goes to bed at night.

	Typical Weekday	*Typical Weekend Day*
MORNING		
AFTERNOON		
EVENING		

2. What activities does your son (daughter) engage in with peers? How much time per day does your son (daughter) spend in the company of peers?

3. How well does your son (daughter) get along with people his (her) own age?

Pre-adolescent Coping with Stressful Situations

1. What were the events or ongoing situations that were most upsetting and stressful for your son (dauther), either at home, with other agemates, or at school?

2. What was the cause of the stress in each situation identified?

3. What was your son's (daughter's) typical way of coping with each of these situations?

	Description of Situation	*Perceived Cause*	*Coping Strategies*
ELEMENTARY SCHOOL YEARS			
JUNIOR HIGH SCHOOL YEAR			

Parent's Perception of the Son's (Daughter's) School Behavior

1. How is your son (daughter) doing at school?

2. How would you rate his (her) current academic performance (poor; fair; very good)?

   Please explain:

3. How would you rate his (her) school attendance (poor; fair; very good)?

   Please explain:

4. How would you rate his (her) relationship with classmates? (poor; fair; very good)?

   Please explain:

5. How would you rate his (her) relationship with teachers (poor; fair; very good)?

   Please explain:

Family Communication Patterns Checklist *

	Family Member(s) Demonstrating Pattern	Frequency of Occurrences Per Session

I. MALADAPTIVE PATTERNS

Commands
Complaints
Defensive Behavior
Interruptions
"Put-downs"
Ignoring
Persistent Negativism
Inflexible Stance
Talking Through a
Third Person
Accusing, Blaming
Preaching
Getting off Topic
Threats
Silent Sulking

II. ADAPTIVE PATTERNS

Supportive Communications
Agreements
Problem Evaluation
Consequential Statements
Humor

*Based on Robin & Foster, 1984.

Family Problem-Solving Patterns Checklist*

Maladaptive Patterns	Family Member(s) Demonstrating Pattern	Frequency of Occurrences Per Session
• Failure or refusal to discuss problem		
• Difficulty with problem definition		
• Difficulty generating alternative solutions		
• Difficulty selecting possible solution		
• Refusal to compromise on a solution		
• Failure to cooperate in planning components of a solution		
• Failure to implement selected solution		

Family Structural and External Problems Checklist*

MALADAPTIVE FAMILY PATTERNS

I. *Power Hierarchy*

- too little adolescent autonomy
- too much adolescent autonomy
- hierarchy reversal (adolescent controls parent)
- disagreement between parents regarding rules
- parent undermines spouse's authority
- other

II. *Dysfunctional Alignments of Family Members*

- parent-adolescent alignment against other parent
- parental competition for alliance with adolescent
- parent-sibling alliance
- other

---

*Based on Robin & Foster, 1984.

III. *Areas of Family Stress External to the Parent/Adolescent Relationship*

- family alcoholism
- marital conflict or divorce
- parent psychopathogy
- seriously ill family member
- sibling's problematic behaviors
- other

Dysfunctional Childrearing Styles Checklist *

Parental Childrearing Style	*Adolescent's Habitual Response Style*
Punitive	
• physical/verbal aggression	• seeks retaliation
	• self-punishment
• punitive guilt-engendering	• extreme guilt
	• approval-seeking
	• adopts victim role
	• fearful obedience
Rejecting	
• adolescent unacceptable	• approval seeking with parents, peers
• lacks affection for child	• excessive demands, tests limits
	• easily offended
	• suspicious of others
	• conduct disorder
Overcoercion	
• excessive parental control	• dependent on others for direction
• excessive parental nagging	• active resistance
	• passive resistance
	• lacks persistence; irresponsible
Overindulgence	
• overprotective	• bored passivity
• low expectations for child	• abdicates responsibility
	• lacks persistence; irresponsible
	• manipulates others

---

*Based on Missildine, 1963.

Oversubmissive
- unable to set limits
- submits to adolescent's manipulations

- impulsive response style
- seeks immediate gratification
- conduct disorders
- self-destructive behaviors
- lacks persistence; irresponsible
- manipulative

Neglecting (due to illness, alcoholism, separation, death, desertion)

- avoids forming close relationships
- lacks empathy
- social skills deficit
- makes excessive demands
- depression
- preoccupied with parental neglect
- excessive striving
- manipulative
- self-blame
- drifting

Perfectionistic Parent
- demands excellence
- withholds approval

- excessive striving
- self-belittlement
- guilt

Parental Hypochondriasis
- exaggerates own and child's illnesses

- uses illness as excuse for avoidance
- failure to take responsibility
- performance anxiety

APPENDIX D:
DAILY ACTIVITY SHEET

WEEK OF:

	Monday	Tuesday	Wednesday	Thursday	Friday	Saturday	Sunday
Morning							
Afternoon							
Evening							

References

Achenback, T.M. (1980). DSM III in light of empirical research on the classification of child psychopathology. *Journal of American Academy of Child Psychiatry, 19,* 395–412.

Alexander, J., and Parsons, B. (1973). Short-term behavioral interventions with delinquent families. *Journal of Abnormal Psychology, 81,* 219–225.

American Psychiatric Association (1987). *Diagnostic and statistical manual of mental disorders.* (DSM-III-R) 3rd Edition, Revised. Washington D.C.: American Psychiatric Association.

Anderson, L. (1982). Understanding and working with the depressed, suicidal adolescent. *Counselling and Human Development, 15* (1), 1–12.

Argyle, M. (1980). Interaction skills and social competence. In: P. Feldman and J. Orford (Eds.), *Psychological problems, The social context* (pp.123–150). New York: John Wiley & Sons.

Bandura, A. (1977). Self efficacy: Toward a unifying theory of behavioral change. *Psychological Review, 84,* 191–215.

Bandura, A., and Walters, R. (1959). *Adolescent aggression.* New York: Ronald Press.

Bandura, A., and Walters, R. (1963). *Social learning and personality development.* New York: Holt Rinehart & Winston.

Baucom, D., and Epstein, N. (1990). *Cognitive-behavioral marital therapy.* New York: Brunner/Mazel.

Beck, A., Rush, A., Shaw, B., and Emery, G. (1979). *Cognitive therapy of depression.* New York: The Guilford Press.

Beck, A. T. (1963). Thinking and depression: 1, Idiosyncratic content and cognitive distortions. *Archives of General Psychiatry, 9,* 324–333.

Beck, A. T. (1976). *Cognitive therapy and the emotional disorders.* New York: International Universities Press.

Beck, A.T., and Emery, G. (1977). *Cognitive therapy of substance abuse.* Philadelphia, Pa.: Aaron T. Beck. Center for Cognitive Therapy.

Beck, A.T., and Emery, G. (1985). *Anxiety disorders and phobias, A cognitive perspective.* New York: Basic Books, Inc.

Becker, W.C. (1964). Consequences of different kinds of parental discipline. In M. Hoffman and L. Hoffman (Eds.), *Review of child development research, Vol. I* (pp. 169–208). New York: Russell Sage Foundation.

Bedrosian, R. (1981). The application of cognitive therapy techniques with adolescents. In G. Emery, S. Hollon, and R. Bedrosian (Eds.), *New directions in cognitive therapy.* New York: The Guilford Press.

Bell, A., Weinberg, M., and Hammersmith, S. (1981). *Sexual preference: Its development in men and women.* Bloomington, Ind.: Indiana University Press.

Bellack, A., and Schwartz, J. (1976). Assessment for self-control programs. In M. Hersen and S. Bellack (Eds.), *Behavioral assessment: A practical handbook* (pp. 111–142), New York: Pergamon Press.

Block, J. (1978). Effects of a rational-emotive mental health program on poorly achieving disruptive high school students. *Journal of Counselling Psychology,* 8, 251–258.

Bloom, M.V. (1980). *Adolescent-parental separation.* New York: Gardener Press.

Bornstein, M., Bellack, A., and Hersen, M. (1980). Social skills training for highly aggressive children. *Behavior Modification,* 4, 173–186.

Bornstein, P., Weisser, C., and Balleweg, B. (1985). Anger and violent behavior. In M. Hersen and A. Bellack (Eds.), *Handbook of Clinical Behavior Therapy with Adults* (pp. 603–630). New York: Plenum Press.

Browne, A., and Finkelhor, D. (1986). Initial and long-term effects: A review of the research. In: D. Finkelhor (Ed.), *A sourcebook on child sexual abuse.* (pp. 143–179). Beverly Hills: Sage Publications.

Catalano, M. (1987). *The chronic pain control workbook.* Oakland, Cal.: New Harbinger Publications, Inc.

Chance, P. (1989). Kids without friends. *Psychology Today,* 23, 29–31.

Chartier, G., and Ranieri, D. (1984). Adolescent depression: Concepts, treatments, prevention. In: P. Karoly and J.Steffen (Eds.), *Adolescent behavior disorders: Foundations and contemporary concerns.* Lexington, Mass.: Lexington Books, D.C.Heath & Co.

Clarke, G., Lewinsohn, P., and Hops, H. (1990). *Adolescent coping with depression course: Leader's manual.* Eugene, Or.: Castalia Publishing Co.

Conger, J. (1977) *Adolescence and youth.* Second Edition. New York: Harper and Row.

Crook, T., Raskin, A., and Eliot, J. (1981). Parent-child relationships and adult depression. *Child Development,* 52, 950–957.

Davis, M., McKay, M., and Eshelman, E. (1982). *The relaxation and stress reduction workbook.* Oakland Cal.: New Harbinger Publications.

DiGiuseppe, R. (1988). A cognitive-behavioral approach to the treatment of conduct disorder children and adolescents. In N. Epstein, S. Schlesinger, and W. Dryden (Eds.), *Cognitive-behavioral therapy with families* (pp. 183–294). New York: Brunner/Mazel.

D'Zurilla, T.J., & Goldfried, M.R. (1971). Problem solving and behavior modification. *Journal of Abnormal Psychology,* 78, 107–126.

Eckman, T. (1976). An educational workshop in conversational skills. In: J. Krumboltz and C. Thoresen (Eds.), *Counselling methods.* New York: Holt, Rinehart and Winston, (495–509).

Eisler, R. (1976). Behavioral assessment of social skills. In M. Hersen and A. Bellack, *Behavioral Assessment: A Practical Handbook.* New York: Pergamon Press.

Ellis, A. (1977). Rational-emotive therapy: Research data that support the clinical and personality hypothesis of RET and other modes of cognitive-behavior therapy. *Counselling Psychologist,* 7(1) 2–42.

Ellis, A., and Harper, R.A. (1975). *A new guide to rational living.* Hollywood, California: Wilshire Books.

Ellis, A., and Grieger, R. (1977). *Handbook of rational-emotive therapy.* New York: Springer.

Ellis, A.E. (1962). *Reason and emotion in psychotherapy*. New York: Lyle Stuart.

Epstein, N., Schlesinger, S., and Dryden, W. (1988). Concepts and methods of cognitive-behavioral family treatment. In. N. Epstein, S. Schlesinger, and W. Dryden (Eds.), *Cognitive-behavioral therapy with families* (pp. 5–48). New York: Brunner/Mazel.

Feldman, P. (1980). The making and control of offenders. In P. Feldman and J. Orford (Eds.), *Psychological problems, The social context* (pp. 185–218). New York. John Wiley & Sons.

Finkelhor, D., and Browne, A. (1986). Initial and long-term effects: a conceptual framework. In D. Finkelhor (Ed.), *A sourcebook on child sexual abuse* (pp. 180–198). Beverly Hills: Sage Publications.

Freud, A. (1965). *Normality and pathology in childhood*. New York: International Universities Press.

Friedman, R., Sandler, J., Hernandez, M., and Wolfe, D. (1982). Child abuse. In E. Mash and L. Terdal (Eds.), *Behavioral assessment of childhood disorders* (pp. 221–258). New York: The Guilford Press.

Goldfried, M.R. (1973). Reduction of generalized anxiety through a variant of systematic desensitization. In: M.R. Goldfried and M. Merbaum (Eds)., *Behavior change through self control*. New York: Holt, Rinehart and Winston.

Goldfried, M.R., and Davidson, G.C. (1976). *Clinical behavior therapy*. New York: Holt, Rinehart and Winston.

Goldfried, M. and Goldfried, A. (1980). Cognitive change methods. In F. Kanfer and A. Goldstein (Eds.), *Helping people change*. New York: Pergamon.

Goldstein, A., and Pentz, M. (1984). Psychological skill training and the aggressive adolescent. *School Psychology Review, 13* (3) (183–214).

Gordon, T.(1970). *Parent effectiveness training*. New York: Peter H. Wyden, Inc..

Grieger, R. (1982). Anger problems. In R. Grieger and I Grieger (Eds.), *Cognition and emotional disturbance*. (pp. 46–76). New York: Human Sciences Press Inc.

Guerney, B., Coufal, J., and Vogelsong, E. (1981). Relationship enhancement versus a traditional approach to therapeutic/preventive/enrichment parent-adolescent programs. *Journal of Consulting and Clinical Psychology, 49,* 927–939.

Guidano, V., and Liotti, G. (1983). *Cognitive processes and emotional disorders*. New York: Guilford Press.

Hadley, J., and Staudacher, C. (1985). *Hypnosis for change*. Oakland, Cal.: New Harbinger Publications.

Hatten, C., Valente, S., and Rink, A. (1977). *Suicide: Assessment and intervention*. New York: Appleton-Century-Crofts.

Herbert, M. (1980). Socialization for problem resistance. In P. Feldman and J. Orford (Eds.), *Psychological problems. The social context* (pp. 39–72). New York: John Wiley & Sons.

Herzberger, S.D., Potts, D.A., and Dillon, M. (1981). Abusive and nonabusive parental treatment from the child's perspective. *Journal of Counselling and Clinical Psychology, 49* (1), pp. 81–90.

Hops, H., and Greenwood, C. (1982). Social skills deficits. In E. Mash and L. Terdal (Eds.), *Behavioral assessment of childhood disorders* N.Y.: Guilord Press, 1982.

Inhelder, G., and Piaget, J. (1958). *The growth of logical thinking from childhood to adolescence*. (Parsons, A., and Milgram, S., Trs.) New York: Basic Books.

Jenkins, R. and Boyer, A. (1968). Types of delinquent behavior and background factors. *Int. Journal Soc. Psychiatry, 14,* 65–76.

Johnson, C. (1982). Anorexia nervosa and bulimia. In: T. Coates, A. Petersen, and C. Perry (Eds.), *Promoting adolescent health: A dialogue in research and practice.* New York: Academic Press.

Kanfer, F. (1970). Self regulation: Research issues and speculations. In: C. Neuringer and M. Michael (Eds.) *Behavior modification in clinical psychology.* New York: Appleton-Century-Crofts.

Kanfer, F. H. (1975). Self-management methods. In F. H. Kanfer, & A.P. Goldstein (Eds.), *Helping people change,* (P. 334–373), New York: Pergamon Press.

Kanfer, F.H., and Saslow, G. (1965). Behavioral diagnosis. *Archives of General Psychiatry, 12,* 529–538.

Kendall, P. C., and Finch, A. J. (1978). A cognitive-behavioral treatment for impulsivity. A group comparison study. *Journal of Consulting and Clinical Psychology, 46,* 110–118.

Kendall, P.C., and Hollon, S.D. (1979). *Cognitive-behavioral interventions: Theory, research, and procedures.* New York: Academic Press.

Kifer, R., Lewis, M., Green, D., and Phillips, E. (1974). Training predelinquent youths and their parents to negotiate conflict situations. *Journal of Applied Behavior Analysis, 7,* 357–364.

Lewinsohn, P. (1975). The behavioral study and treatment of depression. In M. Hersen, R. Isler, and P. Miller (Eds.), *Progress in behavior modification. vol. l.* New York: Academic Press.

Lewinsohn, P. (1976). Activity schedules in treatment of depression. In: J. Krumboltz and C. Thoresen (Eds.) *Counseling Methods.* N.Y.: Holt, Rinehart & Winston.

Lewinsohn, P.M., & Libet, J. (1972). Pleasant events, activity schedules, and depression. *Journal of Abnormal Psychology, 79,* 291–295.

Lucock, M., and Salkovskis, P. (1988). Cognitive factors in social anxiety and its treatment. *Behav. Res. Ther., 26(4),* 297–302.

Mahoney, J., and Arnkoff, D. (1978). Cognitive and self-control therapies. In: S. Garfield and A. Bergin (Eds.), *Handbook of psychotherapy and behavior change.* Second Edition. New York: Wiley.

Mahoney, M. (1974). *Cognition and behavior modification.* Cambridge, Mass.: Balinger.

Mahoney, M. (1977). Reflections on the cognitive-learning trend in psychotherapy. *American Psychologist, 32,* 5–13.

Mahoney, M. (1980). *Psychotherapy process: Current issues and future directions.* New York: Plenum.

Marks, I., and Gelder, M. (1966). Different ages of onset in varieties of phobia. *American Journal of Psychiatry, 123,* 218–221.

Maser, J.D., and Clonniger, C.R. (1989). *Co-morbidity in anxiety and mood disorders.* Washington, D.C.: American Psychiatric Press.

McKay, M., Davis, M., and Fanning, P. (1981). *Thoughts and feelings: The art of cognitive stress intervention.* Richmond, Calif.: New Harbinger Publications.

Meichenbaum, D. (1976). A cognitive-behavior modification approach to assessment. In M. Hersen and A.S. Bellack (Eds.), *Behavior assessment: A practical handbook.* New York: Pergamon Press.

Meichenbaum, D. (1977). *Cognitive-behavior modification.* New York: Plenum Press.

Millon, T. (1981). *Disorders of personality: DSM-III, Axis II.* New York: Wiley.

Minuchin, S. (1974). *Families and family therapy.* Cambridge: Harvard University Press.

Mischel, W. (1984). On the predictability of behavior and the structure of personality. In: R. Zucker, J. Arono, and A. Rabin (Eds.), *Personality and prediction of behavior.* New York: Academic Press.

Missildine, W. H. (1963). *Your inner child of the past.* New York: Simon and Schuster.

Morton, T., Twentyman, C., and Azar, S. (1988). Cognitive-behavioral assessment and treatment of child abuse. In: N. Epstein, S. Schlesinger, and W. Dryden (Eds.), *Cognitive-behavioral therapy with families* (pp. 87–117), New York: Brunner/Mazel.

Musetto, A. (1978). Evaluating families with custody or visitation problems. *Journal of Marriage and Family Counselling, 4*(4), 59–65.

Muuss, R. (1988). *Theories of adolescence,* Fifth Edition. New York: Random House.

Nichols, M. (1984). *Family therapy, concepts and methods.* New York: Gardner Press, Inc.

Nielson, A., and Gerber, D. (1979). Psychosocial aspects of truancy in early adolescence. *Adolescence, 14* (54), 313–326.

Novoco, R.W. (1975). *Anger control: The development and evaluation of an experimental treatment.* Lexington, Mass.: Lexington Books.

Orford, J. (1980). The domestic context. In P. Feldman and J. Orford (Eds.), *Psychological problems, The social context.* (pp. 3-38). New York: Wiley & Sons.

Patterson, G. (1975). *Families: Applications of social learning to family life* (rev. ed.), Champaign, Ill.: Research Press.

Patterson, G. (1982). *Coercive family process: A social learning approach.* Vol. 3. Eugene, Oregon: Castalia.

Patterson, G., and Stouthamer-Loeber, M. (1984). The correlation of family management practices and delinquency. *Child Development, 55,* 1299–1307.

Petersen, A., and Hamburg, B. (1986). Adolescence: A developmental approach to problems and psychopathology. *Behavior Therapy, 17,* 480–499.

Rekers, G. (1982). Psychosexual and gender problems. In: E. Mash and L. Terdal (Eds.), *Behavioral assessment of childhood disorders.* (pp. 484–520). New York: The Guilford Press.

Richards, C. (1985). Work and study problems. In: M. Hersen and A. Bellack (Eds.), *Handbook of clinical behavior therapy with adults* (pp. 557–572). New York: Plenum Press.

Robin, A. (1981). A controlled evaluation of problem-solving communication training with parent-adolescent conflict. *Behavior Therapy, 12,* 593–609.

Robin, A.L., and Foster, S.L. (1984). Problem-solving communication training: A behavioral family systems approach to parent-adolescent conflict. In P. Karoly and J.J. Steffen (Eds.), *Adolescent behavior disorders: Foundations and contemporary concerns* (pp. 195–240). Lexington, Mass.: D.C. Heath.

Robin, A.L., and Foster, S.L. (1989). *Negotiating parent-adolescent conflict. A behavioral-family systems approach.* New York: The Guilford Press.

Robin, A., and Weiss, J. (1980). Criterion-related validity of behavioral and self-report measures of problem solving communication skills in distressed and non-distressed parent-adolescent dyads. *Behavioral Assessment, 2,* 239–352.

Robins, L. (1979). 1 Follow-up studies. In H. Quay and J. Werry (Eds.), *Psychopathological disorders of childhood*. (2nd Edition) New York: Wiley.

Roehling, P., and Robin, A. (1986). Development and validation of the family beliefs inventory: A measure of unrealistic beliefs among parents and adolescents. *Journal of Consulting and Clinical Psychology, 54* (5), 693–697.

Rollins, B., and Thomas, B. (1975). A theory of parental power and child compliance. In: R. Cromwell and D. Olson (Eds.) *Power in families.*(pp. 38–60), New York: John Wiley & Sons

Russell, M., Henderson, C., and Blume, S.B. (1985). *Children of alcoholics: A review of the literature*. New York: Children of Alcoholics Foundation,

Rutter, M. (1986). The developmental psychopathology of depression: Issues and perspectives. In M. Rutter, C. Izard, and P. Read (Eds.), *Depression in young people* (pp. 3–30). New York: Guilford Press.

Safran, J., Vallis, M., Segal, Z., and Shaw, B. (1986). Assessment of core cognitive processes in cognitive therapy. *Cognitive Therapy and Research, 10*, 509–526.

Schrodt, G., and Fitzgerald, B. (1987). Cognitive therapy with adolescents. *Americal Journal of Psychotherapy, XLI* (3), 402–408.

Schrodt, G., and Fitzgerald, B. (1987). Cognitive therapy with adolescents. *American Journal of Psychotherapy, XLI*(No. 3), 492–498.

Schrodt, G., and Wright, J. (1986). Inpatient treatment of adolescents. In A. Freeman and V. Greenwood, (Eds.), *Cognitive therapy: Applications in psychiatric and medical settings*. New York: Human Sciences Press.

Sears, R. (1961). Relation of early socialization experiences to aggression in middle childhood. *Journal of Abnormal and Social Psychology, 63*, 466–492.

Serna, L., Schumaker, J., Hazel, J., and Sheldon, J. (1986). Teaching reciprocal social skills to parents and their delinquent adolescents. *Journal of Clinical Child Psychology, 15* (1), 64–77.

Shaw, B., and Beck, A. (1977). The treatment of depression with cognitive therapy. In A. Ellis and R. Grieger (Eds.), *Handbook of rational-emotive theory and practice*. New York: Springer Publishing Co.

Snyder, J., and White, M., (1979). The use of cognitive self-instruction in the treatment of behaviorally disturbed adolescents. *Behavior Therapy, 10*, 227–235.

Spivak,G., Platt, J., and Shure, M., (1976). *The problem solving approach to adjustment*. San Francisco: Jossey-Bass.

Steinglass, P., Bennett, L., Wolin, S., and Reiss, O. (1987). *The alcoholic family*. New York: Basic Books.

Stuart, R.B. (1971). Behavioral contracting within the families of delinquents. *Journal of Behavior Therapy and Experimental Psychiatry, 2*, 1–11.

Trower, P., Yardley, K., Bridget, B., and Shaw, P. (1978). The treatment of social failure. A comparison of anxiety-reduction and skills acquisition procedures on two social problems. *Behavior Modification, 2* (1).

Vance, P. (1982). The adolescent years: Identification of learning problems. In *Special needs/ Special help: A resource book in special education for the classroom teacher*. Ontario Teachers' Federation.

Weiner, I.B. (1970). *Psychological disturbance in adolescence*. New York: John Wiley & Sons.

Wilson, G. T. (1980). Cognitive factors in life-style changes: A social learning perspective. In P. Davidson and S. Davidson (Eds.), *Behavioral medicine: Changing health life styles.* New York: Brunner/Mazel.

Wolpe, J., and Laxarus, A. (1966). *Behavior therapy techniques: A guide to the treatment of neuroses.* New York: Pergamon Press.

Wright, D. (1971). *The psychology of moral behavior.* Baltimore: Penguin Books.

Zarb, J. (1990). Perceptions and response styles of referred adolescent girls with family problems. *Journal of Youth and Adolescence, 19*(4), 227–288.

Name Index

Subject Index